Always Remembered

*New revelations and old tales
about those fabulous Expos*

DANNY GALLAGHER

Scoop Press
Toronto, 2020

Always Remembered: New revelations and old tales about those fabulous Expos

Copyright ©2020, Danny Gallagher

Published by Scoop Press. For information, please call 365-881-2389.

Printed and bound in Canada by Marquis, Toronto.

Cover design and formatting by Dawna Dearing, First Wave Grafix. Table of contents and chapter layout by Danny Gallagher.

Front cover photo of Gary Carter was taken by Denis Brodeur from Scott Coates' collection. The two photos on the back cover were also taken by Brodeur from Coates' collection.

ISBN: 978-0968-1859-9-5

*To: Charles Bronfman, Stephen Bronfman, John McHale,
Jim Fanning, Mitch Garber, Gerry Snyder*

Table of Contents

Foreword

George Foster of the Cincinnati Reds had lofted a towering fly ball into foul territory and it was headed for me.

I didn't have much time to react and I had a beer in each hand. I wanted to catch the ball for a souvenir but with my hands full, I just ducked and got out of the way. That's my recollection of my first Expos game at Jarry Park in the early 1970s in the company of my brother Jim and Gerry Lepine and Cliff McGrimmon, teammates of ours with the Renfrew Red Sox of the North Renfrew Senior Baseball League.

My passion for the Expos had begun in 1969 when the Expos began playing as a National League franchise. In Douglas, Ontario where I grew up next door to my native Renfrew, I played on a team called the Expos in the South Renfrew Senior Baseball League.

Trying to emulate Maury Wills, who was taken by the Expos in the 1968 expansion draft, I would move the bat up and down in a windmill fashion, practicing and waiting for the pitcher to throw the ball. It was a habit I kept through the 1970 season and then I abandoned it to revert back to my normal batting stance and practice swing.

I grew up listening to Bob Prince on Pirates broadcasts and then Dave Van Horne on Expos broadcasts. For years, I followed the Expos, although I had grown up admiring the Red Sox, especially after the 1967 Red Sox Impossible Dream team almost captured the World Series.

By 1988, my passion for the Expos grew when I joined

the Montreal Daily News. After a few months on the copy desk, sports editor Kevin Boland put me on the Expos beat to help out No. 1 guy Terry Haig. So for close to 32 years, I have written hundreds of articles on the Expos for various publications and I have dished out six books about the Expos.

My first book about the Expos was called You Don't Forget Homers Like That. It came out in 1997 and a year later, it appeared in French. I also wrote two books with co-author Bill Young of Hudson, Quebec.

The first book with Young was called Remembering the Montreal Expos and it was our tribute to the franchise only one year after the Expos had departed for Washington. The second book with Young was Ecstasy to Agony about the 1994 Expos.

Since then, I came out with a book on the 1981 Expos called Blue Monday, which was published by Dundurn Press in 2018. And now this one.

This book keeps the Expos legacy alive. Writing about the past allows you to experience all those feelings in the present – now. And in doing so, it hopefully creates the emotions – energy in motion – that will contribute in some way in bringing back baseball to Montreal.

Fifteen years after Washington took the Expos and started playing as the Nationals in 2005, this book is my tribute to a fallen franchise.

The Expos are gone but not forgotten.

1

Paving the way for Rusty

There have been major-league players, who reported to new teams but never played for them: either as free agents, through trades or through an expansion draft or because they were released.

Remember Jack Billingham? Look at the accompanying photo in this chapter of him in a posed shot by photographer Denis Brodeur in an Expos' uniform.

Billingham was claimed by the Expos from the Los Angeles Dodgers in the 1968 expansion draft and after close to six weeks of spring training, he did come close to actually appearing in a regular-season game for the Expos.

But just when the Expos' inaugural season was about to begin, while the team was playing a spring training game in St. Petersburg, Fla., Billingham was taken aside by manager Gene Mauch and told he had been traded to the Houston Astros with Skip Guinn to complete the Rusty Staub traded that had been made Jan. 22, 1969.

It was later reported that the Expos sent $100,000 in cash to the Astros to complete the trade. The initial trade saw Staub acquired from the Astros in exchange for Donn Clendenon and Jesus Alou.

Billingham had figured he was going to be in the Expos' starting rotation so he made some arrangements to get his belongings to Montreal.

"I remember a funny story," Billingham recalled. "My brother Richie was in the service and he was on leave and the sad part was that was just before he was going to Vietnam. He volunteered to drive my car to Montreal. I'd bought a yellow Chevy station wagon.

"That was when there were no cell phones. When he got up in the New York area, he pulled off to a hotel room and turned on the TV and they said Billingham was traded to Houston. My brother turned around and headed to Houston.

"I called my wife, who was pregnant with our second child. She had a difficult pregnancy. I felt better about going to Houston. I was happy. I'd heard rumours about Montreal. I heard tax-wise that it would be a mess in Canada with the Canadian taxes. I had a bad spring. I didn't have that good a spring training with the Expos. I pitched very poorly. I was hit pretty hard. I was a reliever with the Dodgers and Gene Mauch

Denis Brodeur photo/Danny Gallagher collection
Jack Billingham at Spring Training in 1969

thought I might be able to start the season with Montreal as a starter."

Another factor that unsettled Billingham before he even reported to his new team was general manager Jim Fanning's treatment of him during contract negotiations in the off-season following his draft claim from the Dodgers. It was a wake-up call for Billingham in the days when major-league teams pretty much owned players and there was little or negotiation on possible raises.

4

"Montreal and San Diego were the new expansion teams for 1969 and my pitching coach at the end of the year in 1968 was telling me that if the Dodgers couldn't protect me that I might have a chance of going in the expansion draft," Billingham was saying. "A friend of mine, Larry Guest, who was a sports writer with the Orlando Sentinel, checked the ticker tape to see what was happening on draft day."

On Oct. 14, 1968, Manny Mota was the Expos' first pick from the Dodgers, followed by Mack Jones from the Reds, John Bateman from the Astros and Gary Sutherland from the Phillies. Then Guest informed Billingham, an Orlando native, that he had been picked up by the Expos from the Dodgers, 10th overall, in the first round.

"Larry and I went out on the street and he took a photo of me," Billingham said. "I was kind of excited. I hated to leave the Dodgers because I had spent seven years in the minors with them and then I was 3-0 with eight saves and a 2.14 ERA in my first season in the big leagues."

So with that fancy-dan season under his belt as a rookie, Billingham figured he would get the raise he wanted: $5,000 up to $15,000.

"Jim Fanning called me and said, 'Welcome to the new Montreal Expos.' And he said he was looking forward to having me on the team and he said he would take care of me and he said he would send me a contract," Billingham said. "He sent me a contract. It was for $12,000. I sent it back to him. I didn't like to negotiate in the mail so I called him a few times. I argued with Jim about my salary. I wasn't very happy. He said the Expos had spent so much money on the first-round picks in the amateur draft. I ended up getting a salary of $12,000. I got a raise of $2,000.

"Fanning said, 'Here's a $2,000 raise. That's all we can do. We're an expansion team. If you don't like it, stay home.' He put a knife on a balloon. It didn't make sense. I knew I wasn't going to get a whole lot of money but after the season I had the year before, I was hoping I'd get $15,000 because I had heard they were going to make me a starter. Jim Lefebvre got a $4,000 raise from the Dodgers after he won rookie of the year in 1965.

"I went to spring training. Before spring training, we had a meeting and they knew the players might go on strike. I had a meeting with Fanning and he looked at me and said, 'If you're not here on Opening Day of spring training, we'll fine you $1,000 if you don't report.' I was in my second year in the big leagues and it scared the hell out of me. It was scare tactics.

"Everything is flipped around now. Back then, it was the owners who were in control. They owned us. Now, most of the players and the union are in control."

When I agreed with Billingham that he had enjoyed a stellar season in 1968 with the Dodgers, Billingham replied, "Why didn't you tell Fan-

Fred Whitacre collection

John McHale, Ed Lopat, Jim Fanning and Fred Whitacre in West Palm Beach

ning that?" And we laughed.

Long before Billingham was taken in the draft from the Dodgers, he had impressed the Expos' brass a lot when he made his only start of the 1968 season on Aug. 5 at Dodger Stadium against the Pirates. With the Dodgers pitching staff getting low on rest, manager Walter Alston, on three hours notice, pressed Billingham into action out of the bullpen as a starter. Billingham said Don Drysdale got sick and Alston asked him if he wanted to start. He got a no-decision out of it but the Dodgers won 1-0.

Billingham later heard that even though Montreal had yet to be officially announced as the winner of a National League franchise on Aug.

6

14 because last-minute financing was needed and was provided by Good Samaritan Charles Bronfman, the powers-that-be with the new Montreal team had people out scouting potential players. Apparently so.

Mauch had been fired by the Phillies on June 16 after the club went 28-27 part way through the 1968 season so Mauch was apparently asked by new team president John McHale to do some scouting even though Mauch had not been officially hired. According to online reports, Mauch was hired as manager by the Expos Sept. 5, 1968 but obviously he had unofficially been doing some work for McHale prior to his hiring, as Billingham told me. Weird but true apparently.

Canadian Baseball Hall of Fame
Donn Clendenon

"I had more rest than anybody on the pitching staff. I threw eight shutout innings," Billingham said of his start on Aug. 5. "Gene Mauch and some Montreal people were in the stands. I understand that they liked what they saw, not knowing I was going to start the game."

How Billingham ended up in Houston was interesting. McHale was part of the whole process that went down. As the story goes, McHale, who was the deputy commissioner at the time, had been tabbed to be baseball's new commissioner following the firing of unpopular General William Eckert but as a favour to Bowie Kuhn, a Wall St. lawyer and baseball's legal counsel for years, McHale stepped aside to allow Kuhn to be commissioner in February of 1969.

In return, McHale asked Kuhn to scratch his back. McHale asked Kuhn to allow the Expos-Astros trade to proceed without it being negated, even if Clendenon wouldn't report to Houston. McHale told Kuhn that Montreal wanted to build its expansion team around Staub. So for the next two months, the trade stayed its course but just as the regular season was about to begin, the Astros started complaining because Clendenon was refusing to report. The Astros wanted the trade voided.

Despite protests from the Astros, Kuhn upheld the original trade but ordered the Expos to complete the trade and ruled that Clendenon would remain with the Expos. So instead of Clendenon going to Houston with Alou, the Expos and Astros agreed on this solution: the Expos would send Billingham and Guinn and $100,000 cash to the Lonestar State club.

In fact, Clendenon had temporarily retired. He outright refused to report to Houston because the manager, Harry (The Hat) Walker was a man he detested because he felt Walker was a racist. Walker was white, Clendenon black. Walker had been Pirates manager when Clendenon played there but not only did Clendenon not like Walker, so did many of the other Pirates. There was a personality clash between Walker and most of the players. In the face of a mutiny by the players against Walker, management fired Walker and replaced him with Danny Murtaugh.

The odd thing is that Walker was hired by the Astros and because he was there, Clendenon initially said he wouldn't report, although he did meet with GM Spec Richardson on a possible contract but nothing could be worked out. So on March 1, Clendenon decide to retire, if only for a short time. He resumed his job in the personnel department of the Scripto pen company in Pittsburgh. Clendenon was coaxed out of retirement after friend Monte Irvin delivered an Expos contract offer to him at the Clendenon family restaurant. This followed a meeting Clendenon had with Expos owner Charles Bronfman, Kuhn and several other bigwigs.

In the end, all three players that went to Houston had been acquired the previous October in the major-league draft: Alou, Billingham and Guinn. Odd? Not really, the Expos didn't have much of a roster to begin with because they were starting from scratch. Their inventory of players was low.

Billingham managed a lacklustre season with the Astros, going 6-7 but thereafter, he posted 10 consecutive seasons with at least 10 wins.

Clendenon was also mediocre with the Expos after he decided to unretire and report to Montreal on April 19, 11 days following the completion of the Expos-Astros transaction. He was offered more money as an incentive. He was batting .240 with four home runs and 14 RBI when the Expos dealt him to the New York Mets on June 15, 1969, in exchange for Steve Renko, Kevin Collins and two minor leaguers. Clendenon helped the Miracle Mets to the 1969 World Series championship.

In Houston, Billingham ran into Spec Richardson, who gave Billingham the same song and dance that Fanning gave him when it came to raises.

"We were in Cocoa Beach, Fla. in a back room," Billingham said. "Spec said I can't give you $30,000 but I will give you $29,500. He knew my dad had a Standard Oil gas station back home so he said, 'If you don't like this offer, you can go back to your dad's gas station.' I wanted to reach over and do whatever to him. They threw everything in your face."

Billingham enjoyed his best years with the Reds, helping them to World Series titles in 1975-76. In 1975, in what may have been the most exciting World Series ever played, Billingham was great and so was he in the 1976 Fall Classic. In seven World Series games in total, including three starts for Cincinnati, he went 2–0 with a 0.36 ERA and allowed just one earned run in $25\frac{1}{3}$ innings pitched. How about that?

Billingham came to the Reds in one of baseball's blockbuster trades. Think about this closely: the Reds sent Lee May, Tommy Helms and Jimmy Stewart to the Astros for Billingham, Joe Morgan, Denis Menke,

César Gerónimo, and then minor leaguer Ed Armbrister prior to the 1972 season.

"I like to tell the story that I was in one of the biggest trades Houston ever made," Billingham said. "Morgan was a s-t-a-r with Houston. I was semi-successful with Houston and then I was a throw-in, in the Joe Morgan trade."

But Billingham didn't perform like a throw-in with the Reds. He was superb. Today, he would be making close to $15-million per year as a workhorse, a clone of Steve Rogers, Dave Stieb and Jack Morris. In his last season in the majors, Billingham earned $140,000. His years with the Reds went like this: 12-12, 19-10, 19-11, 15-10, 12-10 and 10-10. Pretty gall-darn good.

When his playing career was over, Billingham was a major-league coach for 20 seasons.

"I had a wonderful career," he said. "I was a player for 18 seasons and a coach for 20."

Because he didn't officially play for the Expos in regular-season play, there was no time for him to be made up with an Expos' baseball card but a compromise was developed and you can see it online. It shows him with a spray-painted Blue hat and the word Expos underneath. On occasion, he gets requests to have that card signed but most of his autograph seekers wants Reds' stuff signed.

And here's an interesting tale involving Billingham and the Expos. In his possession from 1969 until 2015 was a poster that included players taken by the Expos in the 1968 expansion draft. It was very unique. John Bateman, Bob Bailey, John Boccabella, Bill Stoneman, Mack Jones, Larry Jaster and Manny Mota were among the players on the poster.

"I still wish I had it," Billingham told me. "I sold it to a guy I met in a restaurant. I told him I had a poster on my wall in my office. I wanted to sell it for $300 but then I said I was going to settle for $250. My wife pulled it out and we sold it for $150."

2

Digging septic tanks replaced baseball

Bill Seagraves had two options facing him when he went to spring training with the Expos in 1971: give baseball a shot or dig up septic tanks.

He chose the less glamorous job and has never looked back.

Seagraves was one of the first-ever draft picks as the Expos headed into their first season in 1969. He was drafted as a senior out of Edgewater high school in Orlando, Florida but didn't report to spring training with the Expos until 1971 because he decided to play two years at the University of Florida.

"It was my childhood dream to play for the Florida Gators," Seagraves said.

But after two years at U of F, Seagraves dropped out and decided to give the Expos a shot. He travelled across state to West Palm Beach from Orlando with another prospect John Hart, who is familiar to many as the long-time general manager of both the Cleveland Indians and Atlanta Braves. Anyway, Seagraves jumped out of the car and was met by general manager Jim Fanning.

"I went to an office building and I saw my contract with a big Expos logo at the top," Seagraves remembered. "To the left and the right of the contract were all these names so I asked Jim about the names. He said they were the names of all of the owners of the team. I looked at the names and most of them were French Canadians. I said to myself, 'Do they know anything about baseball?'

"Jim was familiar with me. He had scouted me when he worked for the Major League Baseball Central Scouting Combine before he joined the Expos."

Next thing for Seagraves to do was put his uniform on and what he encountered was a Who's Who.

"Anyway, I am nervous, excited," Seagraves said. "I followed this equipment manager into the locker room. It was a special locker room with wooden lockers. I was getting dressed. I was just trying to get my uniform on properly. I was sitting on a bench putting on my sanitary stockings and started to glance around the room. Right next to me was

Don Drysdale, who was an Expos announcer. I couldn't believe it.

"Gene Mauch was there in the clubhouse. Rusty Staub was the only player I saw there. I saw Don Zimmer, a coach, Larry Doby the hitting coach. I was a third baseman and the Expos also had Coco Laboy, who played third but he wasn't a third baseman. Laboy was a natural short-stop but the Expos asked him to play third.

"I thought I was being brought in to play third base. The Expos were in the process of signing Bob Bailey, a big strapping third baseman."

So next thing you know, Doby was telling Seagraves it was time to go and take some BP.

"There were some bats laying on the ground and Larry told me to take one of Bob Bailey's bats because he wasn't there yet," Seagraves said. "The bat was like a tree, it was huge. He was a bull of a guy.

"As I took batting practice with Don Zimmer pitching, I could hear this voice behind me telling me to relax. He said I was OK. I wasn't sure who he was. He was a very small, old man. Curious, I asked someone and it was Eddie Lopat, an Expos' scout, who was a former ma-jor-league pitcher. He was trying to help me."

Seagraves then talked about a fine shortstop he witnessed at the camp.

"He's the best defensive shortstop I ever saw, even the best to this day. Pepe Frias," Seagraves said. "Man, oh man, he was good but John Hart said he would never play in the majors."

"Why is that?" Seagraves asked Hart.

"The front office doesn't like him be-

Canadian Baseball Hall of Fame
Larry Doby

cause he's arrogant and hard-headed," Hart replied.

Frias did play in the majors, playing parts of six seasons with the Expos and then subsequently for other teams.

At one juncture of camp, Seagraves was taken aside by assistant gen-eral manager Danny Menendez, who advised him that the organization had just signed this fellow by the name of Pat Scanlon and that the team wanted Scanlon to play third base. Seagraves was told he might want to try first base and he was also told that he wouldn't start his first minor-league season in his home state of Florida in West Palm Beach.

"I told Danny that Scanlon didn't have a clue about third base," Sea-graves said.

"I got orders from above," Menendez told Seagraves about Scanlon.

"They wanted me to go to upstate New York to Jamestown," Seagraves said. "I said I'm not doing this. So I left for home. On the way, I stopped in Fort Lauderdale to see former major-leaguer Mickey Vernon, whom I knew. I told him what happened. We sat and talked for an hour. He knew everything about my family and the family business. Mickey said, 'You love baseball but you have a heckuva family business.'

"I still have dreams about whether I should have pursued baseball but I made the right decision. In the long run, it was best to dive into the family business. I was born into the family business. I grew up in it. When I wasn't playing baseball, I was digging up septic thanks with my dad.

"I was 22 at the time and I already had two kids. At the time, there weren't many people in baseball making $100,000 a year. I figured it out: I was going to be making $550 a month playing baseball but I would be making $650 per week in the family business."

That family business, now called Your Environment's Solution, is still thriving today. Seagraves is the COO.

Scanlon? He played 120 games in the majors, 73 with the Expos.

Liking Gary Sutherland

Bob Oldis looks back at the original 1969 Expos and picks out one who was his favourite.

"Probably Gary Sutherland," said Oldis, who was a first-base coach for manager Gene Mauch that first season. "He came to play every day, he knew how to play the game. He knew he had to get the guy over, he could hit the ball to right. He couldn't run very good. He was a good kid, he had a really short, solid stroke, a good player.

"We didn't have very good pitching at all. It was unique. We had some very interesting older players like Maury Wills, Rusty Staub, Mack Jones and Elroy Face."

What many people don't know is that Oldis was employed by the Expos right up until they no longer were in Montreal. He was a scout most of the time, recommending the likes of Bill Gullickson and Casey Candaele.

At last word, he was still scouting for the Marlins.

Oldis had been a coaching buddy for Mauch going back to the 1960s, especially the 1964 Phillies, who blew the lead and lost the National League pennant in the remaining days of September.

"We lost 10 games in a row. It was the toughest 10 days I ever had," Oldis told me. "We ran out of gas. It was really tough. We had a six and a half game lead with 12 games to play. The streak started when Art Mahaffey pitched one of the greatest games he ever pitched and we lost 1-0. Frank Robinson was caught stealing second but the runner at third (Chico Ruiz) stole home for the only run."

3

In memory of Le Grand Orange

Rusty Staub was the Expos first franchise hero and Vladimir Guerrero was the Expos last franchise hero.

And in between, there were many other heroes such as Gary Carter, Andre Dawson, Tim Raines and Steve Rogers.

Staub arrived in a complicated trade from the Houston Astros prior to the start of the 1969 season and after things were sorted out, he played three seasons in Montreal, gaining allegiance from fans all across Canada.

After spending some eight years away, his rock star status with Montreal fans remained intact when he was acquired in a trade from the Detroit Tigers in July of 1979. I was there at Olympic Stadium when he made his debut a second time before 59,000 fans. The place rocked.

Staub never did get to play full time the remainder of the season as the Expos fell short of the NL East title.

Staub was the toast of Montreal when he was with the Expos.

Because of his cult status, Staub was elected into the Canadian Baseball Hall of Fame even though he had played only three and a half seasons with the Expos. He was an unusual exception to the unwritten rule that more longevity is needed to get in the door of St. Marys.

I may have been the last journalist to see Staub alive when I was permitted a visit with him in March, 2018 at Good Samaritan Medical Centre in Palm Beach, Florida where he had a home for a few years. I had just walked in off the street. A receptionist gave me his room number. Hospital staff put him upright in his bed from a sleeping position while I told him I had the same given names as him: Daniel Joseph and that I had interviewed him in Belleville, Ontario in the winter of 1970-71 when he did a Bank of Montreal tour across Canada.

I also told Rusty how much he was loved in Canada and by Expos fans. There was no Q & A permitted and no photos allowed. All understandable. He died several weeks later.

"It was the dialysis that killed him," Staub's brother Chuck said to me.

A month after Staub died, his sister-in-law Sam Staub was having

Image supplied by Staub family

drinks at Connelly's Pub in Manhattan with Rusty's two sisters Sue Tully and Sally Johnston. There had been a Celebration of Life for Rusty at St. Patrick's Cathedral and the pub was packed for the party, especially with firemen and policemen. It wasn't surprising that the firemen and the cops were there en masse.

They had grown to respect Staub so much for his philanthropy and work in donating money through the Rusty Staub Foundation and his New York Police and Fire Widows and Children Benefit Fund in honour of those firemen and policemen, who had lost their lives as first responders killed in the line of duty in the tragedy surrounding 9/11/2001.

Sam went over to talk to two people, who were standing by themselves at the bar.

"How are you connected to Rusty?" Sam asked. "The lady replied: 'My husband was in the twin towers.' The man replied, 'My wife was in the twin towers.' Then those two people asked Sam, 'How are you connected to Rusty?' And she replied, 'I'm his sister-in-law.'"

Image supplied by Staub family

Rusty Staub in an undated photo

Sam proceeded to tell the strangers that Rusty had raised millions of dollars for the families of the firefighters and policemen, who lost their lives. The strangers were so immensely full of gratitude when Sam gave them the news about Rusty.

While Rusty was alive, Sam had approached him one time for a memento T-shirt of his playing days with the Expos, Mets, Rangers and Tigers. But Rusty thought beyond baseball. He gave Sam a T-shirt that read Gone But Not Forgotten 9/11/01 and in between the words were images of the fire department and police department.

"It was the coolest T-shirt," Sam told me.

Staub was known as Rusty and not by his given names. You wondered about the story behind Rusty when he entered the world in New Orleans, Louisiana on April 1, 1944? He was supposed to be called Danny.

"When Rusty was born, the nurse said, 'I'm going to bring you little Rusty. Here's little Rusty,'" his brother Chuck related. Staub had red hair, thus the moniker Rusty.

"Rusty and I were very close all the way through in every way, shape or form. We grew up together. I was a year and a half older," Chuck said. "He was a first baseman and outfielder. I was a catcher. They tried to make a pitcher out of Rusty because he threw so hard.

"My father Raymond took us everywhere. He was a school teacher and coach. He'd take us to a park every day. He'd stand on the pitcher's mound and Rusty and I would stand at the back wall. My father would throw us tennis balls. Our job was to run and get the balls where they were hit. My father wanted us to learn and do things right."

Rusty and Chuck were altar boys as they grew up in the strong Roman Catholic faith. As time went on, another inspirational figure came along. It was Firmin Simms, now 91, who saw the two brothers play in a softball game. He was a Chicago Cubs scout and coordinator of baseball for the New Orleans recreation department.

> **Reflections by Rusty Staub**
>
> Just what legacy do you want to leave in this world? You alone can determine that. The legacy you leave will be all you have once you are gone.
>
> We will all be judged the same. It will not be what you got out of life, but by what you have given back.
>
> It is not about how much wealth you have accumulated, but more how you earned and shared it. Avoid at all cost unjust and dishonest shortcuts to success. What will be the long-term consequences of your actions and decisions.
>
> Always be aware of the need of others especially the young and the elderly. Your life and your legacy will be all the better for it.

"He was always a very talented ballplayer," Simms said. He could hit a ball. He had a great love for the game. At the playground, he used to hit the ball over the screen a lot.

"Oh yeah, he was a real good athlete from high school right through professional. He was a good, solid, young man.

"When Rusty was eight or nine years old, I had one of my coaches, Gene Faust, call me one time, and said he had bad news. He said he had hit Rusty in the nose with a pitch at practice. But he got up and started hitting the ball again."

What was even more shocking to Staub and Simms was the news years later that Faust died of a heart attack at the young age of 14. Yes, 14.

In 1960, the Staub brothers played on a New Orleans American Legion Jesuit High School team that won the U.S. Little World Series national championship in Hastings, Nebraska where Kool-Aid was invent-

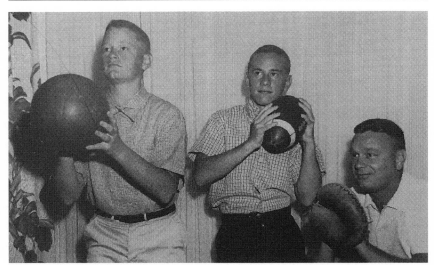

Image supplied by Staub family

Rusty Staub, left, his brother Chuck and their father Raymond

ed in 1927.

Staub and fellow Expos alumnus Dave McNally were opponents in the tournament. McNally suited up for the team from Helena, Montana and was later voted Montana Athlete of the Century. During an amazing 1960 season, McNally was 18-1. But against the Staubs and Jesuit High School, he was ordinary.

Staub would eventually begin his major-league career with the Astros and then made his way to the Expos in a delayed transaction that took a few months to complete.

"The first memory of Rusty was if he would play with us or not," recalled Expos founding owner Charles Bronfman.

Bronfman said Staub's acquisition from the Astros was up in the air but it didn't deter president John McHale, who "engineered" a photo to be taken at spring training in West Palm Beach. It was a stunt dreamed up to convince Major League Baseball that Staub "really meant" something to the Expos in their inaugural season.

"That picture went around the baseball world," Bronfman said in an interview.

In the photo were Staub, wearing Expos No. 10, and McHale, general manager Jim Fanning, Bronfman and commissioner Bowie Kuhn.

A short time later, Kuhn said the Staub trade would stand.

"Rusty was the heart and soul of the Expos," Bronfman said. "He was our first superstar, a cut above everybody else. He always was a very, very decent person, a humanitarian. I was very fond of him. He was a genuine human being. He had two foundations. He gave of himself. He was unique, a very decent character."

Don Bosch played with Staub while with the Expos and shared this story with me: "I was playing centre field and he was in right. There was a ball hit between the two of us and he was pissed off because I caught it. I told him, 'This is my responsibility. I'm the centre fielder.' He had a strong ego because he was a great hitter."

Staub was traded to the Mets following the 1971 season for Ken Singleton, Mike Jorgensen and Tim Foli but eight years later, Le Grand Orange made his way back to Montreal in a trade with the Tigers.

"Montreal was a place he enjoyed very much," Chuck Staub said. "He'd get approached by kids for signings and he never could understand what they were saying so he took French lessons."

Perhaps it's not common knowledge but Staub, fellow Expos alumnus Gary Carter and Mets legend Keith Hernandez were this-close. "Very close", according to Chuck Staub.

Carter had already been in the West Palm Beach area since the 1970s so he arranged for Staub and Hernandez to purchase condos there so they could see each other more often, especially during the winter months.

Prior to dying, Staub had pre-arranged with point men that memorial services or celebrations of life – to be paid on his dime – should be held in New Orleans, where he was born and raised; Houston, where he started his big-league career; West Palm Beach, where he had a winter home; New York City, where he played for the Mets and where he permanently lived for years; and Napa, Calif., where he spent a lot of times with wine connoisseurs and held wine auctions.

Left out of services was Montreal. Same with Shannon, Ireland, where he visited often.

In many of those locales, there wasn't a dry eye when Take Me Out To The Ball Game was played. In some locales, hot dogs and crackerjack were sold. The Jesuit high school band marched into the New Orleans reception.

In New Orleans, Staub had for years spent anonymous time with a priest in one of the churches where he frequently attended masses as a very devout Roman Catholic. When Staub died, the priest told his family that he didn't know who Staub was until he got sick because when they would talk, Staub would never let on who he was because the priest noticed that Staub was "very, very humble."

Staub made it be known he didn't want any eulogies in the five cities marked for services, although some family members and priests did say something. One of the pastors said, "He may not have gotten into the Hall of Fame in Cooperstown but he got into heaven on the first ballot."

When I asked Sally about Rusty being an oversized man and if had something to do with happened in the late stages of his life, she replied, "He put on a lot of weight after 9/11."

What happened on Sept. 11, 2001 rocked and shocked many people around the world, including Staub. Sally Johnston said her brother would never talk about 9/11 but Staub sprung into action. When the twin towers were hit by planes and when he heard the sirens, Staub left his condo near Wall St. and walked the 100 yards it took to get to the awful scene. Somebody told him to go back home and stay there.

But that's when his foundation really sprung into action. For 16 years, that foundation had already been supporting the widows/widowers of police officers and fire officials lost in the line of duty. Prior to 9/11, Staub's foundation was supporting about 200 families but when the planes hit, that number surged to about 800. Nowadays, the figure is around 600.

Years earlier, Staub had found out about a police officer in New York City, whose life was snuffed out in the line of duty. And long before that, his sister's uncle had died in the line of duty in New Orleans. Those deaths were calling cards for Staub to start his foundation. Giving back became his motto, his blueprint, his platform.

The Rusty Staub Foundation devoted much of its funds to the hungry in New York and Staub was the main event behind it, the driving force. At his wish, his own foundation was dissolved when he died. The larger foundation had eclipsed the other one in importance. At its 34th annual fund-raiser in late 2019, the foundation raised a record $4.5-million, boosting the overall sum to $150-million so far, a jaw-dropping figure.

"The foundation grew dramatically in the aftermath of 9/11," said Stephen Dannhauser, who has been the president and CEO of Staub's foundation for many years. "As soon as someone dies in the line of duty and is certified with us, the widow and the children get $25,000 right away and then they receive an annual stipend. We've made major contributions to our historical widows and widowers. When Rusty died, our donor base was totally energized to keep this foundation going.

"A lot of foundations make one-time contributions but we go beyond that and give an annual stipend thereafter. My wife and I attended our first dinner in 1985, introduced by a friend of mine. Rusty knew of me and asked me whether I could get involved. We got to know each other a lot. I was an honouree at the gala in 1996 and became the president of the foundation. Rusty stepped down and became known as the founder and chairman emeritus. He became very close friends with my family, my wife and sons. He was a very much loved man, a really good man, an extraordinary man. He wanted to make a difference in the world. He was a man who really gave back.

"In the first seven or eight months after 9/11, Rusty was basically displaced near the site (of the planes crashing) from early morning until evening, camped out in a conference room."

Two years prior to his death, Staub almost died aboard a plane headed for New York from Ireland when he was found unconscious and slumped over in his seat. He was brought back to life. There was a telling sign that people noticed, something that has not been told in public until now.

"If not for a glass of wine in his hand, they thought he was asleep," Sally Johnston told the author. "There was a person, a female doctor beside him when he slumped. She knew something was wrong. Ironically, a fireman saw him and put him on the floor right out over the ocean. The plane turned around and got him to a hospital. Rusty said he was on borrowed time."

Borrowed time until the early months of 2018. He checked himself into hospital in West Palm that January, figuring he had the flu. The medical staff thought the same thing, realizing there was a flu epidemic catching on in that period of time. He checked himself out for therapy.

Later, it was determined he had lung problems. He checked himself back into hospital.

"They shut his kidneys down and put him on dialysis," his sister said. "He was functioning with dialysis every other day. That year, on Easter Sunday, I said I was coming. He didn't know I was there. He couldn't speak at that point. The last person he talked with was Keith Hernandez. He was very close to Keith. Rusty grabbed my hand and I told him two baseball stories, one about Don Drysdale.

"The other story was about when he was in senior high school. A hitter would get a chicken dinner if you hit a home run over the short right-field fence in New Orleans. Many times, Rusty would be intentionally walked. Behind home plate was a pitcher (Joe Galliano) from another team, who razzed Rusty the whole game, saying Rusty would never hit a home run off of him and he'd never give Rusty an intentional walk.

"So they met up in a game one time at another ballpark where they had a high fence in centre field so home runs wouldn't go into the houses. So Rusty goes up to bat. Strike one and the crowd goes crazy. Strike two and the crowd is really going crazy. Then Rusty hits the third pitch out of the park."

At an appropriate time as he got close to home plate after his trot around the bases, Staub had a few words with Galliano.

Often, Sally would go to many of Rusty's games. Rusty's mother didn't attend games because it rendered her too nervous. Their father requested that Sally give him frequent updates by phone about his son's games. Sally would keep a stash of nickels on hand and after every inning, she would call her dad. Odd but true.

So talented was Staub that he was captain of both the basketball and baseball teams at Jesuit high school. In 1956, he took his playground recreational team to the national basketball championship in Atlantic City, New Jersey.

"It was his first time out of the city of New Orleans," his sister said. "He was known more for baseball. He wasn't going to play basketball in college. The pros (Astros) came in and signed him right out of high school."

Staub made it to the big leagues with Houston in 1964 and enjoyed great success before the complicated trade made between the Astros and the Expos in January, 1969.

"Initially, he was in shock," his sister of the trade to Montreal. "He thought he would be playing in Houston for a long time. But he was ready. There was something that held up the trade and Houston wanted Rusty back but Rusty said, 'I don't want to go back. You've traded me. I'm going to Montreal.' He embraced himself with the people in Montreal. He learned five years of French, he took Berlitz classes. He took French in high school in New Orleans."

Sally said Rusty had a "myriad of girlfriends" in his lifetime but was a lifelong bachelor. She said he dated a wonderful lady Gyslain in New York. I know of at least one another one, Helene Millas, who worked at the Bank of Montreal in Montreal.

Sally was aware of a story written by Stu Cowan of the Montreal Gazette, who interviewed another one of his gal pals, after his death. Her name was Candice Laflamme, who was working in an Expos boutique in the Dominion Square complex where Expos executives had their offices.

Image supplied by Staub family
Rusty Staub as a teenager

Sally said her brother was complex. Isn't everyone complex at one time or another? Don't we all have ups and downs in our lives? It was surprising to hear that Staub got cute with employees and volunteers at the Canadian Baseball Hall of Fame on his induction weekend in June, 2012.

"Rusty was one of these people who hated flying. He was a white knuckler but he had to be on a plane all the time," Sally Johnston said. "He travelled lightly. "I went to his condo after he died and cleaned out his place."

A professional organizer as she calls herself or as her email address suggests Clutter Clearer, she saw that he had put together his own Rusty's Reflections about how people should conduct themselves.

"One time, I visited him in Montreal when he was playing there," Johnston said. "He was in a duplex. He'd be going to the ballpark early. I'd organize his home, suits and clothes, shirts and ties. He came home and said, 'What did you do? Sally, I put everything together because I'm colour blind.' I didn't know he was colour blind. Another time, I went and arranged all of this clothes alphabetically and he went ballistic. He'd leave dishes for me to clean. There were wine glasses all over the place."

4

Saving the day

Some 52 years ago when he gave a speech to members of the Canadian Club in Montreal, Charles Bronfman laid out the heart-break that almost resulted in the 1968 dissolution of Montreal's new Major League Baseball franchise in the National League.

In a 4x6 souvenir booklet containing that dramatic speech given to me by Peggy Bougie of Beaconsfield, Quebec, Bronfman told the club members of the despair he faced in saving the franchise from heading to somewhere below the border.

"For many of the citizens of the City of Montreal, the Province of Quebec and, indeed of Canada, the trauma surrounding the establishment of the Major League Baseball franchise last summer was almost unbearable," Bronfman said in his opening remarks.

In May of 1968, with the help of city councillor Gerry Snyder, Montreal was awarded the franchise but much work was needed over the course of three hectic months to get the project off the ground.

"A feeling of general elation at the announcement of the awarding of the franchise on May 27 deteriorated to complete dejection and it appeared that for lack of suitable playing facilities, loss of sponsors and lack of time, that this franchise would have to be abdicated," Bronfman said. "This on-again, off-again situation was finally resolved at an emotionally charged press conference."

As Bronfman said in his address, "At 4:35 p.m. on Aug. 14, 1968 at the Windsor Hotel in Montreal, Mr. Warren Giles, President of the National league of Professional Baseball Clubs, made the following simple announcement: "Montreal is now a fully-fledged member of the National League."

Bronfman, without bragging, had saved the franchise from going elsewhere by stepping up to provide the major financial support needed to be a major shareholder in the team.

"I am here – not simply as a fan who is enthusiastic about the prospects for Major League Baseball in Canada – but as a businessman, who is only beginning to fully appreciate the economic implications of this move for our city and our country," Bronfman told the Canadian Club.

Denis Brodeur photo/Lesley Taylor collection

Expos majority owner Charles Bronfman

"The type of partnership that exists in this project hopefully is a forerunner of future undertakings in Montreal. The Beaudry brothers, Lorne Webster, Hugh Hallward, Syd Maislin, John Newman, John McHale and I represent a broad spectrum which thus far has become molded into an understanding, action-taking unit."

As he continued his speech, he talked about the impact the Expos would have on the rest of Canada.

"Through our participation in Major League Baseball, young men from all over Canada will be encouraged to think in terms of careers in professional baseball," Bronfman said. "There have been some great Canadian players in the past and there are some today, most notably the great pitcher, Ferguson Jenkins.

"Perhaps our most important contribution is that of our management team itself. As you know, our president and partner John McHale has recently turned down the opportunity of being Commissioner of Baseball to remain here. It is a continuing and great pleasure for us to be associated with John McHale. He is not only an outstanding executive but a very fine human being.

"It is of great interest to note that Montreal, the city that was chosen to break the infamous colour line in Organized Baseball, was also chosen as the first city in the world outside the United States to have a franchise in Major League Baseball. There is no doubt that the outstanding success of Expo '67 had much to do with our selection," Bronfman said.

"On April 8, 1969 at Shea Stadium in New York City, two teams will take the field. After the Star Spangled Banner, fifty thousand Americans will remain standing as for the first time in the history of Major League Baseball, the band strikes up O Canada and our national flag is proudly unfurled. That will be a great day for all of us," Bronfman said in concluding his speech.

For that, he got a standing ovation.

The Economics
of Major League Baseball

An Address to
The Canadian Club Montreal
by
Charles R. Bronfman
President of the House of Seagram
and
Chairman, Montreal Baseball Club Ltd.
February 3rd, 1969

Image supplied by Peggy Bougie
Front cover of booklet of Bronfman's speech

5

Oldest living Expos' player

"Of all time, you mean?" asked the man on the other end of the phone line.

"Yes, you're the oldest living, former Expos' player going back to when they started in 1969," I told him.

"Huh," the man said, very much appreciative but a little disbelieving of what he was hearing.

On April 3, 1969, one of the greatest relief pitchers in baseball history with the Pittsburgh Pirates was released by the Detroit Tigers late in spring training so he went home to North Versailles, Pa.

Not long after he got home to go golf and take up carpentry work, he went to New York City for a visit. While he was there, Elroy Face received a phone call from Pittsburgh writer and close friend Charley Feeney.

Face and Feeney had struck up a trusting friendship that started in 1966 when Feeney became a beat writer covering Face and the Pirates for the Post-Gazette. It was a friendship that lasted until Feeney died in 2014. Both lived in North Versailles about a 20-minute drive from Pittsburgh.

So on the line to New York from Pittsburgh was story-breaking Feeney, who had been kept aware of Face's whereabouts because of his friendship with the player. The Pirates and Expos didn't know where Face was but Feeney knew.

Feeney had the scoop in the paper that Montreal was looking for Face and at the same time, Feeney was telling Face that Expos manager Gene Mauch was interested in working him out at Forbes Field.

As soon as he could, Face was on a plane back to Pittsburgh. The date, as reported by baseball-reference.com in a story done years ago, was April 27.

"I came into the ball park and threw for Mauch," Face recalled. "I threw just a few pitches in the bullpen and he said, 'I can use you in my bullpen.' I was happy to go with Montreal. It still kept me in baseball. It was a new experience, a new ball club."

So for what he recalled was a salary of about $20,000, Face suited

Good and bad of Wills

In a story Montreal Gazette whiz writer Ted Blackman had published the day after the Major League Baseball expansion draft in Montreal Oct. 14, 1968, he mentioned that pitcher Mudcat Grant and shortstop Maury Wills were musical wizards of some notoriety.

"Grant has played here before – not at the ballpark, but at the Esquire Show Bar as a singer after the 1965 World Series in which he starred," Blackman wrote. "The Expos may not win but with ukelele-playing Wills on the squad, they have a terrific twosome."

In the same story, Blackman referred to Wills as a "troublesome" Pirate, who was exposed by Pittsburgh in the expansion draft. Mauch advised Blackman that he didn't think he would have problems with his new but old shortstop. Blackman also wrote that Wills, a star player even though he was getting up in age, would help boost ticket sales.

"I fancy myself as a man who can read players, understand their motivation. I know they have pride and want to play here," Mauch told Blackman. "Believe me, we relied solely on ability with no regard to box-office attraction or position."

Pretty ironic though that Wills turned out to be someone who apparently wasn't enamoured with Montreal and wanted out of town. Ironic, too, that him and Blackman would get into a fight, apparently on a team bus when Wills supposedly slapped Blackman on the face. Blackman wasn't exactly a pussy. He could be an irritant as much as anyone else.

The 1969 season was barely two months old when the Expos traded Maurice Morning Wills back to his first team, the Dodgers. Wills had hit an un-Wills like .222 with Montreal with eight RBI and 15 stolen bases. With the Dodgers, he hit .297 and was 11th in MVP voting on the season. Go figure.

In no uncertain terms, Expos majority owner Charles Bronfman cut to the chase in lambasting Wills in his book Distilled, which was released in 2017.

Yet, teammate Claude Raymond had nothing but admiration for his 1969 teammate.

"As far as I am concerned Maury Wills loved Montreal," Raymond told me. "I remember him being at my pre-wedding party at the restaurant La Catalogne in old Montreal in the winter of 1968 and 1969."

up with uniform No. 14, not the 26 he wore for close to 15 seasons for the Pirates but a digit the Expos gave him because Bill Stoneman was already wearing 26.

"14 was a favourite number of the franchise," Face remembered. "Good things happened, everything seem to happen on the 14th. It was considered their good luck charm. They thought it was a special number, a lucky one. I think they got the okay to become a major-league team on the 14th."

As we looked back and researched, Face was right on. After Charles

Bronfman agreed to pony up and take financial control of Montreal's team, the franchise officially became a member of the National League on Aug. 14, 1968.

And on a further note, the Expos participated in their first expansion draft on Oct. 14, 1968. So how's that for trivia?

According to retrosheet.org, Face's first appearance with the Expos was April 29 and his first win came May 1 against the Mets when he entered the game in the seventh inning to work two and a third innings after taking over from Stoneman.

There was even one game where Face came on in relief in the very first inning and he did his job, getting the Expos out of a bases-loaded jam. Next thing you know, Mauch lifted him for a pinch hitter. This was an anecdote Face volunteered to tell.

"Know what I just did?" Mauch said to Face, as Face told the story. "You're as good to me saving a game in the first inning as you are late in the game."

Face went on to post a 4-2 record in 44 games for the Expos, posted a 3.94 ERA in 59.1 innings and saved five

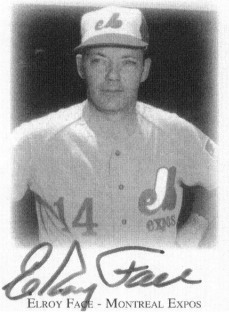

ELROY FACE - MONTREAL EXPOS
Author's collection

games before he got some bad news on what was believed to be Aug. 20, although the exact date isn't known for sure. What is known by checking baseball-reference.com is that Face's last game with the Expos and in the majors was Aug. 15, which ironically was the date of teammate Dick Radatz's last game with Montreal.

By looking at Retrosheet again, it was noted that Face gave up solo homers to Andy Kosko and Bill Sudakis of the Dodgers in two innings of work in that last game Montreal lost 9-2.

"I'll tell you what happened," Face told this writer. "Mauch called me into his office. I was 41 years old, the oldest player on the club. Mauch said they wanted to bring young pitchers up to look at.

"Mauch asked me if I wanted to retire or be released. I said I wanted to be released. If I retired, I would get no money. By being released, they would have to pay me until the end of the season.

"It was fine with me. I was old. I wasn't 30 or 35 years old. I was on my way down. I had 16 years in the big leagues. I figured these kids got to get up here to the big leagues some time."

So Face headed back home to North Versailles, took up carpentry for the remainder of the year and spent more time golfing. The following season, he hooked up briefly with the Triple-A Hawaii Islanders. Then, he hung up his spikes to be a carpenter full-time, retiring as a maintenance foreman from the now-defunct Mayview State Hospital near Bridgeville, Pa.

It just so happened that the year Face left the Expos and the majors was the year the save was officially approved as a statistic but he had been a relief gem of his era for years prior to that.

Hartman was the man

He's believed to be the first draft pick to ever sign a contract with the Expos. His name is Dave Hartman, a native of Austin, Minnesota where Moose Skowron plied his trade for several years in his early days as a professional before going with the New York Yankees.

Hartman actually never played for the Expos nor did he play in the majors but he did duty in Double-A ball for the Expos' farm team in Quebec City called the Carnavals in 1971 when he went 6-10.

Hartman was the 11th overall pick in the amateur draft on June 2, 1968 and somehow, he was the first to ink a contract with general manager Jim Fanning. He pitched most of the 1969 season for the Single-A West Palm Beach Expos.

I made efforts to track him down without any luck. He's believed to be living in Doral, Florida.

"My best memory of Elroy is that he was the best reliever in baseball at the time and he should be in the Hall of Fame because for 10-15 years, he was the best in baseball," said 1969 teammate and Quebec native Claude Raymond. "To me, he was the best relief pitcher I met or saw.

"He had the best forkball I saw in those days. I remember that year before I got to the Expos, I was with Atlanta and Elroy gave up a two-run homer to Tito Francona in the 12th inning on May 16. I got the win.

"Before I got to the Expos, I'd run into Elroy a couple of times and I'd ask him how he threw the forkball. The forkball became a good tool for me. I didn't use it a lot but in key situations. That was my change-up. He had the best forkball in the world. He was such a nice guy, too."

There may be others but with research I conducted, Face, Raymond, Radatz and Lee Smith all recorded their last saves with the Expos. Just another trivia item.

Face is best remembered for his glitzy 18-1 season in 1959 when he won 17 in a row. This all fashioned by a pint-sized, 5-foot-8 pitcher, a self-taught forkballer, who weighed all of about 155 pounds and sometimes only 145 when the sweat and grind of a long season took its toll.

"Everything went my way that year," Face said. "I actually had won 22 in a row. I won the last five games of the previous season. I went 96 games without a loss."

Biggest memory in baseball for Face?

"Probably the 1960 World Series," he said. "I saved three games. It's the only time in baseball history that a player from the losing team in the World Series was voted most valuable player."

Without trying to toot his horn too much, Face thought he should have been the MVP.

"It was a bit disappointing. The winner gets a new Corvette," Face said. "A lot of the writers were from New York so they voted for Bobby Richardson."

Remarkably at age 92, Face has stayed healthy over the years and lives in an apartment on his own in North Versailles. He told me he gets a major-league pension of $2,500 a month and that is supplemented by social security funds, his work pension from the hospital and a state pension.

"Baseball did top up some pension money over the years but they never went back to the 1950s and 1960s," Face said.

But he sounds like a man in his 70s.

"My health is pretty good. I'm taking no medication and I golf three or four times a week," he said. "Nobody believes my age. I have to show them my driver's licence. I don't get many requests for interviews, not too many anymore. People probably think I'm not in good health."

But Face sure is bombarded with a lot of requests for autographs. His mail box is never empty.

"I get three or four requests a day on average," Face said, as a pile of fan mail looked up at him. "On occasion, I get requests for Expos' autographs."

One of those requests came from me and Face said he would send me a card of him in an Expos' uniform with his autograph. I sent him a small cheque to cover the cost of mailing.

"I didn't have an Expos' card from that year but I had 8x10 photos,"

Dynamic Tevans

Fabled Montreal broadcaster and talk-show legend Ted Tevan helped organize the first Expos French language radio crew and his wife Ellie was the first female reporter to cover Major League Baseball in Canada.

Ellie was one of the first women to do sports editorials/commentaries when she plied her trade for Montreal station CFOX and better still, she was the only woman in North America covering MLB on a regular basis. In those days, she faced hardship and discrimination because she was a female.

"She wasn't allowed in the clubhouse so she interviewed the players from the grandstand while the players stood on the field," her son Jay Tevan related.

Face said. "I had a card made up. I had a neighbour, who was a printer and he had them made up. It didn't cost much."

Face's legacy is that he was the pioneer of modern-day relief pitching with the Pirates but his short time with the Expos will never be forgotten.

Peggy Bougie collection

Stoneman also pitched a no-hitter April 17, 1969

Souvenir de la partie
sans point ni coup sûr
de Bill Stoneman
2 octobre 1972

Souvenir
of Bill Stoneman's
No-Hitter
October 2, 1972

Fanning and Hriniak

Jim Fanning was a catcher by trade. So was Walt Hriniak, although he played other positions.

When Fanning managed a minor-league team in Eau Claire, Wisconsin in 1961, one of his players was Hriniak.

Fanning thought so highly of Hriniak that he laid the ground work for Hriniak to be a coach and manager in the minors and majors for the Expos, although it took 10 years.

Hriniak drove in 50 runs for Fanning's Eau Claire Braves but more importantly, Fanning recognized the player's tremendous work ethic. Wouldn't you know it, 10 years later as Expos GM, Fanning signed Hriniak as a free agent on Aug. 24, 1971 and assigned him to the team's Triple-A affiliate in Winnipeg, Man.

Hriniak only played nine games for Winnipeg, batting .304, and Fanning remained impressed. In the 1971-72 off-season, Fanning kept Hriniak on board because he saw coaching and managerial acumen in Hriniak.

In 1972, Fanning assigned Hriniak, 29, as a coach for the Double-A Quebec Carnavals under manager Karl Kuehl. Then when the New York-Pennsylvania League season commenced, Hriniak took over as manager of New York's Jamestown Falcons. Among Hriniak's pupils were Larry Parrish, Jerry White and Gary Roenicke.

Prior to the 1974 season, Fanning announced that Hriniak would be manager of its West Palm Beach affiliate in the Florida State League. But when hitting coach Larry Doby left the Expos, Hriniak was tapped to join the 1974 coaching staff at first base.

Hriniak remained an Expos coach under Mauch through the 1975 season. After Mauch was fired, Hriniak became the hitting coach for the Expos farm team, the Double-A Denver Bears and then manager of the Rookie League Lethbridge (Alberta) Expos. While with Lethbridge, Hriniak served a five-day suspension in July 1976 for "spraying an umpire with saliva", according to a SABR website story written by David E. Shelton.

"Walt was hitting instructor pretty much for the whole organization and he was very good," White recalled.

Taking that Denver hitting job to heart, Hriniak would soon embark on a career that saw him become somewhat of a legend. He mentored many hitters with both the Boston Red Sox and Chicago White Sox. From the Charley Lau school of hitting, Hriniak preached hitting to all fields, among other suggestions. He had some detractors but among those he won over with his ideas were Carl Yastrzemski, Dwight Evans and Frank Thomas.

"Walt was a young manager when I had him at Jamestown," Parrish told me. "He had a lot of energy. He was a hard worker but he was a Mel Didier guy so he had to work hard to work for Mel. He was a disciple of Charley Lau back then. He wound up putting his own twist to it and became a very successful hitting coach."

Roenicke was also a player under Hriniak in Jamestown, remembering Hriniak as a "hard-nosed guy" in what was Roenicke's very first stop in pro ball.

"Years later when I was an Oriole and he was the hitting coach with Boston, we talked hitting some," Roenicke said. "He was from the Charlie Lau hitting philosophy and wanted me to spend a couple of weeks with him hitting. I didn't do that. It probably wouldn't have been good for an Oriole to work with a Red Sox employee."

6

Mayor of Jonesville

Mack Jones was so popular that he had a set of bleachers named after him and he was so popular that he had a way with women.

One social media pundit even suggested that Jones was traded following the 1970 season because he had heard the front office was hearing too many stories about his involvement with women. True or not, we don't know.

On the field, Jones was a special player in the early days of the franchise, not just because of his offensive production but because of historical reference.

"He was the first black player on Montreal's expansion team," said Jones' son Rontae Jones. "It was definitely a great honour, a real honour to have that position. Dad's favourite player growing up was Jackie Robinson. Jackie was definitely a good role model for Dad to look up to."

Dominican-born Manny Mota was the Expos first choice in the 1968 expansion draft, the first man of colour to land with the Expos and Jones, who was born in Atlanta, was the first player of African-American descent. It seemed fitting that Jones would adore Robinson because fans embraced Robinson in 1946 when he played for the Montreal Royals. Some 23 years later, Jones was carrying Robinson's torch as the first black player in the same city at the major-league level.

"My dad was the mayor of Jonesville," his son told me "He just loved the way the people welcomed him. They were very, very nice people. They took him in just like family."

One of those families was the Tevan clan: broadcaster Ted Tevan, his wife Ellie and their son Jay.

On a bad team, Jones was a hit with the Expos. In the Expos first home game at Jarry Park on April 14, 1969, Jones drilled a three-run homer and a two-run triple as the Expos edged the St. Louis Cardinals 8-7 in front of 29,184 fans in a Monday afternoon contest. Jones lays claim to being the first Expos player to hit a home run at Jarry Park.

On top of the crowd of more than 29,000 inside were several hundred fans bundled up outside standing on snowdrifts, trying to get a glimpse of the game. Assembled in the press box and other parts of

Bat boy experience

Before he became a police officer, Mark Bouchard had a rare job many people could only dream of doing, rubbing shoulders with Expos players and staff members.

In short, he was a batboy but he did a lot more than that.

"I spent hours scrubbing shoes. I took balls to the umpires. I met a lot of great players," Bouchard said. "Ron Woods was my favourite. He was a super nice guy. He'd do anything for you. Mack Jones was funny, very easy going, loosey-goosey. Rusty Staub practised his French on us.

"Mike Marshall was tough. He was kind of very intellectual. He liked showing off his muscles. He was kind of stand-offish. Another tough guy was Carl Morton. He was very American. He always wondered why there was an anti-American feeling in Quebec. He'd talk about the Vietnam war, Richard Nixon. He was a bit tough at times. People would roll their eyes when Morton would talk about politics."

Bouchard remembers the time manager Gene Mauch locked the clubhouse after a game, reamed out his players and then, to the shock of everyone in sight paying rapt attention to him, took the vegetable soup canister and threw it on the floor.

"You want soup, here's the fucking soup," said a pissed-off Mauch.

Before becoming a batboy, Bouchard was a vendor at Jarry Park selling popcorn and other stuff but he "hated" the job.

the stadium were about 200 members of the media from Canada and the U.S. who had come to witness the first major-league game ever staged outside of the U.S.

"When I got back to the hotel, I had something like 150 phone calls from the hour of 12 to 6 the next morning," Jones said after the game. "And it was all females. I think I got the record for that."

Left-hander Dan McGinn pitched $5\,{}^{1}/_{3}$ shutout innings in relief of starter Larry Jaster to record the win.

Jones could never duplicate in future seasons what he did in 1969. Following the end of his career, Jones returned to Atlanta and resumed his career in the insurance field. He also resumed coaching youth baseball and football in inner-city parks.

Jones died way too young in Atlanta of complications from stomach cancer at age 65. He was survived by his wife Esther Levon Buggs Hill Jones, daughter Gayle Jones, son Rontae and other relatives.

7

Bateman and his Twitter handle

He's John Bateman's greatest admirer in the world.

Actor Ken Webster, that's who. He's the person behind the @johnny-bateman7 Twitter handle, which has some people fooled and believing Bateman personally is tweeting, except that he has been dead for years. Even I was fooled for a while.

"Bateman's two daughters follow me on Twitter," Webster said.

Webster has been tweeting since March of 2011, dispatching information about many Expos games, especially if Bateman did something of significance. It started as a diary of the 1966-68 Astros and then the Expos from 1969-72 and the '72 Phillies.

Peggy Bougie collection
John Bateman

"Bateman is my favourite player ever," Webster told me. "I was born in Fort Arthur, Tex. and I started following Bateman when I moved to Houston. Rusty Staub is my second favourite player."

Ironically, both Bateman and Staub played for the Expos and Astros. Long before Gary Carter came along to be the Expos franchise catcher, Bateman and fellow Killer Bs John Boccabella and Ron Brand were the toast of Montreal.

"Bateman was an underdog, an overachiever. He hit .230 in high school, wasn't scouted. He played some American Legion ball and became a starting catcher for a major-league team," Webster said, in praise and surprise, maybe shock. "He sent out a bunch of letters and signed a contract tryout in 1962.

"When the Astros were in the pennant race in 1963, Joe Morgan was quoted as saying Bateman was the leader of the team. That was unheard of, a guy like him taking charge of the team."

Denis Brodeur photo/Lesley Taylor collection
John Bateman gets tangled up with former Houston teammate Joe Morgan

Bateman also was hampered by a kidney problem that cropped up after a home-plate collision that left his organ lacerated and put him in hospital for close to 10 days. It was something that caught the Expos front office off-guard.

"This is pretty serious. Oh my gosh," was the Expos reaction, according to Webster.

Because of that problem, Bateman tended to put on weight, making it difficult to contain his largesse.

Bateman was known to hang out with Montreal policemen and when Gene Mauch saw a video of Bateman with the cops, he wasn't happy.

"Bateman was a clubhouse leader," Webster said. "He was a great caller as a catcher, one of the best callers. When Bateman was catching in Philadelphia, Steve Carlton's ERA was 1.60 better than when Bob Boone and Tim McCarver were catching. When John was released in 1972, Carlton was not happy about it."

Bateman also played for Eddie Feigner's The King and His Court softball team as a catcher from 1977-80.

"Bateman was kind of like Dizzy Dean cracking jokes and very funny with the press," Webster said. "He liked to talk thrash in a funny way. He had an unique capacity to insult people without them taking it personally."

8

Roger Savard

Roger Savard was a marketing man's dream, who got things done.

Savard would travel the world to drum up business for Expo 67 which put Montreal on the map.

"He'd pack a suitcase and go to New York, Chicago, Paris, London, the Maritimes, promoting Expo 67," his daughter Peggy Bougie said. "It was his idea to name the Expo 67 pavilions after their countries. He helped set up the German beer garden, he entertained the Queen."

As it turns out, Expo 67 was a barnburner of a success and Savard had a lot to do with it. Prior to that, Savard worked for Quebec's Provincial Transport Enterprises and was responsible for bus service to be extended to Montreal's West island at a time when very few people lived in Dorval and further west.

According to his daughter, Savard named a certain bus company Voyageur. Remember Voyageur, a 48-seater bus that ran mostly between Ottawa and Montreal? I do. Around the same time, Colonial Coach Lines was renamed Voyageur Colonial.

When he was let go by the bus company, Savard got a job, helping to organize Expo 67. From his home in Dorval, Savard, who didn't drive, would head to work by train to the Expo 67 offices at Ile Ste. Helene. He'd leave at 6 in the morning and return home at midnight in a taxi.

So when it was over, a fledgling baseball team in Montreal wanted him to be part of the action. Expos president John McHale knew all about Savard, who was the Expos director of marketing from 1968-1984.

"Everyone knew my father when Expo 67 closed," Bougie said. "John McHale said, 'Who better to promote the Expos than my father?'"

Savard finally got a car and drove to the ballpark, namely Jarry Park. Rarely did his wife Edna and his children see him.

"Sometimes, he'd never come home," Bougie said. "He'd sleep in his office. He was a go-getter, he made the phone calls, planned all of the big events. On weekends, he'd sit in a big chair at our cottage up north and sleep the weekend away."

Savard's life ended up too soon at a very young age. One morning, Savard, 65, told his wife that he wasn't feeling that great so he went to bed and lay down. He died.

Denis Brodeur photo/ Peggy Bougie collection

The late Roger Savard was the Expos group director of sales and marketing from 1969-84. Here he is second from left. To his right is Marc Cloutier, who was the team's director of stadium operations. The lady is Linda Breault, Cloutier's assistant and the man on the right is Ron Piché, one of Cloutier's assistants. The man with the moustache is unknown. Cloutier believes the ceremony in question in this photo had something to do with his birthday. He thinks this photo was taken around 1970.

"He was always a large man and drank a lot," his daughter said. "As children, we rarely had supper with my father. He was a prisoner of war. We used to hear him yelling at night, screaming sometimes. We didn't know how much he had suffered from the war. He was laid to rest in the veterans' cemetery in Beaconsfield."

9

Injuries hurt Foote

Barry Foote was some fine baseball player in college in the late 1960s, so good that the Expos took him No. 3 overall in the first round of the 1970 draft of amateur players on June 4. He was much ballyhooed.

His future manager Gene Mauch called him "The next Johnny Bench." But they sure were big shoes to fill. He just never lived up to all the hype but he enjoyed the run.

"I think I got the most money of anyone who was drafted that year," Foote was telling me. "I was an all-star every year at the minor league level. I was the third pick in the country."

Foote fought hard to get $100,000 out of the Expos but no dice.

"We held out for a long time until the end of June, the first part of July. We talked with Jim Fanning and Mel Didier," Foote recalled. "My father Amby and my mother Sue were with me when I signed. The whole crew was trying to get me to sign. We wanted at least $100,000. We didn't get that. I was a scholarship athlete, a scholastic person. I had planned to go to college at North Carolina State. That was my backup plan."

At spring training in 1971, Foote was working out when another prospect Bill Seagraves saw him getting down on himself.

"One day as I headed to a backfield for some workouts, I ran into this player, a big strapping guy with freckles from Lumberton, North Carolina," Seagraves said. "He had been signed for $90,000 And back then, it was a lot of money. Barry Foote started crying like a baby saying he was playing so bad that he thought the Expos were going to release him. He had red hair and freckles. He was crying like a baby. We were laughing and he didn't like it when we were laughing. We told him, 'They just gave you a bunch of money.'"

Point of all this was that Foote was going nowhere and that he wasn't going to be released.

"He was putting too much pressure on himself," Seagraves said.

While playing for the Expos' minor league affiliate, the Quebec Carnavals in 1972, Foote was selected as the catcher for the Eastern League All-Star team. He made his major league debut with the Expos on Sept.

14, 1973. He was a mere 21.

Foote replaced John Boccabella as the Expos catcher in 1974, collecting 11 home runs, 60 runs batted in, a .414 slugging percentage and a league-leading 12 sacrifice flies in 125 games. He also led National League catchers with 83 assists. Foote was named to the 1974 Topps All-Star Rookie Team.

"I certainly had a good year," Foote said.

For the 1975 season, Foote was anointed the head catcher by the Expos and a fellow by the name of Gary Carter was dispatched to the outfield.

Foote got hurt, Mauch was fired and Karl Kuehl came in to manage in 1976, a disaster.

"The Expos made a mistake in getting rid of Mauch," Foote said. "I never heard the reasons why."

To add to his woes, Foote ran into knee and back problems which stymied his career.

"I had chronic bad problems that really hurt my career. I had issues with my back," Foote said.

"Until he signed. For someone from a population of 5,000, coming to Montreal to join the big-league team was quite an experience. Looking back, my biggest memory is the culture shock when I ended up in Montreal. It really was cosmopolitan in the 1970s more than it is now. Fashion wise, it was the cutting edge of fashion. It was a great cultural growth period for me then."

Foote is president and CEO of Pura Aqua Solution.

Coco robbed of ROY award

Most people don't know him as Jose Laboy but they sure do know him as Coco. One day when he was just a baby in Puerto Rico, Laboy was called Coco by a very good friend of his mother.

"I don't remember the person's name but I was called Coco, Coco, Coco as in coconut. You are like a coconut," the 1969 Expos hero was telling me on the phone.

The name has stuck to this day.

"I will always remember Bill Stoneman, Rusty Staub, Mack Jones, Bobby Wine. Those guys were friends and helped me a lot," Laboy said.

Laboy's legacy is his dream season of 1969 in the Expos inaugural season when he hit 18 homers and drove in a team-high 83 runs, establishing himself as a fan favourite. He won't forget that three-run homer against Mets Canadian-born reliever Ron Taylor as the Expos prevailed 11-10 in Montreal's very first franchise game.

What he did in 1969 resulted in him finishing second in Rookie of the Year voting. It was a travesty because he did much more than winner Ted Sizemore of the Los Angeles Dodgers. Was this discrimation against Montreal by the U.S. writers? Sure sounds mystifying.

Sizemore, a singles hitter at best, hit four homers, drove in 46 runs and batted .271. How could he have won top honours? Hrrrmph.

Laboy tailed off in 1970 with five homers and 53 RBI and then he was reduced to part-time status with the Expos from 1971-73. He couldn't master the curveball but his Expos legacy remains in excellent standing.

10

Case of two Taylors

Everyone knows about Dave Van Horne's voice and tenure with the Expos but do you remember Russ Taylor?

Quietly forgotten, Taylor actually became a member of the Expos broadcast team before Van Horne got the call to be the principal play-by-play man.

"What I heard recently was that my dad was hired on by the Expos before they hired Dave," said Taylor's daughter Lesley Taylor. "Dave Van Horne talked about how my dad took him under his wing and introduced him to Montreal and Canada.

"Everybody was happy in the Montreal media that my dad got the gig. People were worried that it was going to be an American."

Taylor was born in 1926 in Montreal and began his career in radio as a engineer in the early 1950s. He would help announcers get set up properly with audio, the underdog in the broadcast booth. He slowly worked his way up through the ranks. He learned on the job.

One of his early gigs was broadcasting the Little World Series in Williamsport, Penn. and he went on to cover the Montreal Royals Triple-A team.

"My dad was very connected, very central to the sports world in Montreal, not just in baseball but in sports," his daughter said. "He had a very strong background."

Van Horne was quick to praise Taylor for helping him adjust to his new and exciting role as Expos broadcaster, confirming that Taylor had been hired before he was signed by president John McHale.

"No question about that," Van Horne said. "Russ was actually hired in March of 1969 prior to my hiring. I was hired several weeks after him. We had never met and I went from the station in Richmond, Virginia to Tampa St. Pete's. We were broadcasting a couple of exhibition games at Al Lang Field. We formed a bond right away because we loved the game. He was a reporter covering the Montreal Royals and I was close to the International league with the Richmond Braves. We had that in common. We hit it off right away.

"Russ was gregarious and fun to be around. It was an expansion team, a dream come through. We were excited about the opportunity

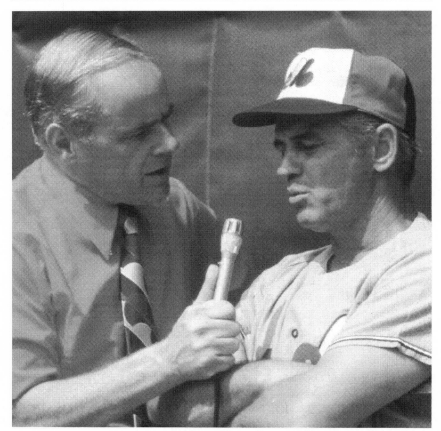

Denis Brodeur photo/Lesley Taylor collection

Russ Taylor interviews Expos manager Gene Mauch

after three seasons of minor-league ball. John McHale wanted an American broadcaster to work with Russ. So Russ was the one who filled me in on the baseball history in Montreal and the province of Quebec. He brought me up to date on that. But it went beyond that, he filled me in on the political scene in Montreal and throughout Canada. What I lacked in knowledge of Canada from a political standpoint, he made me feel comfortable. He was a terrific teacher in all aspects. Of course, I was introduced to the finest pubs and eateries in Montreal."

Because of his knowledge about Montreal, Taylor is credited with being a savior of sorts when Montreal's new baseball franchise was diligently searching for a place to play home games. It was Taylor, who suggested to visiting National League president Chub Feeney and other officials that Jarry Park be used.

"The Expos didn't have a stadium and Dad said, 'I think this would work.'"

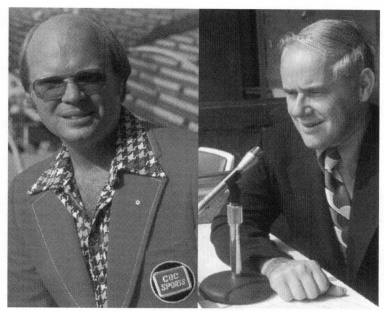

Denis Brodeur photos/Lesley Taylor collection
Dave Van Horne, left, and Russ Taylor were broadcast partners

As Van Horne recalled, "Absolutely, it was Russ who suggested to the powers-that-be that Jarry Park, when all else was failing, was available. Russ said the ballpark in the southwest corner of Jarry Park might be available and that they should have a look."

As Van Horne recalled, Duke Snider just did TV with him from 1973 to 1976, joined the radio booth in 1977 while Taylor became Director of Broadcasting and did radio games when Van Horne was on TV. The late Tom Cheek, who would later became a stellar announcer with the Blue Jays starting in 1977 and doing 4,306 consecutive games at one point, broadcast games with Taylor from 1974-76 when Van Horne was doing TV.

"On Aug. 10, 1977, we were in Philadelphia for a doubleheader. It turned out to be one of the longest in terms of time," Van Horne said. "The doubleheader started at 5:20 p.m. and ended at 3:23 a.m. Duke and I did TV for the first game, and up to 11 p.m. for the second game when CBC pulled the plug. Then it was back to radio for the duration in relief of Russ.

"When it ended, I asked Russ what he did to pass the time when not on the air that night and he said, 'I sampled every flavor of ice cream available in the press room!'"

Eight days later, the Expos fraternity was dealt a severe blow when Taylor died suddenly of a heart attack at home while he sat in a chair reading a newspaper.

"He died on his birthday at the age of 51," his daughter Lesley said. "He was young. He wasn't old but he was an old 51. He looked a lot older than he actually was. It was still a shock. My mom (Pamela) was several years younger in her late 30s. My dad was an Irishman and liked to drink. He was a little heavier and had the family history of men in his family who had died earlier of heart attacks."

Gallivan stuck to hockey

Legendary Montreal Canadiens announcer Danny Gallivan was approached by the Expos to see if he was interested in spot duty behind the microphone.

"Russ Taylor offered him the job," Dave Van Horne said. "Danny was a great encyclopedia with great experience. Russ didn't have to sell Danny. Russ wanted to incorporate Danny into the role but Danny decided he didn't want to tarnish his reputation as a hockey broadcaster."

Taylor's daughter Lesley said her father discovered Gallivan while he was in Halifax and convinced him to come to Montreal

Gallivan knew his baseball because he was a pitcher on the St. Theresa's parish team from Sydney, Nova Scotia that won the Maritime Intermediate Baseball Championship in 1937. Gallivan started the deciding game against the Pugwash Maple Leafs in the best-of-three series and pitched a three-hit gem while striking out 11 batters.

In 1938, Gallivan was invited to a New York Giants training camp as a pitcher, but an early injury to his arm ended any thoughts of a big-league career.

Whatever the case, Van Horne was shocked that morning to find out his partner in the booth was gone.

"It was a terrible time. I remember that morning getting the call. I was in disbelief," Van Horne said. "I remember going to his home right away. I saw Danny Dooner, the owner of the Hunters Horn Irish Pub on Peel Street, who was close to Russ, and I talked with him and I told him I just felt I wasn't going to be able to work that night. But Danny said he felt Russ would have wanted me to work. It wasn't easy without Russ and it was a very, very tough night from a personal standpoint."

Mrs. Taylor, the daughter of Montreal broadcaster Christopher Ellis, was left to care for three children on her own: Lesley, Christopher and Carolyn, while working as a full-time secretary at Lower Canada College, where she was employed for over 20 years. She died at 78 on Aug. 30, 2019.

According to her obituary, "Pam started a widows support group in Notre-Dame-de-Grâce (NDG), was host to many grateful international students who considered her "a mum away from home and had a deep spirituality that guided her through the vicissitudes of life."

Talking of popular announcers, remember Claude Mouton, the public-address announcer, who worked for the Expos from 1969-73? Remember his booming pauses and emphasis of name, especially in announcing John Boccabella's surname? Bocc-a-bel-la. The pronunciation is not lost among avid followers of the Expos.

Mouton's first association with Major League Baseball was as master of ceremonies at a City of Montreal function for visiting club officials during the National League expansion draft meetings held in Montreal in October, 1968. Earlier, he had been an announcer at bicycle races before landing a job as a sports announcer at radio station CKAC.

Mouton would later become the long-time PR director of the Canadiens. One of the lasting impressions, shocking at that, was seeing him outside the Canadiens' dressing room one night before he died of cancer. A sprout of green hair shot out from his head, a sign I heard linked him to cancer. It was a jarring sight. He died at the young age of 63 on March 30, 1993, a little more than a month following Gallivan's passing.

•••••••••••••••••••••••••

And there was Chuck Taylor, who was a pretty solid reliever with the Expos from 1973-76.

After going 4-2 with a 1.77 ERA in 1973 in 20.1 innings, Taylor enjoyed The Season of All Seasons for himself in 1974 as a member of the Expos pitching staff.

Expos postcard photo supplied by Taylor family
Chuck Taylor, his wife Joyce and his son Chris

Taylor appeared in relief 61 times, posting a 6-2 record and a 2.17 ERA in $107\frac{2}{3}$ innings. He ranked ninth in the league in game appearances, fifth in the league in saves with 11 and sixth in the league in games finished with 39.

In 1975-76, Taylor wasn't quite as good but was respectable.

"We loved Montreal. We had good friends there. We were very happy to be there," said Taylor's widow Joyce. "He loved the ballpark. He really liked manager Gene Mauch. He was outstanding. He was a good manager."

46

Taylor never enjoyed another season like that in the big leagues. After Chuck's retirement from baseball, he and Joyce purchased the Western Auto/Ace Hardware Store in Smyrna, Tenn. and operated it for 10 years. At a very young age of 48 in 1991, he suffered a cardiac arrest which resulted in a gradual decline over the years.

"He didn't smoke or drink. He exercised two hours a day. He was out running and collapsed," his widow said. "He went into shock. He was shocked in the ambulance and he came back. After that, he started to get mentally impaired and it got worse."

Taylor died in 2017.

11

A screwball with a screwball

Expos general manager Jim Fanning made a dandy trade to acquire reliever Dr. Mike Marshall, a bull of a pitcher, from the Houston Astros on June 23, 1970.

Then he would trade Marshall a few years later to the Dodgers for Willie Davis, a trade with debatable results.

"I sloughed Marshall off Houston for Don Bosch," Fanning told me decades later.

In other words, Fanning pulled a fast one on the Astros and it was one of the best trades Fanning ever made. It was a steal. Fanning pulled the wool over the eyes of Houston GM Spec Richardson. Granted, up to that point in his career, Marshall had been somewhat ordinary with the Detroit Tigers, Seattle Pilots and Astros.

After a brief stint with the Expos farm team the Winnipeg Whips, Marshall joined the Expos in 1971 under manager Gene Mauch.

"Marshall had fantastic stuff, the best screwball I've seen in my life. You would see him on a cold night at Jarry Park and no sweatshirt, just a short-sleeved uniform top," Fanning said.

And of course, he had those mutton-chop sideburns. He was an eccentric curmudgeon, a grumbling kvetch, a screwball with a Phd but that screwball baffled many a batter.

The screwball, or screwgee, is meant to act as the opposite of a curveball or slider and breaks away from the batter.

Marshall was just astounding on the mound most of his tenure with the Expos. What he did during those three and a half years, you would never see anyone do in the majors nowadays. Relievers pitch what maybe two innings at the most in this modern day and age.

It's too bad long-ago relievers such as Marshall aren't considered for Cooperstown for merely having finished so many games. It was said that Marshall had a rubber arm.

Marshall was so-so in 1970-71 with the Expos but picked it up a notch in 1972-73. In 1972, he went 14-8 with 18 saves and a glittering 1.78 ERA in 116 innings of work. And then in 1973, the stats went like this: 14-8, 2.66 ERA, 31 saves in 179 innings. He was chosen Expos

MVP.

"He was given a new Cadillac at the end of season, but he refused to accept it unless the Expos paid the taxes," former teammate Ken Singleton told me. "I'm not sure how that standoff was settled.

"Mike had an air about him that he was smarter than the rest of us and he probably was. After all, he had a degree in Kinesiology. Nobody else on the team could make that claim. He and I did not have much in common and did not interact all that often. He did his job and I did mine."

I reached out to Marshall in 2019 at the phone number and email I got for him but there was no reply. It would have been neat to take up on his intellect.

"I ran into Gene Mauch, and Gene Mauch was not intimidated by anybody. My intelligence didn't bother him. He loved it," Marshall told a reporter years ago. "He liked to talk to me about strategy, pitching strategy and training strategy.

"These are things that he didn't have in his educational background, but he was insatiable for information. And that just formed a friendship. I mean, imagine a manager asking me questions. He put me in charge of everything that happened: the pitch selection, the defensive alignment, everything."

Marshall was traded to the Dodgers for Willie Davis in December of 1973. The Expos apparently weren't too pleased when they heard that Marshall had criticized several teammates. Not only that, Marshall had apparently threatened to retire to finish off his doctorate degree and he had some strong union comments. So Fanning had some excuses to deal Marshall away.

To his credit, Davis was exceptional in his only season with the Expos, his second-best behind his 93-RBI campaign with Los Angeles in 1970. Davis hit .324, hit 12 homers and drove in 89 runs. Pretty gall-darn good.

But Marshall was exceptional, too, with the Dodgers in one of the most astounding performances by a relief pitcher in MLB history: 208.1 innings pitched, 106 games, 15-12 record, 21 saves, 2.42 ERA.

12

Botched trade

When Rusty Staub was deemed expendable by the Expos prior to the 1972 season, who came in to take his place in right field for the Expos?

A classy player by the name of Ken Singleton, who was the centre piece of this trade April 5, 1972 but also the centre piece of a really bad Expos transaction a few years later.

Singleton stepped in to be everything the Expos wanted in an offensive player when they acquired him, Tim Foli and Mike Jorgensen from the Mets for Staub. The Expos saw that Singleton showed promise when he hit 13 homers and drove in 46 runs for the Mets in 1971. In 1972, Singleton improved to 14 homers and 50 ribbies in his first season with the Expos. It was around that time that Singleton began experiencing itchy skin because of the Expos uniforms.

"I had sensitive skin and in 1972, the Expos wool uniforms caused me to break out in hives," Singleton told me in late 2019. "Not pleasant to say the least. I took Benadryl and that helped some. Side effects were drowsiness so I could not take the pills before a game. That discomfort I would not wish on anyone.

"Change of temperature would also bring out the hives especially on colder game days and then going into a warm clubhouse. The change to double knit uniforms helped me later in the season, but, not completely."

By 1973, Singleton had become explosive, either from the left side or the right side at the plate. He played all 162 games for the first and only time in his prestigious career. He collected a career-high 123 bases on balls, including 13 intentional passes. But his important statistics were the ones most people look at: 23 homers, 103 RBI and 100 runs based on 692 plate appearances. Just a phenomenal season when the Expos made their first stab at making the playoffs in their fifth campaign of operation.

"The 1973 season was my first big season in MLB," Singleton was telling me. "Playing every game did not seem like a big deal at the time. Being a switch hitter, I expected to play every day. I think a few things stand out for me regarding that season. I became the first Expo to drive in 100 (103) runs in a season.

"I led the league in On Base Percentage (.425), although at that time, it wasn't regarded as a major statistic. We did not even bring up that fact in contract negotiations. Nowadays leading the league in OBP is worth millions of dollars. Times have certainly changed."

Dariush Ramezani Illustration
Ken Singleton

They sure have. Singleton's amazing On Base Plus Slugging (OPS) of .904 was equally as astounding. OPS is the chic sabermetric statistic calculated as the sum of a player's on-base percentage and slugging percentage. An OPS of .900 or higher puts the player in the upper echelon of hitters.

"I will say I could have not made such great strides as a player without the help of hitting coach Larry Doby," Singleton said. "He taught me that I could hit for both power and average because I had a good batting eye. That year, a .302 batting average with 23 home runs and 123 walks made me Doby's best student. The team also had a good year. We hung in until the final weeks of the season. A good year for a young franchise."

Indeed.

After a 5-4 win over the St. Louis Cardinals in the first game of a double-header at Jarry Park on Sept. 17, the Expos were tied for first place in the NL East. They lost the second game that day and the next six after that, but weren't mathematically eliminated from the playoffs until the final weekend of the season.

Bob Bailey hit 26 homers. Rookie pitcher Steve Rogers went 10-5 with a 1.54 ERA. Reliever Mike Marshall chalked up 23 saves and threw an almost unheard of 179 innings. Part-time player Boots Day was a major contributor with 13 pinch hits. Part-time catcher Bob Stinson delivered some clutch hits.

"It reminds me of an anecdote," Sylvain Roy of Montreal said in a Facebook near the end of 2019. "I never left a game before the last pitch no matter the score, except one time. In 1973, I attended a game with my mother. She tried to convince me to leave since the fifth inning.

"I finally agreed to leave in the bottom of the ninth with the Expos losing 6-2. I followed the bottom of the ninth on the 83 bus. Bob Stinson, who had difficulties hitting his weight, hit a grand slam to tie it 6-6 and the Expos went on to win 7-6!! I didn't talk to my mother for a month!!"

Some people playfully called the '73 Expos the Jarry Juggernaut. Gene Mauch's crew sure shocked the baseball world that season. To nobody's surprise, Mauch was named NL manager of the year.

"That was a very exciting time," Day told Montreal Gazette sports reporter Ian MacDonald years ago. "We weren't all that great, but we were right in it until the last day."

Photo from 1974 Expos program
Ken Singleton

In 1974, Singleton's offence fell fallow and leaner than what he collected in 1973. He managed only nine homers and drove in 74 runs and batted .276, although he played in 148 games.

On Dec. 4, 1974, the Expos shocked their fans and the clubhouse by trading Singleton and pitcher Mike Torrez to the Orioles for veteran pitcher Dave McNally, Rich Coggins and Bill Kirkpatrick. Like Singleton's explosive season in 1973, this trade was explosive.

"I think management traded Ken because they thought he was making too much money," catcher Barry Foote said in an interview.

When the Orioles and Singleton agreed to a contract for the 1975 season, his salary was $67,000, compared to the $55,000 he earned in 1974. There were also rumblings that the all-white trio of Mauch, general manager Jim Fanning and president John McHale weren't too

Denis Brodeur photo/ Scott Coates collection
Dave McNally pitched briefly for the Expos in 1975 before quitting

thrilled that Singleton had married a white French Canadian gal a few months prior to the '74 season.

"As I look back on the trade to Baltimore after the '74 season, it was the break of my career," Singleton told me. "I got to play for an outstanding team for 10 seasons. A winning record every year. Two World Series, three All Star games and I played with several Hall Of Fame players and for a Hall Of Fame manager (Earl Weaver).

"I've made lifetime friendships with many of my Oriole teammates and we remain very close. A close knit team has a lifelong bond as 1983 World Series champions. If the Expos did not want to pay me, that's their problem. Remember the Expos did not want to pay Rusty Staub and that's how I got to Montreal. It was never a problem in Baltimore. I was in the top 10 percent of players in the game and was paid as such in Baltimore.

"If the Expos traded me because I married a French Canadian woman, that's also their problem," Singleton added. "Nobody is going to tell me how to live my life. Funny story, after I was traded to the Orioles, we played the Expos during spring training in Miami. That night, I hit a home run off David Palmer.

"My wife and young sons were seated just in front of Jim Fanning. Late in the game, my wife said to the boys it was time to leave. They did not want to go and said, 'Dad might hit another home run.' My wife looking directly at Jim Fanning said, 'We have seen what we wanted to see, it's time to go.' By that time I was an All Star player. I think she was rubbing it in."

The Expos thought McNally would give their pitching more credibility. He had won a head-turning 181 games with the Orioles. He was a proven left-hander. He was only 32. In 1974, McNally was 16-10 and in his prime. He was a four-time 20-game winner over consecutive seasons. Remember the Baltimore starting rotation of McNally, Mike Cuellar, Jim Palmer and Pat Dobson?

McNally boasted great success with a two-seam fastball, a four seamer and a breaking ball.

"Damn good lefty pitcher," Expos majority owner Charles Bronfman recalled.

> **NcNally case led to salary explosion**
> Thank Dave McNally in part for helping to pave the way for the modern era's explosion in baseball salaries.
> After quitting the Expos in June of 1975, he helped file a grievance along with Andy Messersmith against Major League Baseball regarding the game's reserve clause which bound players to teams for the life of their playing time in the big leagues.
> When arbitrator Peter Seitz ruled in McNally's favour in the landmark contract case, he became a free agent and modern-day players began to reap the benefits of his efforts.
> When McNally quit the Expos, the Expos kept him on their reserve list while suspending him at the same time.
> "A lot of today's players should know about McNally, Messersmith and Curt Flood to go along with Marvin Miller," McNally's 1975 teammate Larry Parrish told me in October, 2019. "Those guys made the sacrifices that let these guys make millions today."
> Ironically, McNally didn't resume his career despite his win in court. He stuck to selling cars.

McNally shockingly left the team on June 9, sporting an un-McNally like 3-6 record. He started the season 3-0 but lost his next six decisions. His last game was June 8 when the Expos lost 5-2 to the Padres at Jarry Park in the first game of a doubleheader.

McNally pitched six innings in that game and in his last inning of work, he gave up a two-run homer to also-ran unknown Dick Sharon after Dave Winfield singled and was balked to second. McNally's last pitch was a called third strike to Padres pitcher Joe McIntosh. McNally must have muttered, "Dick Sharon?"

McIntosh had beaten his childhood hero and fellow hometown idol and Billings, Montana native.

"He was my boyhood hero ever since he signed with Baltimore when I was 10-years-old," McIntosh told MacDonald.

Poor McNally. He had been taken out of a comfortable routine that pleased him immensely in Baltimore. He had posted an impressive record of 181-113 with the Orioles and he was going to another team, a Canadian city, a new league with unfamiliar hitters.

He also had to hit because the NL has a no-designated hitter rule. In 1973-74, McNally didn't bat because the AL had a DH rule.

McNally had pitched for the Orioles from 1962-74 and was starting all over again. I guess when he saw that there was very little talent with the Expos, he decided to move on.

"Dave was the consummate professional. A real nice guy with the kind of personality you would expect of someone from Montana," batterymate Barry Foote told the author. "I think after his success in Baltimore, he wasn't too interested in playing for what was an expansion team earlier. Plus, he wasn't throwing that good for us at the time he left. He probably didn't want to go through a whole year in a different country while he was struggling."

So the day after McNally was beaten by McIntosh as the Expos prepared to open a three-city trip to California, he told McHale that he was quitting. He apparently hadn't told any of his teammates about his plans.

Research by this writer at the Toronto Reference Library of Montreal Gazette microfilm showed that McNally didn't dislike Montreal but he was distraught that he wasn't living up to his capable standards set out with the Orioles.

"The time has come when I can't do a creditable job for the money that I am getting," McNally told MacDonald, who tracked him down. "There is absolutely nothing wrong with my arm. Look, I was being paid good money by the Expos, damn good money. I didn't do the job. I know in my heart that I tried as hard as I could every time I pitched. I did my best. It wasn't there."

According to Baseball Reference, McNally was the Expos highest paid player at $115,000, although some reports pegged the salary at $125,000.

But Mauch didn't accept McNally's thoughts.

"It's quite a blow to me," Mauch told MacDonald. "I think his action now in retiring is premature. David called me. We talked for a long time."

By all accounts, McNally was a prized teammate.

"I played gin rummy with Dave on all the flights," recalled 1975 teammate Don DeMola. "We were on the tram out to the plane (after a game). Looking around, I didn't see Dave. I was anxious to get my $20 back (from a card game). I said to Woodie Fryman, 'Where's Dave?' 'He quit.'

"Dave didn't fare too good in the National League. Gene Mauch had a meeting. He told us Dave packed it in. 'He left $85,000 on his stool' is the way Gene put it.

"Dave was a wonderful man. He wore a toupee and acted like it was nothing, unlike Singleton, who also had a hair piece but was very vain."

McNally hadn't actually signed a contract for the '75 season so he was renewed but he told MacDonald that he was not miffed by the contract dilemma when he headed to the mound every game.

"I'm quite positive that the contract problems had no effect whatsoever on my pitching, none at all," McNally confided to McDonald. "Look, I'm sorry I'm leaving like this. Tell the people in Montreal I'm real sorry I let them down. Everyone was great to me."

Of the estimated $115,000 he was slated to earn in '75, McNally had already taken in about $30,000 in the first two and a half months with the team.

"I didn't feel right by stealing money from the team," McNally bluntly told MacDonald.

McNally returned to his hometown of Billings and joined brother Jim as operators of the Archie Cochrane car dealership. He was far from washed up but he never pitched in the majors again. McHale did travel to Billings to try and talk McNally out of retirement but McNally didn't budge.

"Dave was quieter than I was," Jerry White said. "Veteran players didn't really say much to the younger guys."

McNally could have pitched a few more years and probably earned a place in Cooperstown but it was of no interest to him. He was content in the car business. That's the puzzling aspect of that whole scenario is that McNally didn't want to play beyond the 1975 season.

"It was tough to give up a pitcher like McNally, who has contributed so much to us," Orioles GM Frank Cashen told reporters on trade day.

"I've learned that when I was traded to Baltimore, the Expos were given the choice of Richie Coggins or Al Bumbry," Singleton said. "The Expos took Coggins which turned out to be the wrong choice. Al became the far more productive of the two and a big part of what we did during our time together in Baltimore. Al also remains one of my best friends and golfing companions along with several other former Orioles."

Kirkpatrick never played in the majors, while Coggins participated in a few games that season before he was dispatched to the Yankees June 20. That trade sure was a disaster for the Expos. McNally left June 8 and Coggins was traded 12 days later.

Torrez had great career

Equally as maddening for the Expos in this trade involving Dave McNally and Ken Singleton was how Mike Torrez fared with the Orioles and other teams after being dumped by the Expos.

The trade was utterly a disaster for the Expos. Expos manager Gene Mauch and Torrez had feuded during the pitcher's time with the team from 1971-74 so it wasn't a surprise that Torrez was shown the door.

Torrez was an outstanding 20-9 for the Orioles in 1975 and proceeded to post a 185-160 lifetime record in the majors. His mark with the Expos was 40-26. The Expos gave up on him too soon.

"Mike was a good sinker-slider pitcher, who didn't get along real good with Gene Mauch," Foote said. "He was a good teammate and went on to have a good career with Baltimore, Oakland, the Yankees and Red Sox. He was a World Series champion with the Yankees. I always liked Mike and was happy to see him do good in his career."

13

1976 disaster

If the 1974 trade involving Ken Singleton and Dave McNally was a disaster or the Expos, then the 1976 season was even worse.

The Expos lost 107 games.

In what president John McHale would later call a mistake, the Expos fired manager Gene Mauch after his seventh season following the 1975 season. He had a lengthy run so he couldn't complain but his replacement Karl Kuehl, a mere 39, was in over his head, trying to be a military general and disciplinarian.

Guys like shortstop Tim Foli balked at Kuehl and there were confrontations galore. Foli wanted to be the manager. Players weren't too happy that they had to shave their faces. Kuehl had played and managed in the Cincinnati Reds organization, which for years had a policy of shaven-faces only.

"Poor Karl Kuehl," was something majority owner Charles Bronfman would often throw into any comments about 1976. Kuehl was promoted from Montreal's Triple-A team in Memphis, Tenn. Earlier, he had spent two seasons with the Double-A Quebec Carnavals as manager.

Kuehl had begun his managerial career as a young 21-year-old for an independent team in Salem, Oregon and by the time he had reached the majors with Montreal for his only big-league season as skipper, he had 18 years managing experience so the Expos front office felt he deserved a chance.

Kuehl tried to keep an even keel but never made it through the entire '76 season. He was fired in early September and replaced by Charlie Fox.

Before the regular season even started, Kuehl had gone after Foli during spring training and ordered him to shave his moustache before a certain game would begin. Foli complied. But there were others who balked at the moustache script on occasion and even president John McHale went ballistic at their confrontational attitudes.

Then on May 28 at Veterans Stadium in Philadelphia, Foli took Kuehl to task over some strategy.

Expos third baseman Larry Parrish was concise and clear in recalling that particular episode when Kuehl came to the mound to discuss some strategy with pitcher Fred Scherman and catcher Gary Carter. And of

Denis Brodeur photo/Peggy Bougie Collection

This was a special occasion at Jarry Park during the 1976 season as the Expos honoured two Canadian medal winners at the 1976 Winter Olympics in Innsbruck, Austria. The two athletesa with flowers are Kathy Kreiner on the left and Cathy Priestner. Kreiner won bronze in the women's giant slalom and Priestner captured silver in the 500-metre race in speed skating. The Expos from left to right are Larry Parrish, Steve Rogers, Tim Foli, José Morales and Woodie Fryman. The three gentlemen in the suits are unknown.

course, Foli, Parrish, second baseman Pete Mackanin and first baseman Andre Thornton joined the huddle.

According to research of this game in the fourth inning by the author in the Montreal Star and from retrosheet.org, beat writer Bob Dunn wrote that Foli saw Greg Luzinski warming up with his bat in the walkway near the Phillies' dugout and figured the big slugger would come in as a pinch-hitter. Foli tried to motion to Kuehl to show him that Luzinski was likely to come in but Kuehl ignored him and in the end, another batter, Ollie Brown, stepped to the plate with Mike Schmidt on second with a double and two out. Brown was intentionally walked with first base open and Jay Johnstone on deck. Johnstone lined out to end the inning.

"Karl is telling him (Carter) one thing and Foli the other," Parrish recalled some 43 years later. "Carter didn't know what to do. It was whether to pitch to Brown. Karl wanted to walk Brown and Foli was saying no. I was brought up where if a coach or manager said something, you did it even if you didn't agree. But Foli challenged Karl on the mound.

"I think Foli was correct in his thinking but I wasn't used to that. I don't remember who our pitcher was (it was Scherman) but Karl had a meeting after the game and said Foli wouldn't play again until he apologized to him and the team. Tim wouldn't do it so he didn't play. But Pepe Frias was a backup and made a couple of errors that cost us and McHale told Karl to get Foli back in the lineup."

After the game in Philly, Foli was oh-so very critical of Kuehl. Ouch.

Bad seasons for the Expos	
Season	Record
1969	52-110
1976	55-107
1998	65-97
2000	67-95
1999	68-94
2001	68-94
1971	71-90
1970	73-89

"He's incapable of managing," Foli told reporters. "He can't manage the team, not by himself. He's a rookie. I'm not a puppet. I'm not a dummy. I've worked hard to play the kind of shortstop I play."

Expos outfielder Jerry White took exception to Foli confronting Kuehl.

"That's like kicking a horse. You're not used to seeing stuff like that," White told me 43 years later about Foli's antics. "That was like a no-no. You wouldn't do that to your parents so why the manager? Karl got me to the big leagues. He was the guy who taught me a lot in the Instructional League and in the minors.

"Some guys didn't like his discipline but he was trying to help. It was a very interesting year. Karl was trying to win. I have to really thank him. He'd tell me, 'Learn the strike zone.' So we'd work at it every day. He helped me with that strike zone. He got me to the big leagues."

Despite Kuehl's frailties as manager, Carter thanked Kuehl during his induction speech in Cooperstown in 2003. And White was very supportive of Kuehl. White enjoyed a pretty nifty season in 1976, thanks to Kuehl, who inserted White in the starting lineup for most of the season.

Never did White play so much in the majors as he did in his rookie year with 304 plate appearances, two homers, 21 RBI and 15 stolen bases. He was never able to swat away that sobriquet of fourth outfielder, though. What I didn't know until recently is that White played in parts of 10 seasons with the Expos but strictly as a part-timer. His official service time in the majors with the Expos and other teams is only about seven seasons.

White also played under Kuehl in Triple-A at Memphis and with the Quebec minor-league team so it's no surprise he had the greatest of admiration for Kuehl. The '76 season was a rather unusual season because Foli and Parrish were the only position players to suit up on a regular basis.

Despite his bad act, Foli played in 149 games and batted .264 with a team-leading eight sac flies. He became the first Expo to hit for the cycle when he pulled the feat April 21-22. The game was continued on the 22nd because of rain and Foli finished off the cycle with a home run.

Parrish played the most games, 154, producing 11 homers and 61 ribbies while batting .232.

"Yes, it was a long year but at that age, I was just glad to be in the big leagues," Parrish told me.

Like White, Ellis Valentine was playing his rookie season in 1976 on a platoon basis with other outfielders, including Carter. Barry Foote handled most of the catching duties that season but ultimately was replaced down the road by Carter.

"We were all kind of young. We came up together," White said. "It's just that things didn't gel. When you get in a rut, you keep losing. It was hard but Karl wasn't down on people. It's just that we were young. Most of us had average years, including me.

"My goal was to be rookie of the year. I thought I had a chance. I was playing every day from both sides because I was a switch hitter. Winning rookie of the year would have been cool. And then something happened. There was a big drop (in production). I could have had more stolen bases if I had played more."

When Fox became manager, White saw him reduced to bench status.

On the pitching ledger, Steve Rogers may have gone 7-17 but his ERA was sparkling at 3.21. Woodie Fryman, who would later shine as a reliever, was a solid 13-13 as a starting pitcher. The other two main pitchers, Don Stanhouse and Don Caritthers, went 9-12 and 6-12, respectively. Dale Murray was solid out of the bullpen in 81 appearances with a 3.26 ERA after what was a stellar season in 1975 when he went 15-8. Those were the days, my friend, when relievers logged a lot of innings.

The seeds were sown for a great nucleus of players that would shine in the coming years for the Expos: Parrish, Rogers, Valentine, Carter, Warren Cromartie and so on and so on.

"As I was saying, Karl was a big part of all of our success because we came through Karl," White said.

So true. Kuehl was a teacher and a mentor. He's the type of guy who was solid as a coach and as a minor-league manager but not as a big-league skipper. Ironically, Kuehl would go on to be a coach for years with the Minnesota Twins, including a good run under Mauch, his Montreal predecessor.

"They should have let Karl finish the year," White said, but on the other hand, he added, "Gene would have done a better job. I would never forget those guys, Gene and Karl. Gene taught me how to dress. We had to dress up (for road trips) and Gene was a sharp dresser. I always noticed what he was wearing. Montreal was also a fashion city."

Looking back, White couldn't help but volunteer to mention his good friend Valentine. Despite Valentine's descent into drugs in later years, White never dropped him as a friend. Valentine was dear to White as he was to Parrish, Dawson and many others who came up through the Expos organization.

Valentine got caught up in the wrong crowd in the late 1970s and early 1980s and took too many sniffs of cocaine. He also rebelled against practice, telling me one time it was all about "I, Self and Me." It's believed that the late Montrealer Bobby White supplied the Expos' players with all or some of the cocaine they needed.

"Ellis was my idol," White gushed. "Anytime I think of him, I kind of tear up. He was a very good friend, my first roommate. They put me in a room with him in the winter of '72 in the Instructional League. He could do anything and everything. He could hit with two strikes, he could hit to right, he could hit for power, he could run, he could throw. Man."

And then White sighed and paused to say: "He was funny. He kept people in stitches all the time, he kept the game fun."

14

Big Steve Renko

When the Expos traded Steve Renko May 17, 1976 to the Cubs along with Larry Biitner in exchange for Andre Thornton, he was more than happy to depart.

The big guy from Kansas City, Kansas had enjoyed a good run with the Expos but he wasn't too enthralled with 1976 rookie skipper Karl Kuehl.

"I didn't care for the new manager. I didn't dislike him but there was no communication with the things he was doing," Renko said of Kuehl. "It was time to leave. Gene Mauch was one of the best managers I ever had. He was a pitcher's manager. He was 2-3 innings ahead of everyone else. I was under Gene for a long time.

"The day of the trade, (GM) Jim Fanning called me and said I needed to get down to the Expos office at Dominion Square and sign some papers. The Canadiens had won the Stanley Cup and there was a parade downtown. I couldn't get within 10 blocks of the Expos office. I had to park and walk. The Cubs were in town so I just changed clubhouses."

Back on June 15, 1969, Renko had joined the Expos in the trade that saw Donn Clendenon shipped to the Mets. Going to the Expos with Renko were Kevin Collins, Bill Carden and a player to be named later (Terry Dailey). Expos Inside Out author Dan Turner reported that the Expos were offered this fellow by the name of Nolan Ryan but said no. They opted for Renko instead.

"I'd met the team on the road in Pittsburgh after the trade," Renko said. "My thought is that this was the big leagues. People were excited. When we got back to Montreal, the first guy I saw at the end of the clubhouse was Dick Radatz. I did recognize him. I knew who he was. I had already met the other guys."

Renko was a three-sport star at Kansas State in football, baseball and basketball. The most famous teammate he had was Gale Sayers, who went on to become one of the NFL's greatest running backs with the Chicago Bears. Sayers still lives in Lawrence, Kansas, only a "short ways away" from where Renko resides in Kansas City. Renko sadly reports that Sayers' health is worsening with Alzheimer's, which his family blames on repeated blows to the head during his playing days.

"I loved playing whatever sport was in season," Renko said, when I asked him which sport he liked the most. "Basketball was fun. I had a lot of fun playing football. It's the most disciplined sport there is. It's 11 guys. If one guy breaks down, the whole team breaks down."

In the end, baseball won out for Renko. He became one of the Expos greatest pitchers in their early bad days. Not only that, Renko was a solid hitter and was often used by Mauch in the seven hole in the batting order, not the customary ninth spot for pitchers. He batted .292 in 1972, .273 in 1973 and .278 in 1975. Although he only batted .210 in 1971, he drove in a career-high 12 runs.

Dariush Ramezani Illustration
Steve Renko

Renko's most noteworthy seasons with the Expos saw him go 13-11, 15-14, 15-11 and 12-16. That's why I nominated him a few years ago for the Canadian Baseball Hall of Fame. One performance stood out more than any other.

"I was fortunate to pitch a game in 1971 in Montreal where we won 4-0. The Expos were honouring the hockey player, Jean Beliveau, who was retiring that year," Renko said. "The fact that we won 4-0 and his number was 4 was unique. I met Jean and I knew a lot of the Canadiens."

I scoured through retrosheet.org to find details. I went looking for a 4-0 score and it was June 9, 1971. He threw a complete-game one hitter, beating the Giants at Jarry Park, the only hit being a second inning single by Dick Dietz. Renko even hit a run-scoring double.

"I was happy to have played in Montreal," Renko said. "It was great. What I didn't like was the snow. I stayed there two winters."

Denis Brodeur photo/Lesley Taylor collection
Steve Renko in his days with the Expos

15

Good-feel story

How David Palmer ended up with the Expos is one of the good-feel stories in franchise history. He was signed as a free agent back in 1976 at a time when management claimed it had no money to give him a bonus.

"Like hell and they had no money," sniffed Canadian-born Bill Mackenzie, who was instrumental in signing Palmer and who felt bad that he had to tell the pitcher there was no funds kicking around to sign him.

Palmer was signed out of a tryout camp in his hometown of Glens Falls, New York and showed up late by an hour, according to Mackenzie but Mackenzie didn't send him home.

"Am I too late to try out?" Palmer asked.

"No, you're pitching. You can go down there and work out," Mackenzie told him.

"It was an open Expos tryout camp," Palmer remembered. "I struck out three or four guys that I faced and when I was finished pitching, I put my sneakers on and I was going to leave like the other guys but someone said they wanted to talk with me and possibly sign me. I still had another year of high school. Then I was invited to Montreal to pitch on the side at Jarry Park at a big tryout camp."

Palmer was signed shortly thereafter and the organization dispatched him quickly to its rookie-league affiliate in Lethbridge, Alberta in the summer of 1976. His time there was not a good one. He suffered through a disaster of a season: 0-5 record and 7.20 ERA in 45 innings of work.

"We sent him out the first year and he was shelled. We were saying, 'This was going to be quick. He gets no money and he walks,'" Mackenzie said.

When Palmer reported to spring training in 1977 in Daytona Beach, this is where it got even worse.

"One night before spring training, I was playing a video game and I ripped the nail on my index finger of my throwing hand," Palmer said. "I was at the very point of being released out of baseball on what I had done in Lethbridge. After that injury, I had to use my little finger more and I never threw my fastball straight.

"I threw a cutter. I had to hold the ball off-centre. I had to put no pressure on the index finger. It was sore enough but in a couple of days, it was fine. For whatever reason, from that moment on, that fluke injury worked out pretty good."

Thanks to the Expos, who saw potential in him, Palmer stepped up his game. And just think, in 1978, after he had pitched in his first major-league game with the Expos, McHale pulled out what Mackenzie said was a $20,000 cheque and gave it to Palmer.

"It was the bonus he never got when he signed," Mackenzie said, smiling.

"I was very generous on John McHale's part. I was more than happy to get it," Palmer related. "I don't know if they ever made an excuse. I wasn't going to quibble about it."

Palmer began his big-league career in 1979 as a September call-up and proceeded to be a gall-dang decent pitcher with the Expos, going 10-8 in 1979 and 8-6 in 1980 before running into arm problems that sidelined him for the entire 1981 season, forcing him to miss the team's playoff run in 1981.

When it was determined that Palmer would not pitch in 1981, general manager John McHale pursued free-agent Ray Burris and beat out other suitors.

Burris received offers from other teams but decided on the Expos' offer of $325,000. The date was Feb. 18, just a few days prior to spring training.

"I had elbow surgery in Los Angeles with Dr. (Frank) Jobe," Palmer said. "The arm never responded enough to pitch in 1981. It was such a great year for the Expos and the city of Montreal in '81."

Palmer may be best known for his five-inning perfect game as part of a double header April 19, 1984.

"Steve Rogers pitched the first game and I pitched the second game," Palmer said. "There were rain delays before the second game before we could warm up. I had to sit an hour and 15 minutes because of the delay.

"I would have to say putting on the Expos uniform every day was a highlight. One of my favourite moments with the Expos was hitting a home run in Philadelphia. It was kind of cool to have my father and brother there to see it.

"Bill Gullickson and I were like brothers. We played together in the minor leagues. We roomed together on the road. We were best friends."

16

Losing out to the Bues

Dale Murray was one of those Expos relievers who found himself one of the best in 1974. He accumulated this pretty nifty ERA of 1.03 on a bad Expos team in the course of throwing 69.2 innings.

We don't know for sure but that 1.03 has to be one of the lowest ERAs in big-league history for relievers with at least that many innings.

In 33 games, Murray finished 23 and collected all 10 saves that season in the month of September.

He had been drafted out of Blinn College in Brenham, Texas and spent 1972 with the Expos Double-A team, the Quebec Carnavals. In 1975, he slipped a bit with an ERA of 3.96 but what was remarkable was that he was 15-8 in 63 games. That 15-8 sounds like the record put together by a starting pitcher but he was a reliever. That was in the days when relievers threw a lot of innings, unlike today where pitch counts prevail and middle relievers or closers don't throw much more than an inning or two.

Murray reverted to 1974 form in 1976 when the Expos went a disastrous 55-107. For him to excel in a season of disaster was extraordinary. He appeared in a National League leading 81 games, saving 13 games and finishing with an ERA of 3.26.

No wonder the Expos used Murray as bait along with fellow reliever Woodie Fryman when they made a stunning, headline-grabbing trade with the Cincinnati Reds on Dec. 16, 1976. The Expos acquired elite first baseman Tony Perez and reliever Will McEnaney. Perez was the key to the deal. It was odd that it was only a 2-for-2 deal because Perez was worth much more than that for the Reds. Perez had spent 12-plus seasons with the Reds and was one of the keys to their World Series titles in 1975-76. Some said Perez was the heart, soul and leader of those Reds teams.

But the Expos never forgot how good Murray was so they re-acquired Murray, this time from the Yankees in late August for the stretch drive in 1979. It was ironic, though, that Murray might be best remembered for coughing up a home to a guy by the name of Willie Stargell. In this their first run at a record above .500, the Expos had worked their way to the high echelons of power in the National League East.

Courtesy Pittsburgh Pirates

Willie Stargell feasted on Expos pitching during his career

For 10 consecutive seasons from the beginning of the franchise, the Expos had always posted a record under .500 until 1979.

On Sept. 18, long before the end of the season in the 11th inning, Stargell connected off Murray for a two-run homer at Olympic Stadium to give the Bucs a 5-3 win. Stargell hit a 2-2 pitch high to right-centre.

In his game story, Ian MacDonald of the Gazette joked that a man of Stargell's age should have been tucked away "comfortably in bed", insinuating that the slugger should have been retired by then. Stargell proved that age, 39 at the time, was no enemy of his.

It was a game that took six hours and 10 minutes and included three rain delays. Larry Parrish and Chris Speier convened makeshift teams to play touch football underneath the stands. Other players went to the clubhouse to play cards or backgammon. Expos manager Dick Williams protested the game in the sixth inning because the umpires resumed play while rain was still falling.

Murray had entered the game in the 10th inning and got through it unblemished with a 1-2-3 outing. Know what the Pirates did? They complained to umpire Doug Harvey that Murray might be doctoring the ball. So Harvey checked Murray's glove and belt for any pine tar or any foreign substance. Nothing surfaced.

In the 11th, Pirates pinch hitter Mike Easler singled and was promptly

Canadian Baseball Hall of Fame
Dale Murray

replaced by little known pinch runner Alberto Lois. Up to the plate stepped Stargell, who was believed by some to be not in his heyday anymore, that he was perhaps at the end of his career. Murray got two strikes on him and then gave The Starge something to hit. Game over, one minute after midnight.

Pops still had pop in his bat. Tim Burke of the Gazette wrote that big, burly, huge Dave Parker was The Body of the Pirates but that Stargell was The Soul.

With that mystical windmill practice swing bobbying back and forth, a tactic learned from Pirates alumnus Pie Traynor, Stargell was fearsome. He used a 36-inch, 36-ounce bat, long and heavy.

Back on May 20, 1978, Stargell connected for the longest home run at Olympic Stadium when he deposited a Wayne Twitchell offering to the upper deck in right field, a stroke estimated at 535 feet. The Expos paid tribute to Stargell by painting the seat where the ball landed in Pirates yellow. Following the 2004 season when the Expos were shipped to Washington, that seat made its way to the Canadian Baseball Hall of Fame in St. Marys, Ont.

Following that blast by Stargell, Twitchell told reporters he was awestruck at the beauty of the hit and the sound.

"It was like trying to watch a tracer bullet. You could hear it when it hit," Twitchell said. "I was kind in shock. He made perfect contact. This ball made it to the upper deck in a heart beat."

And don't forget the home runs he would hit into the public pool at Jarry Park beyond the right-field scoreboard from 1969-1976. From what I see online, the Expos presented Stargell with a life preserver to "commemorate all the swimmers he chased out of the pool."

Stargell, like Mike Schmidt of the Phillies, was an Expos Killer. During his career, Pops tagged 37 home runs and drove in 110 runs.

Some people may have thought Stargell was near the end of the line but he did propel the Pirates to the World Series in 1979 even if that We Are Family jingle annoyed some people.

By 1980, those fears about Stargell's career coming to an end started coming through. He was no longer the same hitter with 11 homers and 38 RBI. By 1982, he was out of the game.

Funny thing about how the '79 season ended was that both the Expos and Phillies finished 8-6 in their last 14 games following Stargell's home run. If only the Expos had fared better in those last 14. Too bad they couldn't have gone 10-4 in their last 14. But the Expos were at a disadvantage because they played 13 of their last 16 games on the road, including five doubleheaders. They did go into Shea Stadium for a twin bill Sept. 19 and swept the Mets.

For part of one day, the Expos did in fact take a temporary lead of half a game over the Pirates. That was on Sept 24 as part of a doubleheader in Pittsburgh. The Pirates took a half game lead by winning the first game 5-2 and then the Expos won the nightcap 7-6 with closer Elias Sosa nailing down his 18th save.

In the game the Expos took a temporary lead on Sept. 24, they trailed the Bucs at one time 6-3 but they rallied with the help of part-timer Duffy Dyer's run-scoring single and a two-run double by John Tomargo, another BUS squad member, off seemingly unbeatable Pittsburgh closer Kent Tekulve. Tomargo was called on to pinch hit by manager Dick Williams and came through by outfoxing the submariner Tekulve.

Up to that point, Tekulve had not blown a save in 91 appearances. Can you imagine? Holy shoot. Tekulve had owned the Expos for several seasons because they had only one full-time left-handed hitter in Warren Cromartie.

Ellis Valentine then drove home Rusty Staub with the winning run. Staub had worked Pittsburgh pitchers for four bases on balls. So with five games to go, the Expos were in first place. Although he didn't play much in his short stint back with the Expos following a trade with Detroit, Staub did make some contributions of note.

On Sept. 25 and 26, though, the Expos lost 10-4 and 10-1 to the Pirates in the third and fourth games of the four-game series. The Expos played many of their remaining games without the injured Gary Carter, who had hurt one of his thumbs.

"We had a great year, The Pirates had a powerhouse," outfielder Jerry White remembered.

Denis Brodeur photo/author's collection
Ellis Valentine

It was a season of great memories. One memory that stood out was May 19, 1979 at creaky, old Veterans Stadium. It may have been the turning point of the season for the Expos, at least one of the turning points to show that they weren't just going to roll over and die.

72

Courtesy Pittsburgh Pirates
**Willie Stargell (top), Tim Foli (bottom left) and John Milner (top right) help
celebrate Pittsburgh's 1979 World Series win**

It was a game where the Expos took the game by the balls and won
10-5 after being down 4-0. Larry Christenson went to the mound for
the Phillies to face Steve Rogers. It was the infamous game where the
Phillies' marketing department did the unthinkable by introducing ug-
ly-ugly, all-burgundy uniforms. They were wearing these special uniforms for the first time. And the Phillies hated how they fit and how
they looked. The event was called Saturday Night Special, a nod to the
cheap handguns then called by that name.

Christenson had no use for Carter, even though they played winter
ball together. In the second inning, Christenson came in hard against
Carter and the catcher fell to the dirt. In the fourth, Christenson went
to 0-2 on Carter again and then decided to throw some chin music.
Carter couldn't get out of the way and got hit on the helmet. It was a
beanball. Carter took exception and took after Christenson.

"It was an infamous game. Carter came running to the mound, he got
three-quarters of the way and pulled a sharp right to first base," Chris-

tenson said. "I'd thrown down my hat and glove. He stands on first base, pulls up his sleeve and he was jeering at me. I said, 'Get over here, we're supposed to be in a fight.' I really wanted him. He didn't show up.

"I never, just never liked Carter. Gary and I just had something."

And that "something" was no admiration for each other.

"He always hit me pretty good until I learned to entice him into over-thinking," Christenson said. "He rubbed me the wrong way. Carter and Steve Garvey were not my favourite players. Carter would pull his sleeve up, which pissed me off. One other time, I hit him and he ran hard to first like Pete Rose. I said, 'You're not Pete Rose, you're Gary Carter.' I was like Bob Gibson, not talking to hitters, I wanted to keep the edge. Gary was chirpy and he'd look at me in the batter's box. He'd look at my batting average. Real stupid stuff."

Yes, that tugging on his sleeve was one of Carter's idiosyncrasies, something that begged of showing off or boasting. He would take his right hand and pull on his left top near the shoulder. Sometimes, he could be seen pulling on both sleeves between swings. Check it out some time online. Carter would tell me years later why he did that.

"Doing that was just something to get comfortable at the plate," Carter explained. "It got you into a comfort zone and got you mentally prepared. I didn't realize all those things in the batter's box until I bought a video-replay machine for $1,200 in California in 1980.

"That's when those machines started coming out. I would see myself on the machine tugging on my sleeve and I noticed that when I was in the on-deck circle, I'd go through this routine of putting the donut, pine tar and resin on my bat."

But getting back to that beaning of Carter: it fired up the Expos because they came back and won the game 10-4.

17

So close and yet so far

People will talk forever about the home run that stymied the Expos from going to the World Series in 1981.

Expos fans will never forget the home run Rick Monday hit off of Steve Rogers in the ninth inning of Game 5 of the NLCS to send the Dodgers to the World Series against the New York Yankees.

But almost as devastating in Expos lore is the home run Stan Bahnsen of the Expos gave up to Mike Schmidt of the Phillies on Oct. 4, 1980. It was a heart-breaker. The Expos had come so close to a playoff berth and didn't make it.

The only difference in the two games was that Rogers' effort took place in post-season play but Bahnsen's faux pas left the Expos so eerily close to the post-season on the next-to-last game of the regular season.

The Expos had led the 1980 game 4-3 after eight innings, thanks to Jerry White, a hero a year later for the Expos in that same 1981 series against the Dodgers. White hit a two-run homer and added a sacrifice fly to power the Expos in the game against the Phillies.

Just to tell you how crazy and surreal this game was, let's go into the Expos fourth inning when White hit his home run. Expos pitcher Steve Rogers was a cat with nine lives in that inning. He was picked off base, not once, but twice in the same inning, but escaped like Houdini because Phillies pitcher Larry Christenson committed errors in both cases, allowing Rogers to advance a base.

Rogers led off the inning with a base on balls and then was promptly picked off by Christenson but in the ensuing rundown, he made it to second when Christenson threw the ball away. On second, Rogers again was picked off by Christenson. But Christenson screwed up again, throwing the ball away in a rundown and Rogers made it to third.

Unreal.

Then White, like he did against southpaw Jerry Reuss in the 1981 playoffs, hit a homer off of Christenson to left field. The Montreal Gazette said it was the biggest day of White's career. But a year later, that best game was replaced by his go-ahead three-run homer in Game 3 of the NLCS.

National Baseball Hall of Fame, Cooperstown, N.Y.

Mike Schmidt was an Expos killer during his career with the Phillies

"It was a good curveball that I hit," White recalled of his blast against Christenson. "I thought we had the game won. Our momentum was going in our favour."

Christenson couldn't remember specifically what happened during those episodes with Rogers on the basepaths and neither did Rogers. You're talking some 40 years ago.

"Danny, I will be honest I had to look at Retrosheet to even approach having a memory of that game," Rogers said. "Being picked off twice may have caused me to have a mental block."

In the top of the ninth, Bob Boone came through mighty in the clutch, delivering a game-tying, two-out, Punch and Judy single to put the Phillies back on even footing at 4-4. It was enough to have Expos fans pull hair out of their heads.

This was a game that saw injury-recovering Larry Parrish strike out four times. Parrish, Andre Dawson and Gary Carter went a combined 2-for-19.

Parrish was the epitome of frustration because he could hardly swing the bat with any pop because of a broken wrist he suffered when hit by a pitch earlier in the year. His follow through on his swing was very much negated but he decided to do his best.

"It was the best start I ever got off to and then I broke a small bone in my wrist. It took over a year for it to heal," Parrish said.

The Expos, especially pitcher Woodie Fryman, were upset in the inning that saw Boone hit the single to centre. Fryman had walked Rose on four pitches. That didn't help. Bake McBride hit a grounder to Rodney Scott, who tagged Rose in the baseline before firing to Warren Cromartie to complete what looked like a double play. For some reason, first base umpire Dick Stello ruled McBride safe. Schmidt then chopped a grounder to Parrish, who fired to first.

"Schmidt appeared to beat the throw but Stello called him out, a case perhaps of evening up for the previous call," Montreal writer Brodie Snyder wrote in the Sunday Express. McBride moved to second with two out, paving the way for Boone's heroics. Now if Stello had called McBride out to make it a double play, it may have changed the course of the game.

"It's too bad we had to lose that kind of a game," Fryman told reporters following the game. "I needed an out, and I couldn't get it. I walked Rose but thought we had the double play. We didn't get the call."

Said Williams: "I thought we had a guy out at first but then we got a break. We didn't think we had the play on the next guy (Schmidt) but they called him out."

Because of an injury, Ron LeFlore was only used as a pinch-runner that game. During most of the regular season, he had been a very dramatic player. He only hit .267 with a mere four homers and 39 RBI but he was dynamic on the basepaths, plundering a franchise-record 97 stolen bases in 116 attempts. He was a pain in the ass to the front office and some of his teammates but his breath-taking speed more than made up for his indiscretions.

And future Hall of Famer Tim Raines was barely an Expo that season, having gone 5-for-20 in very limited duty. He, too, like LeFlore, was used only as a pinch-runner against the Phillies. Raines was deemed too inexperienced to be playing a full-time role in such a pivotal game. He was only 20 at the time.

The game included three hours of rain delays. There was a crowd of 50,794 rocking Olympic Stadium. The night before, 57,121 crammed the spaceship for a game the Phillies won 2-1 as Dick Ruthven (17-10) outduelled Scott Sanderson (16-11). This was the golden age of Expos baseball.

The Expos had gone into the showdown series red hot. They had taken two out of three from the Phillies at Veterans Stadium and then they waltzed into St. Louis to sweep a three-game set at Busch Stadium.

This was a game delayed numerous times by rain. During one of those delays, Christenson had entered the clubhouse undeterred by the cold, nasty weather. In fact, he loved unpleasant Mother Nature.

"The cold weather, the rain delays, I liked them," Christenson told me. "The longer and colder and later it go, I felt better. I didn't care for afternoon games much. I had more energy and strength for night games. If we played at 2 or 3 in the morning, I would have been a 40-game winner."

So as the rain pelted down in the midst of pressure within the confines of the Phillies scheme of things under abrasive, loudmouth manager Dallas Green, Christenson immersed himself in a 700-page novel written by Robert Ludlum, waiting for the rain to stop. It was called The Bourne Identity.

Remember Ludlum? A theatre critic and producer by trade, his niche in life was sculpted by writing. He wrote 27 thriller novels and he was the author who made the fictional character Jason Bourne famous.

Christenson and Phillies lefty Steve Carlton were intellectuals on a Phillies team, a cast of characters, that was rough and tough in the mould of Green, a towering man, who delved in profanity to make a point. On plane trips while many Phillies played cards and did a lot of yelling, Christenson and Carlton listened to music and read fiction in a back corner, mind and soul stuff. They would often go to Barnes & Noble and buy books.

While Christenson loved Ludlum, Christenson said the outcast, reclusive Carlton isolated himself in dystopian fiction and romance novels such as Atlas Shrugged, the 1957 tome by Ayn Rand, her fourth, final and longest book.

"I've read all of Ludlum's novels. The Bourne Identity was a great book that came out in 1980," Christenson was telling me. "They made a movie out of it quite a while ago."

That's right, with Matt Damon the star. The Bourne Identity took pressure off in the midst of a series and turmoil that centered on Green. The Phillies had produced great teams from 1976-78 and didn't get to the World Series.

Observers wondered if the teams from 1976-78 were better than this 1980 squad. Green had been appointed Philly manager on Aug. 31, 1979 following Ozark's tenure of close to six years at the helm. Ozark's squads finished with identical 101-61 records in 1976-77 and then they went 90-72 in 1978 before tapering off with a lacklustre season in 1979 before he was fired.

"There was a lot of pressure in the locker room. It was turmoil. Dallas had stormed on the year before from Danny Ozark," Christenson said. "He was nothing like Danny Ozark, the players' manager. Dallas was a screamer and hollerer. He was screaming, yelling and hollering. The players didn't get along with Dallas. Dallas just did not like me. I didn't have the manager's support. I had elbow surgery in the middle of the season and had five bone spurs taken out of my elbow."

Expos manager Dick Williams was known to be a bit of screamer himself but Green's tantrums amounted to verbal abuse.

But back to one of those rain delays as Christenson immersed himself in The Bourne Identity.

"I was getting near the end of the novel when somebody said the game was about to resume. I told them I still had a few pages to read," Christenson said.

Christenson and Rogers didn't last long. Rogers was out after four innings, Christenson threw 4.2 innings.

In the 10th inning, Bahnsen had set the Phillies down in order 1-2-3. In the 11th inning, Pete Rose led off with a single. Bahnsen got McBride to pop up behind the plate to catcher Gary Carter, bringing the feared Schmidt up to the dish. The Expos Killer, as he was known.

Williams could have elected to intentionally walk Schmidt. It isn't often that someone will be walked with a man on first. Sure, a dangerous hitter would likely be walked if first base was open. But Rose was not on second. He was on first.

In the on-deck circle was a nobody, Don McCormack, who had one previous MLB at-bat. Schmidt had already hit 47 homers on the season, heading into that at-bat. Scary stuff indeed. Oh, oh. So why not walk Schmidt to put men on first and second and one out with McCormack due up?

With Boone and Bob Dillard already out of the game, McCormack was the only Phillies catcher available so it was unlikely he would have been replaced by a pinch-hitter. Neither pitching coach Galen Cisco nor Williams made an attempt to even convene a round table on the mound with Bahnsen, Carter and the rest of the infield.

So Schmidt was allowed to take his whacks. Could the Expos not have earned a lesson from the night before? Schmidt had hit a sacrifice fly and a solo homer as the Phillies took a one-game lead on the Expos with a 2-1 victory. The Expos decided on mediocrity and decided to pitch to Schmidt.

This was on a day when Reuben's two-location restaurant business, still thriving, in downtown Montreal was advertising in the Gazette that you could get a charcoal broiled rib steak for $6.49, including a salad, potato, pie and tea or coffee.

So Bahnsen went 2-0 and then Carter called for a curveball. Bahnsen shook his head. Carter put the one finger down and Bahnsen nodded his head. Bahnsen grooved it and Schmidt hit a no-doubter into the left-field stands, giving the Phillies a 6-4 lead for one of the biggest home runs of his career.

"It was a blast, it was a bomb," Christenson said of Schmidt's homer.

The funny thing is this: McCormack comes up and hit a single off Bahnsen. Go figure.

"In those days, the manager wasn't as analytical and calculating as they are these days," Christenson said. "I do recall that Dick Williams in the dugout made a decision not to put Mike Schmidt on but if first base was not open, you can't really put the blame on Williams."

As Rogers said, he had no recall of the Schmidt-Bahnsen match-up. Neither did Parrish.

But if you were the manager, wouldn't you have walked Schmidt to pitch to McCormack? The purists would say not to walk a batter in that situation because it would have put Rose in scoring position. Of course, the big reason Bahnsen was allowed to stay in and face Schmidt is that the slugger was for 5-for-20 lifetime against Bahnsen prior to that AB.

And even more lucid was the fact Schmidt had only managed one hit in his previous 13 at-bats against Bahnsen. So there, that's the percentages that came into play: Bahnsen had basically owned Schmidt. Career-wise against the Expos, Schmidt was massive with 57 homers and 161 RBI, including 26 homers and 70 RBI in Montreal.

Even more revealing was a guy warming up in the bullpen for the Expos: Sicilian Italian John D'Acquisto, who like Bahnsen, also boasted some off-the-charts statistics against Schmidt. I had been tipped off about D'Acquisto, not aware that he had been warming up.

So taking advantage of the fact that we were Facebook friends, I sent D'Acquisto a note about what he thought of the game for this chapter, not knowing his dominance of Schmidt. He went on to reveal that he, like Bahnsen, had tied up Schmidt most of his career in matchups. In his revealing book Fastball John, D'Acquisto has a chapter on that very scenario of him warming up and it's called Game 161.

Unfortunately, Williams didn't realize how good D'Acquisto was against Schmidt. D'Acquisto had been plucked by the Expos Aug. 11, 1980 from the San Diego Padres in a 1-for-1 trade that saw minor-league slugging legend Randy Bass head west.

"Mike Schmidt hit .191 off me, in a lot of ABs from 1973-1980," D'Acquisto told me as he sent me Baseball Reference stats to confirm what had transpired between the two players. "Williams was not told about the successes I had with Schmidt. He told me I should have told him. I told him, 'Not my job, skip.' In my opinion, that was the difference.

"Schmidt struck out eight times, had four hits and didn't record a home run in the eight years that we faced off."

Wow, pretty impressive. So whether it was Bahnsen or D'Acquisto, the Expos had the right match up against Schmidt.

Bahnsen threw his first pitch down low and then went to the outside corner and thought he had a checked-swing strike. In video I saw, Carter asked home-plate umpire Bruce Froemming to appeal the play with Stello, who spread his arms wide to signal no strike. Then Bahnsen grooved one for Schmidt.

"It wasn't a good pitch but I figured he'd been sitting on my slider," Bahnsen understated to reporters following the game. "I accept the loss but we had chances to win. Everybody is disappointed. Heck, I sure am. I've been on six second-place teams but never a winner. Maybe next year."

Canadian Baseball Hall of Fame

Stan Bahnsen

In the bottom of the 11th, reliever Tug McGraw retired the side in order. The Phillies had clinched the NL East. The game that originally was scheduled to start at 1 in the afternoon finished at 9:05 at night because of the delays. For the Expos, the cry was Wait Until Next Year.

"The celebration was on, guys were coming in from the bullpen with heavy gloves on," Christenson said. "I was looking into the dugout for Gary Carter. He had a scowl on his face. There were doldrums in the Expos dugout. It was a wild game, back and forth."

Many Expos stared into their lockers and as Montreal Gazette columnist Michael Farber wrote, also "stared into their hearts." Instead of sipping and spraying champagne, Expos players drowned their sorrows in beer.

The game between the Expos and Phillies the following day was meaningless because the Expos were out of the race.

"Sunday's game was irrelevant," Christenson said. "A few guys were hung over. Greg Luzinski was eating ribs from the Bar-B Barn. We were still in party mode. We were having a lot of fun."

Getting immersed in the Phillies' fun the day after Game 161 was pitcher Randy Lerch but as he got on a trainer's table for some treatment, he got the shock of his life when team owner Ruly Carpenter walked by and said, "Hey Blade (his nickname), don't celebrate too much, you might not be part of the post-season roster.'"

When Lerch heard that, he said, "I was destroyed."

White hit a walk-off, three-run homer in the 10th inning as the Expos won 8-7 in Game 162. Only 30,104 showed up. Another 25,000 stayed at home because the game didn't mean anything.

"Somebody asked me why didn't I hit that home run the day before," White said. "I did. I told him I hit a home run to put us ahead on the Saturday."

The Phillies went on to beat the Houston Astros in the NLDS and then beat the Dodgers to advance to the World Series where they beat the Kansas City Royals.

"Dallas, the pissy-ass manager, goes down in Phillies lore by winning the World Series," Christenson said. "It was twice as wild in the Houston series. We had four extra-inning games. I bombed in the World Series. My arm was dead. Without Pete Rose, we don't win in 1980. People argue about that, whether the 1980 team was better than the teams from 1976-78."

Jay Daniel of Indianapolis paid tribute to the 1980 Phillies in his book Phinally, a reference to the Phillies semi-dynasty in the mid-to-late 1970s. Daniel said the 1979 slide by Philadelphia showed the team "to be vulnerable" and cost Ozark his job.

"Farm director Dallas Green took over and immediately challenged a team that was immensely talented but was perceived to be soft," Daniel said in an interview. "The battles between Green and some of his players didn't cease until they hosted a World Series trophy on Oct. 21."

Unlike Rogers, who has faced the music umpteen times with the media and authors about Oct. 19, 1981, Bahnsen has mostly shied away from talking about his difficult moment. For Expos fans, it's akin to Ralph Branca giving up the big home run to Bobby Thomson on Oct. 3, 1951. Or Ralph Terry of the Yankees allowing Bill Mazeroski's blast Oct. 13, 1960. Or Mitch Williams allowing Joe Carter's walk off Oct. 23, 1993. Just devastating.

Bahnsen had joined the Expos in 1978 and while he was so-so in his first season with Montreal, he kicked into high gear in 1979-80. He had been a starting pitcher for most of his big-league career but switched to the bullpen later on. In 1979, he was terrific. In 1980, he was also pretty solid.

As a starter, Bahnsen produced these won-lost records with the Yankees: 17-12, 9-16, 14-11 and 14-12. With the White Sox, his stats included seasons of 21-16, 18-21 and 12-15. And get this: he threw 16 shutouts and collected 73 complete games. Holy shoot. How many pitchers nowadays come remotely close to 73 CG? Bahnsen was a workhorse.

As I researched Montreal Gazette microfilm, I saw that Expos majority owner Charles Bronfman came into his team's clubhouse and told Bahnsen, "I hope you will be back next season."

Sure enough in the off season, the Expos weren't down on Bahnsen because they gave him a three-year contract worth $1-million.

In late 2019, Bronfman told me, "The pitch that Mike Schmidt hit out, I was there. My shoulders slumped as soon as he hit it. I knew that was that and the season was essentially over for us. I was some sad."

With moisture welling in his eyes, Williams told the media following Black Saturday that Montreal fans deserved better than what happened. Prior to the game, those fans had given the team a standing ovation for two and a half minutes.

"The best fans in the world are up here in the northeast in New England and Montreal," Williams said.

Fryman was down on himself and admitted at 40 years of age, his chances for post-season success was running out.

"This might be my last chance," Fryman said.

Just a few days earlier, Fryman had told the Gazette that the '80 season was his best in the majors: 7-4 record, 17 saves and a 2.28 ERA.

"I could always throw strikes and when you're relieving, that's what you have to do," Fryman said.

But Fryman was kicking himself because he walked Rose on four pitches in the ninth inning Oct. 4. At the same time, Williams came to the lefty's defence.

"Woodie was certainly overworked in the bullpen," Williams said.

As Gazette city columnist and sometimes Expos beat writer Ted Blackman revealed in a news-section piece, Quebec-born former major leaguers Claude Raymond and Ron Piché had been scheduled to throw out the first pitch in the first two games of the NLCS. Even more startling was this: Blackman told his readers that some 10,000 souvenir pennants had been made up and they said: Montreal Expos 1980 National League East Champs. They had been waiting to be put on sale. But alas, they were dispatched to a dumpster or bonfire.

All because of Schmidt. The Big Game Hitter.

In an interview I did with Schmidt years ago, he said 1980 was a big season for him and he honed in on his at-bat with Bahnsen.

"Stan Bahnsen owned me that year," Schmidt told me. "He took me too lightly. After throwing two sliders for balls, he let a fastball over the plate and the rest is history. I'll never forget that moment."

Said Christenson: "Schmitty was quite the player. Boy, what a great defensive player. He went through some tough times but Pete Rose was the secret key to making Schmidt believe in himself."

Lerch, like Christenson, had nothing but praise for Schmidt.

"Mike had so much ability. He was a great, great player. He was such a streaky hitter," Lerch said. "He'd go on a tear and literally nobody could get him out. He'd come up to the plate and they would walk him. Sometimes, he couldn't borrow a hit."

Expos fan Michael Brown of Plattsburgh, N.Y, located about two hours south of Montreal, attended the Black Saturday game with his mother and father and was devastated.

"After nearly freezing to death and cursing Mike Schmidt under my

Photo submitted by Dave Van Horne

Dave Van Horne, middle, poses with former Expos Tommy Hutton, left, Jeff Reardon, Tim Wallach, Bill Gullickson and Steve Rogers in this setting in Palm Beach Gardens a few years ago.

breath, it was the longest ride back to Plattsburgh forever from an Expos game," Brown said almost 40 years later. "I remember my mom saying as only a mother can, 'It just wasn't their day and better luck next year.' I love my mom dearly but she just didn't understand the struggle Expos fans go through, probably because she was busy raising two kids so I guess she gets a pass.

"However, on a Monday afternoon in October a year later, she didn't say anything. I think it took her a year to understand."

Expos BUS Squad leader Tommy Hutton poses with his father George at Dodger Stadium where the elder was an usher. Hutton formed the Broke Underrated Superstars squad in the late 1970s as a tribute to the part-time players who would take long bus trips in Florida while the established players usually stayed behind at the spring-training base. Among the others on the BUS squad were Jerry White, John Tomargo, Ken Macha, Duffy Dyer and Tony Solaita.

Photo submitted by Tommy Hutton

18

Gully strikes out 18

In the heat of a pennant race on Sept. 10, 1980, Bill Gullickson dug down deep into his reservoir of pitches to establish a nice piece of Expos history.

He struck out 18 batters to lead the Expos to a 4-2 victory over the Chicago Cubs.

"I'd throw a fastball down the middle and they didn't swing at it. I'd throw a curveball in the dirt and they would swing at it," Gullickson was saying about his success that day close to 40 years later. "I thought I had a good, hard breaking ball. I had a little change-up that I barely ever threw. Gary Carter called a good game."

While pitching to Lenny Randle in the sixth inning, Gullickson thought maybe his time was up.

"It was a tight game and if I had ended up walking Randle, I think Dick Williams would have taken me out," Gullickson said. "But I struck him out on a curveball. I just wanted to keep going."

In the euphoria of the clubhouse following the game, Carter was effusive in his praise for Gully's performance which surpassed the 15-strikeout effort by Mike Wegener of the Expos in 11 innings in 1969.

"The big thing was he was getting ahead in the count all the time," Carter said. "He had an excellent slider and that's what most of the guys were striking out on."

The irony of Gullickson's strikeout gig was that he was never known as a strikeout pitcher.

Gullickson made his Expos debut in 1978 and later combined with similarly aged pitchers Scott Sanderson, Charlie Lea and David Palmer to become the envy of the majors and mentored by the staff's ace: Steve Rogers. They were all right-handers.

For many years, the Fab Four were members of the Expos staff at the same time as Rogers, although Palmer was hurt during a portion of that term, missing the 1981 and 1983 seasons. Rogers had started his Expos career in 1973.

Along with the traditional fastball, Rogers taught his four young'uns how to effectively master a curveball and slider. The slider was Rogers' out pitch and the four younger guys tried to emulate him.

"My best memory in hindsight is that we all looked up to Steve Rogers," Gullickson said. "We'd see him and say, 'We used to watch you pitch and try to be like you.' We wondered how he was so successful. Let's watch him. He was the catalyst. We knew what we had to do and be successful. We were all younger than Steve. Nowadays, you never see five right-handed starters."

When Gullickson started experiencing a sore arm from throwing the curveball too much, he praised pitching coach Galen Cisco as "the best", teaching him "a little cutter, a cut fastball. It really helped."

Sadly, only three of those five are still alive: Gully, Palmer and Rogers. Charlie Lea died of a heart attack in 2011 and Sanderson died of cancer in 2019. When the topic of Sanderson was broached, Gully said, "Oh my God, how sad is that?"

Gully looked at the photo of the 1981 NLDS-winning team that lost out to the Dodgers in the NLCS and said, "A lot of the guys are dead."

Woodie Fryman is also gone from the photo along with managers Dick Williams and Jim Fanning and coaches Pat Mullin, Steve Boros and Vern Rapp.

As a further aside as he studied the photo, Gullickson said, "Holy shit, we had a great team."

Gullickson has learned to cope with Type 1 diabetes since 1978 but instead of taking daily doses of insulin, he has taken advantage of advice from a specialist and modern-day technology to change his insulin and wear an insulin pump on his stomach. The pump is a computerized device that delivers insulin through a thin tube that goes under your skin.

"Things are much more advanced," Gullickson said.

And as for those rumours that Pete Rose declined to bet on games that Gullickson threw for the Cincinnati Reds, Gullickson said, "I never heard anything about it. I love Pete. He was the best. I had a great time in Cincinnati."

19

Blue Monday

From 1979-82, the Expos had talent coming out of their wazoo. They carried a quasi-dynastic feel.

"Call it tough luck," said Ken Macha, a backup Expo from 1978-80, talking about the lack of success by those squads in the late 1970s and early 1980s. "I just look back at those teams. It was unfortunate to be in a division where the eventual World Series champions won. You had some premiere players that were very good. The most talented guy was Ellis Valentine. He could hit the breaking ball and the fastball. He had a tremendous arm."

How about those 1981 Expos? The 1981 squad came closest to winning the National League pennant, only to lose to the Dodgers on Blue Monday, Oct. 19, 1981.

The Expos carried a 2-1 series in the best-of-five NLCS on the strength of Jerry White's three-run homer in Game 3. Olympic Stadium shook after White's homer and the euphoria spread to the streets of Montreal afterward.

"I was there when White hit that home run off of Jerry Reuss. It was bedlam," said fan John-Patrick Foy.

"I was at that game and I remember the stadium floor shaking so much," Rosso Anticus said. "I thought the place would crack."

Said Brian Gerstein: "I felt like a kite flying in the air. It was the high point for me as an Expos fan. I was convinced we were going to play the Yankees in the World Series, was already looking ahead for pitching match-ups."

The Expos had so much momentum following White's homer and it got deflated in the days to come. They managed to scrounge up only two runs, one in each of their last two games. The Dodgers won 7-1 to tie the series 2-2 and then they won 2-1 in Game 5. Just a brutal ending. Devastating.

For the third October in a row, the Expos had suffered misery with teams so talented. Bench player turned full-time player Rick Monday hit the biggest home run of his career to lead the Dodgers into the World Series by outduelling Steve Rogers in the 1981 series finale.

"It brings back memories of sitting in the nose bleeds and my friend

Photo montage by Catherine Gallagher/photos courtesy MLB Productions
Steve Rogers and Rick Monday moments before Monday's famous home run

Sheilah saying, "Oh no worries, Rick Monday!" And then the crack of the bat and the stadium gasped and went silent," recalled Chantal Bunnett, who later became an Expos scoreboard employee. "My mom even came to that game. My brothers, my mom, me and my two best friends were there. I swear we were in the rim of the stadium in right field but it was exciting to be there."

White was the hero in Game 3 but he didn't like the way Game 5 ended when he was the last out against reliever Bob Welch. In my latest interview with White following several ones he gave me for my 264-page book Blue Monday, he volunteered to say he was disappointed at what he did. And what was that? He swung at the first pitch. He had always been a man of patience and this strategy against Welch was surprising, considering that the two previous batters, Gary Carter and Larry Parrish, earned consecutive walks against Fernando Valenzuela, prompting Welch's entrance. White should have at least taken one pitch from Welch.

The Dodgers, especially second baseman Davey Lopes, were playing White to pull. Lopes was playing way over close to first and not even close to second. Lopes moved to his left, scooped up White's hit and threw the runner out in a very close play as first baseman Steve Garvey made sure by hanging on for the out with a big stretch and holding the glove up in the air.

"I always took great pride in taking the first pitch," White told me last year. "I'm a pretty good, better hitter with two strikes. It was a sinker. It looked like a fastball. It was a half swing. It wasn't really a good swing. They were playing me in the hole. If I had two strikes, I'd try to hit the ball up the middle. But on a first-pitch fastball, I was always trying to pull."

Several hundred reporters receive credentials for the final series. It was the golden age of baseball, the golden age of newspapers, although in 1980 the Ottawa Journal that employed me for two years closed and went out of business, leaving the Citizen as the only daily paper in Ottawa.

For the games in Montreal between the Expos and Dodgers, the Citizen sent three reporters: sports editor Eddie MacCabe, Expos beat writer Bob Elliott and general news reporter Greg Weston.

"The Citizen sent me to Montreal as the reporter who knew the least about baseball," Weston told me. "The last thing I did that week was finish filing a full-page color story at about 10 p.m.

"I was alone in the stadium and I stood up in the upper press box and heaved the computer in a beautiful arc. It exploded as it hit the seats below. I remember the computer was called "Mary." I renamed it "Hail Mary". Then I joined the others on Crescent St and we drank until 5 a.m."

Denis Brodeur photo/Perry Giannias collection
A disconsolate Jim Fanning and Tommy Lasorda are shown in this rare photo moments after the Dodgers eliminated the Expos in 1981

Let's get this straight, though, the Expos would not have made it to the NLCS without Steve Rogers. He outduelled Lefty Carlton not once but twice in the NLDS as the Expos won the series 3-2. That was vintage Rogers. Rogers came up big in Game 5 in intimidating Veterans Stadium. Sure Rogers gave up the home run to Rick Monday but the Expos would not have advanced without his heroics against the Phillies. And do we forget Wallace Johnson's two run triple that allowed the Expos to clinch a playoff spot Oct. 3?

"Steve was a battler, a competitor," Phillies pitcher Larry Christenson said. "You could take it all the way to the bank with Steve Rogers. He was a road warrior. He stepped it up against Carlton. He had fire in his eyes. The Expos had tough, pretty strong hitters. They were an expansion team that became a powerhouse team."

In the end, the Expos played two full playoff series, playing 10 games, winning five and losing five, the most difficult loss being on Blue Monday. Against the Dodgers, the Expos scored a mere 10 runs. In each of their three losses, they only scored one run.

"I like to think '81 was the year that started the coffin job," said Ottawa-based Expos fan J.P. Allard. "If they win the Blue Monday game, then they probably win in '82 and possibly '83 and then we don't have to witness The Kid win a championship in '86 and The Hawk win MVP in '87."

Denis Brodeur photo/ Perry Giannias collection

Rick Monday is hugged by Tommy Lasorda after the Dodgers won Game 5

20

Cops got wrong guys

It was around mid-day on a summer day in 1981, an off-day for the Expos, and close friends Andre Dawson and Jerry White went shopping.

It was a two-fold mission: they were going to look for some clothes for White's new baby girl, Noella, and they were going to search for a ball of knit for Dawson's wife, Vanessa, who did a lot of sewing, a lot of knitting and would make many quilts sandwiched around family time.

"Jerry and I used to hang out so much. He was a role model for me," Dawson was telling me in late 2019.

According to White, they had completed part of the mission for clothes for his daughter but they ended up in the knitting department of Eaton's, a famous department store in downtown Montreal.

As he told the story to me, White mused about how odd it was for two men looking for a ball of knit.

All of a sudden, they were approached from behind and hit in their backs with guns drawn by two police officers, who were not in uniform but in plainclothes.

"We were looking around for whatever we were looking for. I thought it was (teammate) Rodney Scott fucking around because sometimes, he'd put a finger in your side," White explained. "They had guns in my back. I turned around, you know what, Danny, I thought it was some guy joking but someone stuck something in my back."

Then White and Dawson discovered these two white guys, apparently undercover officers, were serious but when they found out they were Expos, they decided to let the two teammates free.

"I told them we weren't thieves," White recalled. "I was pissed. I was mad. What the hell. I was shocked. I told them, 'You said something derogatory. You don't do something like that.' I've never been treated like that ever. I think it was a case of mistaken identity. They figured they had the wrong people. It happened so quick. It was all hush-hush. If you didn't bring it up, I forgot it happened. I bet the players never knew. It happened and never brought up again."

Said Dawson: "They said to put our hands on the partition in front of us and not to turn around. We didn't know what to think of it. We thought it was a teammate stunt but then we heard a French ac-

Russ Hansen photos
Andre Dawson (left) and Jerry White are close friends

cent. We did as we were instructed. It was not good. They said we fit the description of two robbery suspects. They said this is a mistake. These are not the suspects. They recognized who we were. There was a piece in the newspaper but it didn't go into much detail about what happened. They said it was a little incident with the police."

White remembers that apparently someone from the police department called the Expos afterward and explained to general manager John McHale what happened. White said McHale came into the clubhouse and apologized to White and Dawson.

"From what I remember, it was overblown but I don't want to minimize how they felt," said Mark Bouchard, a former Expos batboy, who was a Montreal police officer during the period when Dawson and White were suspected of wrong doing. "Someone in the store obviously called in the info and it snowballed from there. That being said, sometimes when you're intercepted by police, the best thing is to fully cooperate and complain later.

"And the reason guns were pulled is that the info said the suspects were armed. Obviously not true but you don't know until you check. Like I said, they had reason to be pissed. But sometimes the story goes deeper than that and you have to find out why."

Liking Wallace Johnson

Kavin Adams played in the minors with a slew of teammates who went to the major leagues. That cast included Wallace Johnson, Tim Raines, Terry Francona, Brad Mills, Tim Wallach, Razor Shines, Roy Johnson, Dave Hostetler, Jerry Manuel, Bobby Ramos, Brad Little, Bill Gullickson and Tony Phillips. So I asked Adams who he admired the most. "Wallace Johnson," he said. "He was very genuine and down to earth as a person and he maximized his talent through hard work." Wallace is best known for his two-run triple that helped clinch the Expos first playoff spot in 1981.

21

1982 team fell short

Near the end of spring training in 1982, Expos GM John McHale made a controversial trade, swapping third baseman Larry Parrish and outfield prospect Dave Hostetler to the Texas Rangers for first baseman and designated hitter Al Oliver.

Parrish was a revered clubhouse leader, who had a knack for being a liaison between white players and black players. Figuratively, he sat between the blacks and the whites. He was the conduit. But on the field, he was also a leader, a clutch hitter and fancy-dan fielder.

A big reason Billy DeMars wanted to join the Expos as a coach for the 1982 season was Parrish, who likewise had pushed for the Expos to bring DeMars into the fold.

"I was also the third-base coach with the Phillies so I got to know Larry because he played third. We'd always get talking about hitting," DeMars explained from his home in Clearwater Beach, Fla. "I always liked Larry because he was a very good third baseman and he was a good hitter with tremendous power. So I get to spring training and they traded him before the season started."

DeMars couldn't believe McHale had traded Parrish. Of course, Parrish himself was floored and so were his teammates and many fans. The trade was made so that Tim Wallach could come in and play third instead of staying most of the time on the bench like he did in 1981.

But there was another reason why McHale made the trade: the Expos were lacking left-handed hitters besides Warren Cromartie.

"I was thinking of it later after the trade that, 'Why not put Parrish in right field? Why didn't we do that?' He had a great arm," DeMars said. "I think it would have been an excellent move. Gosh, he would have been successful in right. That was too bad."

What happened, though, is that when spring training started, Fanning sidled up to DeMars and said, "Hey, can you help Tim Wallach?"

So through DeMars' magic and patience, Wallach flourished after his rookie season of 1981 when he managed four homers, 13 RBI and a .236 average in 212 at-bats as a part-time player. The Expos felt Wallach could do more and DeMars worked with him.

And without DeMars having to look the stats up, this is what he correctly remembered from the top of his head, "Wallach went out and hit 28 homers and had 97 RBI. He showed up with the pitchers and catchers at spring training and we worked together every day the whole season."

Early in this season of great expectations, the Expos got rid of three

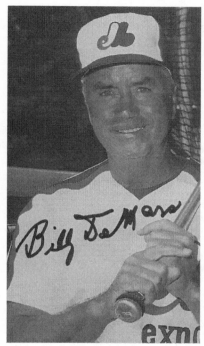

players within days of each other in May. The first release was part-time player Rowland Office on May 5. Then on May 7, second baseman Rodney Scott got his walking papers. When pitcher Bill Lee heard about his to-this-day good friend, he went ballistic in the clubhouse and decided to drown his sorrows at a pub near Olympic Stadium and didn't return to the park until late in the game. For what he did, Lee was given the heave-ho by general manager John McHale on May 9. Lee, 36, never played again in the majors. Then On May 22, backup infielder Jerry Manuel was traded to the San Diego Padres for Kim Seaman.

Ron McClain, the Expos trainer from 1980-2004, dealt with so many players during his fine career. He calls a spade a spade about Scott and Lee. McClain was indeed very candid. Even though Dick Williams was gone as manager late in the 1981 season and his replacement Jim Fanning was managing again in 1982, McClain brought up Williams as part of a talking point.

Author's collection
Billy DeMars

"Scott and Lee were part of the rotten-apple syndrome," McClain told me in 2019. "They should have been dumped long before that. You don't poison a team like that with them. John McHale let Dick Williams dictate who was on the team.

"They traded Tony Bernazard to the White Sox in 1980 and kept Rodney. The best player was Bernazard. Boy, Bernazard looked great. He could hit, hit for power. The real topping on the cake was when Bernazard had some good years with Cleveland. Rodney couldn't hit, although he could run, bunt and steal. They could never trade Scott because nobody wanted him.

"Scott barely wanted to come to the ball park," McClain said. "Instead, he wanted to get high and party. He didn't work at his hitting.

Milner left us too young

John Milner loved his cigarettes. He was a chain smoker, who took a liking to the Ultra King variety.

It's very likely the nicotine caused his lung cancer and his ultimate death. He died way too young in 2004 at age 50.

The one-time Expos outfielder/first baseman used to drag on cigarettes in between innings in the hallways leading to dugouts in the major leagues. Or even sneak in a few puffs on the bench or near the dugout, either at home or on the road.

"Very taboo," former Expos trainer Ron McClain said, in referring to players he recalled smoking tobacco. "Bryn Smith, Jeff Reardon, Stan Bahnsen. There really were not many smokers in my time."

Milner also got caught up in "riding the white horse," the expression used to describe people, who used cocaine. Milner testified in court in 1985 at the Pittsburgh Drug Trials that he snorted cocaine in 1982 with Tim Raines and Rowland Office while all three were with the Expos.

"He was a recreational user," Milner's sister Sharon told me about his cocaine habit.

Milner had a pretty decent career as a first baseman, outfielder, pinch hitter and offensive thrust with the Mets and Pirates before finishing his career with the Expos in 1982. Some say Milner should have been sent in as a pinch-hitter for Jerry White in the bottom of the ninth inning of Game 5 of the 1981 NLCS when Dodgers manager Tommy Lasorda brought in right-handed reliever Bob Welch to pitch.

Hammer was Milner's nickname in honour of his growing-up hero, Hank (Hammer) Aaron.

"My memory of John Milner was one of a grizzled veteran who didn't talk much but commanded the room when he did," said teammate Wallace Johnson. "He spoke of his playoff experiences with the Pirates and we were all ears."

Damn, if the manager didn't like him. If he came to the park late, he knew Williams was behind him. If he came to the ballpark late, he'd still be in the lineup. He might have been a really good player if he had the attitude of Raines, Dawson and Carter and guys like that. One time before a game even started, he went on the field and said to one umpire, 'How are you doing, fat boy?' He was thrown out before the game even started."

Word had gotten around that Scott was lazy and had a penchant for doing drugs. Teams didn't want to deal with him. When Cool Breeze was released, he was picked up shortly thereafter by the Mets but he never played again in the majors. He was only 29 in 1982.

As a man who started his Major League Baseball career as a trainer with part-time work with the Cincinnati Reds, McClain said he sat back and compared the "championship calibre Reds" organization to people who didn't fit the mould. Scott and Lee wouldn't have fit in with the Reds.

"He would take visine to wake up every day," McClain said of Scott.

"He just woke up before leaving for a night game. You don't sleep when you are high on cocaine. So you go to bed around 8 a.m. and wake up around 3 p.m. BP was at 4:30 p.m. You do the math. Everyday. Messed up but that is how he lived his life. Him and Ellis."

As for Lee, McClain said, "Nobody wanted him after he was let go. When nobody wanted him, it tells you he wasn't worth a damn. Some of the coaches wanted to dump him. He was hurt a lot. It doesn't mean I didn't like him. He was extremely funny, extremely smart but not good for the team. We still have very good conversations. I've laughed my ass off."

Lee arguably could be the most popular Expos player of all time. Right up there anyway with Gary Carter, Andre Dawson, Tim Raines, Steve Rogers and Vladimir Guerrero.

One noteworthy event that season was pretty unique. Joel Youngblood got two hits on the same day for two different teams in two different cities. Playing for the Mets, Youngblood hit a two-run single off of Cubs pitcher Ferguson Jenkins and before the end of the game, he was traded to the Expos. Somehow, he caught a cab to the airport and took a plane to Philadelphia to try and get to Montreal's night game. He made it. In the seventh inning, he singled off Phillies ace Steve Carlton.

Canadian Baseball Hall of Fame
Dick Williams loved Rodney Scott

To this day, Youngblood is still the only player in baseball history to get a hit for two different teams in two different cities on the same day and they came off of future Hall of Famers.

The Expos couldn't quite pull it off at the end with the Cardinals winning the NL East, followed in second place by the Phillies. The Expos finished third at 86-76, way below expectations.

"Jim Fanning took the losses so hard. He used to get migraine headaches," DeMars said. "He was in such terrible pain. He took the managing really, really hard."

As far as Wallach goes, DeMars even knew without looking it up that Wallach had hit four homers in 1981. And to this day, DeMars and Wallach have remained in touch. Each Christmas, Wallach sends DeMars a card.

When I asked DeMars who his all-time favourite player was while he was with the Expos, he quickly said Wallach.

"Tim and I are pretty damn close. He was a very good player and he's an excellent person," DeMars said.

"Billy was one of the smartest and hardest working coaches I ever played for and a great person as well," Wallach said in a text message.

In Philadelphia, Montreal and Cincinnati, DeMars had a special project. In Montreal, it was Wallach. In Philadelphia, it was Larry Bowa. In Cincinnati, it was Eric Davis.

"Larry Bowa had not been a good hitter whatsoever but we worked every day and he ended up getting 2,191 hits," DeMars said. "Same thing with Eric Davis. He got better. He got up to 27 homers and then 37 the season after. I was very patient with the guys. I worked with them on basic fundamentals. I never, ever told them they had a bad day in the batting cage or in a game. I always left the kid with a good thought in his mind."

Canadian Baseball Hall of Fame
Bill Lee

Despite the negativity associated with the Parrish-Oliver trade, Oliver posted the best season of his big-league career in 1982 with a league-leading .331 average to go along with 22 homers, 109 RBI. The Expos got solid offence from Gary Carter, whose stats were similar to Wallach's: 29 homers, 97 RBI, .293 BA. Andre Dawson batted .301 with 23 homers and 83 RBI.

In the pitching department, ace starter Steve Rogers shrugged off the huge disappointment of the 1981 Blue Monday caper to miss the 20-win mark with a superlative 19-8 record and a glittering 2.40 ERA. Three younger pitchers in Bill Gullickson, Scott Sanderson and Charlie Lea all won 12 games. David Palmer also got to start 13 games and finished at 6-4.

At the all-star game held in Montreal, the Expos had five representatives: Oliver, Dawson, Carter, Raines and Rogers.

A huge disappointment that season was Ray Burris, who couldn't capitalize on his outstanding pitching in the 1981 NLCS when he allowed only one run in 18 innings of pitching against Dodgers rookie phenom Fernando Valenzuela. Burris finished at 4-14 with a gaudy 4.73 ERA. Now, if he had won 12 games like Gullickson, Sanderson and Lea, the Expos would have won the NL East. That's how you can assess Burris' work.

Another significant factor in the Expos' third-place finish was the puzzling performance by Tim Raines, who fell short of his wonderful

1981 rookie season. He hit a subpar .277 with a mere four homers and 43 RBI, leaving him with an Expos career-low OPS of .723, the sabermetric stat calculated as the sum of a player's on-based percentage and slugging percentage.

On the upswing, Raines did steal 78 bases but the joke was that he often put cocaine in his back pocket and slid in head-first so that the cocaine vials wouldn't fall out. What was remarkable was this: despite missing six games in 1982, some of which was blamed on absenteeism or tardiness to the park because of the cocaine addiction, Raines managed what was somewhat phenomenal: a career-high 731 plate appearances.

His decline in '82 was indeed blamed in part on his admitted use of cocaine. After the '81 season, Raines went back home to Sanford, Fla. and got messed up with the wrong crowd, taking advantage of his celebrity status. This cocaine habit carried into 1982 spring training and the regular season. He went into rehab following the '82 season and kicked his habit. In the 1990s, Raines admitted to me that because of his drug use, "I felt like Superman."

Oliver was the kingpin star of the Expos, making his teammates and fans try to forget about Parrish. Funny thing, though, Oliver was supposed to have been traded to the Yankees by the Rangers not long before he was traded to the Expos but there was a stumbling block. That stumbling block was the late Oscar Gamble, who somehow was able to reject a deal to Arlington after Rangers GM Eddie Robinson and Bill Bergesch of the Yankees had agreed on a deal. Gamble wasn't a 10-and-5 player, meaning he had 10 years in the majors, the last five with the Yankees. If he did, he had rights to turn down the deal.

"What happened was that the deal was made. The Yankees and Rangers had made a deal for me to go to the Yankees but Oscar Gamble vetoed the deal," Oliver said. "The deal was already made a week before the trade to Montreal. Something strange about this was that Oscar and I had the same agent: Howard Mandel.

"Then the Expos came into play. Montreal was a team that had a chance to win. The Expos were close the year before so I knew I was going to a good team. I fit right in with those guys. We had a lot of fun, a lot of laughs. I really enjoyed playing with those guys. All along, I knew we had a team that should win the division. The Cardinals were a little better in more areas than we were."

"The reason '82 stood out was that I finished first in quite a few categories. That was the first time anyone had done that since Stan Musial in 1969. That's what I was told," Oliver said in looking back. "That's what made '82 better than 1980. 1980 was a pretty good year also. The biggest thing about 1982 was the all-star game played in Montreal. I received a standing ovation."

While with the Texas Rangers in 1980, Oliver batted .319, his OPS was .838 and he drove in a career-high 117 runs. He went crazy, playing in 163 games, one over the limit, the 163rd game being a playoff game to decide a playoff spot.

What Oliver was keen about revealing is that few people knew that he played the entire 1982 hurt. Can you imagine what he would have done if he was completely healthy? A bum left shoulder hindered him.

"Probably the most difficult thing in 1982 when I came to Montreal, people don't realize it, even to this day some of my teammates didn't know that I had a shoulder injury," Oliver said. "I asked Andre Dawson four years ago or so, if they knew what was wrong with my arm and he said he didn't know. There were times when I was throwing that my arm would lock up. The fans never booed me, never. I felt love for the Expos fans.

"Nobody really asked me about my shoulder. I was never a complainer. I can't remember how I got the injury but all of a sudden in 1981 I had trouble throwing. Something just popped up. Then in spring training in 1982, I had a hard time throwing. So they sent me to see Dr. Frank Jobe in California, who at the time, was the specialist for Major League Baseball. He x-rayed my shoulder and found a bone spur was there. He said if I was 26 instead of 36 that he would have probably suggested surgery. He gave me some exercises to do."

And it helped that McClain and assistant trainer Mike Kozak would attempt to give some comfort before every game by stretching out his arm and shoulder.

"When Al Oliver was traded to us, he could hardly lift his arm above his ear and we tried to improve his range of motion," McClain said. "It was a real gradual process. It was like pushing against a wall. It hurt him like heck. There was a bone formation in there. He was trying to get another couple years out of his body. He could hardly throw the ball to home from first. Once a game, because teams knew he had a bum arm, they would bunt to him."

Oliver more than made up for throwing problems with what he did at the plate. His Rangers manager Tom Grieve once said he had never seen a player hit the ball as hard as Oliver did. He hit screamers. If he played today, they'd be telling us how fast the ball was coming off the bat in miles per hour. In his heyday, there were no speedometers in major-league parks.

"I knew I was capable of having a year like that," Oliver said of 1982. "My batting average wasn't too much higher than I hit before. I always hit a lot of doubles. It was one of those years. As I say, I hit the ball hard. I was known as one of the best hitting hitters in baseball when I came to Montreal. I never really worked at it. It always came natural but at the same time, I never took it for granted."

22

Ron (Opie) Howard suits up for the Expos

It was hours before game time as the Expos got ready to take on the Dodgers at Chavez Ravine in 1982.

Writer and actor Jimmy Ritz of Happy Days TV fame was talking with Expos hitting coach Billy DeMars, his close friend. DeMars and Expos equipment manager John Silverman would occasionally stay or eat at Ritz's house in the L.A. area.

In the course of a conversation, one thing led to another and Ritz told DeMars that he was bringing actor and movie director Ron Howard to the game. Almost immediately, DeMars said he would arrange for a field pass at Dodger Stadium for Howard and Ritz.

As things moved forward, DeMars was then asked, "Any chance you could arrange for Ron to get in an Expos' uniform before and during the game tonight?"

So DeMars pondered the request and told Ritz he would run it by manager Jim Fanning. Gentleman Jim quickly agreed and DeMars arranged for Silverman to issue Howard a uniform.

"I had asked Ron if he was free to come to the game and he said, 'Oh, I would love to come to the game,'" Ritz recalled.

"Ron's dream was to be on a bench during a major-league game," DeMars said in an interview. "Jimmy wrote a couple of episodes for Happy Days which Ron was an actor in, playing Richie Cunningham. I got introduced to Jimmy years earlier when I was a coach with the Phillies and we became good friends."

In a photo that has been circulated on social media, Howard is seen in an Expos' uniform and hat, beaming at the camera in the presence of a number of Expos' players, including Dan Norman, Scott Sanderson and Jeff Reardon. One other photo is also in DeMars' possession: Howard and DeMars posing on top of the Expos' dugout. It was taken by Ritz and given to me.

When one of the photos was broached in a phone conversation with DeMars, he surprisingly said, "I'm looking at the photo right now."

The photo is on DeMars' wall at his residence in Clearwater Beach, Fla. and it brings back great memories for him. Ritz lives in Oldsmar not far from where DeMars lives. The photo shows the Expos in what

Photo submitted by Billy DeMars
Ron Howard (left) and Billy DeMars before an Expos game in 1982

appear to be 'home' white uniforms but they are actually grey or light blue designed for 'road' games.

Howard spent eight seasons as Opie Taylor on the Andy Griffith Show in the 1960s. Happy Days was a television hit, beginning in 1974, but a year prior to its inauguration, director George Lucas of Star Wars fame had picked Howard to star in his 1973 feature film American Graffiti.

Howard was 28 at the time he donned the Expos' uniform and by then, he had stepped away from acting to concentrate on directing. And by the sounds of it, Howard actually looked like a ballplayer and hit like a ballplayer, not some guy up there flailing away hopelessly. He caught and threw like a normal ballplayer would.

"Ron dressed up in an Expos' uniform for batting practice," remembered Expos trainer Ron McClain. "He took BP, shagged balls in the outfield, took ground balls and so on. The plan was that he would be a batboy and he might have for one inning. I can't remember. He had a good stance and swing. He was a line-drive hitter. No power but he looked like he could do it in his younger days."

All the pre-game rituals went without fanfare because there were few if any fans around and Howard had the time of his life. He was acting out a dream but when the game began, there was a commotion. Photographers covering the game got wind of Howard's presence. The end result was negative. It was one of the few times in baseball history that an umpire ejected a celebrity from a game.

"Photographers found out and started taking pictures. The whole situation got messed up. By the second or third inning, I had to tell Ron to get off the field. He was having an absolutely great time. There was a game to be played and the umpires didn't like the commotion. It ruined the night for me and Ron," DeMars said.

"When photographers realized it, they kept taking pictures," McClain said. "Soon, the umps noticed and realized something was going on in the dugout. I do know the umps ruined it by tossing Ron out of the dugout. They said it was causing a distraction to the game.

"They thought he would have to have a job in order to sit in the dugout. The umps didn't buy it. No visitors are allowed in the dugout so he had to leave. So he left. He went back to the clubhouse and got dressed. He loved the experience, though. It was a fun day for awhile. He enjoyed the on-field, pre-game experience, I know that. He was a good guy. He loved baseball," McClain said.

"Ron didn't make a big deal out of it, of having to leave. He was just happy," Ritz said. "When the press got involved, Jim Fanning was thinking this may be getting out of hand, that it might get a bit hairy. To be very truthful, if the press hadn't caught on, Ron would have been there in the dugout the whole game. It was the first time, to my knowledge, that Ron had been in a big-league uniform. At one time, Jim Fanning had Ron's name on the lineup card as an extra and then he scribbled it out. It was a fun day,"

As Sanderson said in an interview a few days ago, he remembered most of all the sheer joy in Howard's face.

"He had this huge excitement, a smile on his face that wouldn't leave," Sanderson told me in 2017. "He had a grin on his face all day long. I remember him being so excited that he was talking a mile a minute. It was funny to watch. He was a bundle of nervous energy.

"He was just like a kid, he wanted to ask questions. He just wanted to talk. It makes you chuckle. We were pretty excited to have him join us. He was acting like a Little Leaguer. There was a game going on but it was nice to see someone take an interest in the game."

One Facebook member, musician Terry Edmunds, posted that Howard would occasionally bring his kids Bryce, Jacelyn, Paige and Reed to games in Montreal over the years.

"Ron was a big baseball fan and him and his kids would drive up from N.Y. state a lot to watch the games," Edmunds wrote. "Seems Richie (Cunningham) got it, the cool vibe that was the Expos. He always wanted to hang out with the coolest."

Online reports say Howard sold his 17,200 square foot, Victorian-themed mansion on the New York/Connecticut border for $27.5-million in 2014. The Howard property on Converse Lake had an address in

Armonk, N.Y. but part of it fell in tony Greenwich, Conn.

As a map shows you, a trip to Montreal by the Howard clan would have been on a direct line on I-87 North for about six and a half hours. Howard was born in Oklahoma but moved to southern California with his family at age 4. He and his wife Cheryl bought the New York/Connecticut property, which included a sports barn, in 1985 to raise their family. When the kids were grown up, Howard and his wife moved the family back to California.

We contacted Howard's office to see if he might talk about his Expos' experience but his PR handlers said there was no way we could get an interview unless we got an agent or lawyer to intercede. We also wrote a postal letter to Howard's business address of Imagine Entertainment in Beverly Hills, Calif. but we never heard back. We also tweeted him a note.

Howard is still going strong these days as a director, movie producer and story teller. One of his latest projects was called Solo: A Star Wars Story.

"Ron Howard was an excellent person, just like you and I. A great kid," DeMars said.

"I'd been in the Phillies' dugout in uniform myself for 10 years," Ritz said. "I was with them when they won the World Series in 1980. I'd met Billy DeMars many years prior to that. Ron also got to be in a White Sox uniform in the 1980s on at least two occasions when Tony La Russa was the manager. Ron and I have a long history with various teams.

"Ron was a huge Dodgers' fan. Sandy Koufax was his favourite. Ron played organized ball. He had a pretty normal childhood even though he was acting. He played Little League and he played on our Happy Days softball team. Here's a funny story: one time when we were in Anaheim and shagging balls, we were with the White Sox before a game and a batter hit a shot to left field and Ron bumped into the wall and caught the ball and one of the players said, 'Opie, yes.'"

How close are Howard and Ritz? Howard was best man at Ritz's wedding in 1982 around the time Howard suited up for the Expos.

McClain said it wasn't uncommon that celebrities would want to take batting practice with the Expos.

"We had several celebrities take BP over the years," McClain said. "I had New York Knicks trainer Mike Saunders help shag balls for extra hitting and then coach Joe Kerrigan would let him hit for about 20-30 swings. I remember Mike Fitzgerald hitting him fly balls off a fungo bat, taking him up against the wall at Shea Stadium. He said, 'I can't believe I am out here where Darryl Strawberry, Willie Mays and Duke Snider stood.' He was thrilled. He spent 30 years as the Knicks' trainer."

23

Bill Virdon becomes manager

After a disappointing finish to the 1982 season, the Expos went looking for experience in a manager and they settled on Bill Virdon, who had been the Houston Astros skipper for many years.

Virdon was old school but then GM John McHale thought he would be the guy to push the team back into post-season play and eliminate the country-club atmosphere that permeated the clubhouse.

"I made them work," Virdon told me a few years ago.

Virdon was a hard-nosed guy, who wanted to be a disciplinarian. He tried to get players to shave their beards, especially reliever Jeff Reardon. But Reardon responded by telling Virdon that he was more intimidating on the mound with his beard. So Virdon relented.

Virdon was dealt a severe blow when his pitching coach and confidant Mel Wright was diagnosed with cancer during spring training and died May 16. Virdon then brought in Joe Kerrigan, who took advantage to partake of a long career in that position with the Expos, Red Sox and Phillies.

Virdon also banned alcohol on team flights and in the clubhouse. That edict posed a problem for players such as alcoholic pitcher Randy Lerch, who had joined the team in a swap from the Brewers Aug. 14, 1982. The official wording of the deal was that he was sold but he never found out what exactly was involved. The Expos likely sent money to the Brewers in exchange.

"I tell you what, I started on beer and then I started on the hard stuff," Lerch told me about his addiction. "It was tons and tons of vodka, pretty much straight. Sometimes, I'd put in cranberry juice. At the end, I was drinking a quart of vodka a day."

Yikes. Lerch quit drinking "at the end" because he was advised that he had cirrhosis of the liver. That was in 2016. He has a new lease on life. He has never felt so good in his life. He had a liver scan in the fall of 2019 and he said he's doing fine.

"God has blessed me one day at a time," Lerch said. "The drinking almost killed me. I have arthritis and I've had two hip replacements."

But it was amphetamines or "greenies" as he calls them that got him on the fast track to erosion of his body. It wasn't just booze. He said an unidentified Phillies teammate told him that he should start on the greenies as a starting pitcher.

"I won't mention the name but he was an older successful, established player," Lerch said. "I started the greenies and then started the drinking because it would make you feel so superior. The drinking would keep you alert and it would allow you to sleep. I never started another game without being high on greenies. I went from being a top prospect to an average major leaguer. I started drinking alcohol and it snowballed into worse and worse."

Photo submitted by Frank Albertson

Hockey legend Wayne Gretzky paid a visit to an Expos game in 1982 and batboy Frank Albertson was tickled pink. Albertson ended up giving this bat to Gretzky to keep.

So checking Lerch's stats, he would have been on greenies for nine games he started for the Expos in 1982-83. He said he didn't use greenies if he was pitching in relief. Funny, though, greenies never entered into the equation about the '82 Expos, only cocaine. Lerch said he never got involved with cocaine while with the Expos. He said he wasn't aware of other Expos who were on greenies.

Whether high on amphetamines or not, Lerch looked at those 1982-83 Expos squads as being exceptional.

"That 1982 team was the best I ever played on as far as talent goes," Lerch said. "That team was amazing. It was comparable to that great team in 1981 I was on in Milwaukee. We had Molitor, Simmons, Bando and we ended up losing in the Yankees in the ALCS."

The 1983 Expos squad was a team trainer Ron McClain called the best of the lot from 1979-83. By June 13, the Expos had moved into first place and remained there through the all-star break with a 41-36 record. Later in the season, they went on a 10-3 tear that put them back in first place again after they had faltered.

The Expos scuffled during most of September and finished a disappointing third with a 82-80 record. McHale brought Virdon back for 1984 but he never finished the season. For the final few weeks, beginning Aug. 30, Jim Fanning was back as manager.

"When you get fired, you're never happy no matter where it is," Virdon told me. "We had several pretty good clubs with guys like Andre

Dawson, Gary Carter and Tim Raines."

As we went to press with this book, Virdon is the oldest surviving Expos manager at 88. Felipe Alou is next at 83.

In the 1984-84 off-season when Canadian born Murray Cook took over as GM, one of the first moves he made was to bring in former Brewers manager Buck Rodgers, who had managed the Expos farm team in Indianapolis in 1984 to a 91-67 record. Rodgers was Hollywood-handsome, charismatic, eloquent, quotable and a great communicator, who was honest with players on where he stood with them.

And there was a bombshell coming.

Looking for prized glove

When Mike Sullivan's father died when he was only 12, he said his uncles paid extra attention to him.

"My uncles were amazing and one of them took me to countless Expos games," Sullivan said in an interview. "We'd arrive early and try to get signatures from my idols."

In particular, the Calgary resident had a glove signed by Tim Raines, Andre Dawson, Ellis Valentine, Gary Carter, Warren Cromartie and manager Dick Williams around 1980. It was dear to him that he owned such a glove.

"I was lucky enough to have brief chats with them when they signed," Sullivan said. "Carter was my idol. I was a catcher for many years when I was growing up on the south shore of Montreal."

One day while he was playing a game at Rabastaliere Park on Rue Goyer in St. Bruno, Quebec, some crook lifted the glove out of his Adidas bag and Sullivan hasn't seen it since.

"That was over 30 years ago and I often wonder if the person who has it feels some anxiety about owning it," Sullivan said. "I wish I still had it."

24

Shocking trade

It was Dec. 10, 1984 and Mike Fitzgerald was resting at home in California when the phone rang.

Expos GM Murray Cook was on the other end telling Fitzgerald that he had been acquired by the Expos in a trade with the New York Mets. Fitzgerald was in a daze.

"It was a Monday afternoon. I was shocked when it happened," Fitzgerald was saying recently. "Murray Cook was saying I had been traded but he couldn't give me any info on who was I traded with or who I was traded for. Murray said he was happy and excited to have me."

Then the phone rang again. This time, the caller was someone with the Mets.

"They told me how much they loved me and they traded me," Fitzgerald said in an interview. "They couldn't tell me who I had been traded with or traded for."

Then word got out. Gary Carter was swapped by GM Murray Cook and president John McHale to the Mets in exchange for Fitzgerald, Hubie Brooks, Floyd Youmans and Herm Winningham. A blockbuster. Holy shoot.

Fitzgerald revealed that Brooks found out about the trade while he was watching the NFL Monday Night game. Can you imagine? Fortunately, the Mets reached Fitzgerald before the NFL game went on air. When we checked, the Los Angeles Raiders beat the Detroit Lions 24-3 that night. With his homestate Raiders playing, there was no denying Brooks would be sitting in front of the television.

There was hesitancy on the part of the Expos and the Mets to go into detail about the trade early that day because Expos GM Frank Cashen had to visit Carter at his home in Palm Beach Gardens, Florida to coax him into accepting the trade. Carter could have vetoed the trade because he was a 10-and-5 player, meaning 10 years in the majors, the last five with the same team.

In fact, Cashen would say years later that it took 10 phone calls and several face-to-face meetings with Carter to clinch the deal at the winter meetings.

"He [McHale] didn't want to do it," Cashen told reporters. "I thought the possibility of getting him was slim and none. We needed a hitter and a catcher and he fit the bill completely. I hung in there for a long time, much longer than you do for an ordinary kind of trade."

When most players get traded to Montreal, they don't particularly embrace the idea and Fitzgerald initially entered into that mindset.

"It caught me off-guard. I thought it (Montreal) was as far away as I could be in California," the catcher said. "I didn't look at it (trade) as an opportunity."

Fitzgerald had become content with the team that drafted him in 1982 and had enjoyed a pretty decent season in 1984, batting .242 with two homers and 33 RBI in a part-time role. He was no match offensively for Carter but he became known as a master caller, expert pitch framer and a catcher who pitchers loved to be involved with. Fitzgerald was that blessed in handling a pitching staff. He was an underdog part-timer, who still meant a lot to the teams he played for.

"It's a poker game," Fitzgerald said. "Everyone can catch the ball but behind the plate you're trying to get the most out of your pitcher or pitchers and winning the game. Even if you go 0-for-5 or 3-for-4, the important thing is winning the game. Whether you hit .200 or .300, there are intangibles behind the plate.

"Sport Magazine, in the early onset of baseball numbers, had a stat about me that fortunately when I started games, said that my numbers were real good. It was before stats were coming in. It was before WAR was the thing. The fact that I started a game behind the plate, my team won more games. Nothing against them (other catchers) but my numbers were better. Some of the other guys were saying, 'Why are they playing him (Fitzgerald)?' So you could say the bottom line is that you ask a pitcher to do something and he does it and you get an out. It's the confidence developed between the pitcher and catcher."

25

Face of the franchise

Peggy Bougie of Beaconsfield, Quebec tells an interesting story about a teenager, who had been drafted by the Expos in 1972 out of Sunny Hills high school in Fullerton, California.

Bougie's father Roger Savard, the Expos group director of marketing and sales, went to Dorval airport in suburban Montreal to pick up the stud prospect, who told Savard that he was going to stay at the Queen Elizabeth Hotel in downtown Montreal. Savard said no.

"Don't be ridiculous," Savard told the player. "Get your bag and come up north."

So Savard brought the kid up to his cottage in Morin Heights, 30 miles north of Montreal, and Savard's children were tickled pink.

"My sisters and I rushed up to him to shake his hand. His hand was absolutely enormous, just an enormous hand. He had huge, thick sausages for fingers," Bougie said, smiling. "My father nicknamed him the Kid."

His name: Gary Carter.

In an informal poll I conducted on Twitter and Facebook in September, 2019, I asked Expos fans, who they thought was the Face of the Franchise, considering so many great players donned the Expos uniform from 1969-2004. Getting the majority of votes among 180 respondents was Carter.

There are stories galore about Carter, whose other nicknames included Camera or Kodak because he often smiled and there wasn't a camera, microphone or notepad he didn't like. Some teammates like Andre Dawson resented him for wanting to be smiling much of the time.

"Here's a funny story," Barry Foote was telling me. "Carter was a sort of a mischievous young guy. He'd get on the older guys when they were playing cards."

This would have been 1975 and one of the card players was huge Steve Renko, who finally had enough of Carter's shenanigans one day.

"Hey, kid, I'm trying to finish this card game," Renko told Carter.

As Foote told the story, "Renko picked Carter up and put him upside down in the garbage can."

When I asked Renko about that story, he replied, "I don't recall that.

Photo submitted by Carter family
Gary Carter was one of the most popular Expos of all time

Principals in trade Dec. 10, 1984	
Player	Follow up info
Gary Carter	Died of brain tumour Feb. 16, 2012
Mike Fitzgerald	Sells insurance in Los Alamitos, California
Herm Winningham	Baseball coach in Orangeburg, S.C.
Hubie Brooks	Lives in California
Floyd Youmans	Uber driver in Nashville, Tenn.

Gary was a big guy himself."

Bobby McLaughlin of Huntsville, Alabama absolutely adored Carter. McLaughlin has some 1,700 pieces of Carter memorabilia, mostly cards. Imagine that. There is one piece McLaughlin would love to get his hands on. It's obscure for sure.

"It's the white whale of my Gary Carter collection," McLaughlin said. "I've been searching for years for a Gary Carter 1976-77 Expos Redpath sugar packet. From what I've been able to gather, these were available at several locations around the Montreal area in the late '70s, including Tim Hortons. Finding one of these would mean more than I could ever explain. I've collected Gary Carter stuff for almost 30 years and this is the one item that I've never been able to find that was made during his playing career."

I made some enquiries on McLaughlin's behalf about this nadir and I even emailed Redpath but I had no luck.

Late-night host David Letterman was so enamoured with Carter that when Carter showed up in a Hollywood studio in the 1980s to do an interview in the same studio building as his, Letterman went looking for an impromptu interview with Carter while still on the air.

I've seen the footage as Letterman left his seat on the set of the studio, as cameras rolled. It was during a taping and the footage shows Letterman walking into a back room. He soon saw Carter standing with someone else. Carter and Letterman waved at each other.

From what I could see in a video, though, Carter and Letterman never stopped to talk about a possible interview. Letterman was this-close to Carter and never made a pass at him for an interview. Carter was in the building to do an interview with someone else. Somehow, Letterman didn't seem to find it polite to barge in and try and talk with Carter 1-on-1. It appeared Letterman was actually trying to find a go-between, a producer of some sort, to see if an interview could be arranged.

Letterman returned to his seat for his taping and used his right hand in a waving motion, meaning to say the interview possibility was squashed. He was very much disappointed. That was the power and the glamour of the Carter brand.

In 1982, the Canadian television network CBC's Fifth Estate fashioned a segment called The Montreal Expos Golden Kid. That same year, when Canadian Prime Minister Pierre Trudeau spoke at a gala during MLB's all-star game in Montreal, he referenced Carter's brand, his baseball magnetism and the importance of the Expos in Montreal's scheme of things in Canada.

"It's tough to be a prime minister in a country when you know Gary Carter could be elected tomorrow," Trudeau joked, as gala onlookers chuckled. "There are 25-million people in Canada. Most of them are Expos fans, the rest of them go around lighting candles for the Blue Jays."

Carter was traded by the Expos in December of 1984 to the Mets because management, especially majority owner Charles Bronfman wasn't thrilled about him getting an eight-year contract worth $16-million several years earlier.

"When Carter was traded, it took some of the Expos out of me," said Expos fan Michael Ng of Markham, Ont.

When Carter returned to the Expos by way of a waiver claim from the Dodgers Nov. 15, 1991, Expos fans for the most part embraced the deal. Their hero was back even if he had little left in the tank. His last hit, a double over the head of Dawson on Sept. 22, 1992, was the stuff of legends, the stuff of movies. When that happened, he decided he would not play another game.

Numbers retired by the Expos		
Player	No.	Date
Rusty Staub	10	May 15, 1993
Gary Carter	8	July 31, 1993
Andre Dawson	10	July 6, 1997
Tim Raines	30	June 19, 2004

On July 31, 1993, Carter's No. 8 was retired by the Expos before 36,558 fans. Another momentous night.

"When I was with the Phillies and you played against Gary, you hated him," his former teammate and close friend Tommy Hutton told me. "But as a teammate, you realized he was genuine along with everything he did. I was with him on the golf course when he got the call he was elected into the hall of fame. He wanted to get out of the house to be ready (for the call)."

When Carter died, it was a knockout punch for Hutton, who was Carter's neighbour in Palm Beach Gardens. It was no surprise then that Hutton delivered the eulogy at Carter's funeral.

It wasn't long after Carter's death that it was speculated that the cause of his brain tumour was extensive cell-phone use.

Did Carter's use of cell phones pressed against his head lead to his tumours and ultimate death?

Did chemicals from the artificial turf Carter played on at Olympic Stadium and in U.S. parks lead to those tumours?

Could something like quasi-concussions lead to those tumours? Yes, we are aware knocks on the head can lead to dementia but what about tumours themselves? Carter played in close to 2,056 games as a catcher for the Expos and other teams. Could the mere theory of him pulling a mask over his face and part of his head for close to 20 seasons have some bearing on his brain problems? Balls rattled off his mask and he collided every so often with runners coming home. He played the dirtiest position in the game.

The answer to all these theories? Possible.

Carter was busy, busy in the aftermath of his brilliant playing career so it wasn't uncommon for him to have a cell phone stuck in one of his ears as he talked about upcoming appearances, autograph sessions, chatting with family members, former teammates or his players on the baseball team he coached at Palm Beach Atlantic University in south Florida.

Before and after his funeral in February of 2012, people were chatting outside the church and the theory was thrown out that excessive use of his cell phone was a contributing factor, maybe not 100%, to his brain tumours.

Friends of Carter say he was one of the very first people to purchase a mobile phone when they became available decades ago. He was on the phone often.

"The story about the cell phone was talked about but the family didn't want to admit it," said a close friend of the Carter family. "My wife was at his funeral and this is what came up was his use of the cell phone. You see where there are cases where cell phones are a factor."

It is known that cell phones emit radio-frequency energy, a form of non-ionizing radiation, from their antennas. Tissues, such as ears and the brain's lobes, nearest to the antenna can absorb this energy.

In May 2011, Carter was diagnosed with four malignant tumours in his brain after experiencing headaches and forgetfulness. He tried every available form of treatment and travelled far and wide to U.S. markets outside his south Florida residential area for opinions and treatment options in a valiant attempt to beat his devastating illness.

Duke University in Durham, North Carolina, the home of the famous Durham Bulls' minor-league baseball team, is believed to be the only medical institution that publicly revealed it had treated Carter and this information was disclosed, with approval from the Carter family. Duke staff said Carter was suffering from Stage 4 cancer.

At the time, Allen Friedman and Henry Friedman, co-deputy directors of Duke's Preston Robert Tisch Brain Tumour Centre, said in a statement: "The results of biopsies performed on the tumour in Gary Carter's brain have conclusively shown that Mr. Carter has a glioblastoma. While surgery is not a good option given the location of the tumour, we discussed an aggressive treatment plan with Mr. Carter and his family, which will include chemotherapy and radiation. Mr. Carter's youth, strong physical condition and fighting spirit will be to his advantage as his treatment commences."

Some nine months after the diagnosis, Carter was dead.

Jeff Reardon, a teammate of Carter's with the Expos from 1981-84 and a neighbour of his in Palm Beach Gardens, Fla. from 1981-2012, said he hadn't heard anything about the cell phone connection.

"No, but I know he was on that phone a lot," Reardon said. "He told me he started to write a cheque for something and said he forgot how to write and I think six months later, he was gone."

After a number of attempts, I got in touch with Dr. David Ashley, the director of pediatric neuro-oncology for Duke's brain tumour centre since 2017. He's considered an international leader in pediatric brain tumour research and the former chair of medicine and director of the Andrew Love Cancer Centre at Australia's Deakin University.

Although he didn't speak about Carter specifically due to confidentiality reasons, Ashley deflected the theory of cell phones contributing to brain tumours.

"It's an absolutely difficult thing to prove," Dr. Ashley told me. "Brain tumours can happen to anyone. It's just one of those things. There is no one thing that causes brain tumours. There's no evidence that cell phone use can lead to brain tumours. There was a Scandanavian study done a few years ago that concluded that cell phone use was not a meaningful cause."

Now, what about the chemicals in artificial turf?

"What was the commonality between Gary Carter and other major-league personnel?" asked Russ Hansen, a Canadian who got to know Carter for close to 35 years.

"Gary Carter, Tug McGraw, Dick Howser, Dan Quisenberry, Johnny Oates, John Vukovich, Bobby Murcer, Ken Brett and Darren Daulton all died of glioblastoma and all of them played or coached or managed on artificial turf," Hansen said.

All were in their 50s except for Murcer, 62, and Quisenberry, 45. All gone too soon.

Hansen wonders if there were chemicals causing the tumours. The New York Times zeroed in on the possible link in a story published in August of 2017, shortly after Daulton died. Daulton, McGraw and Vukovich all played on the artificial turf at Veterans Stadium in Philadelphia. There certainly was irony but The Times story didn't reach any conclusions. Like the five Phillies, Carter was exposed to and ingested carcinogens.

Hansen befriended Carter after the catcher invited Hansen to come to an Expos game in August, 1978 to do photography for the Carter family. At the time, Hansen was living in Gananoque, Ont., located about a three-hour drive from Montreal.

As for concussions having some sort of effect leading to tumours, former Expos trainer Ron McClain has never heard of this theory.

"I do not know of any reason," McClain said. "Concussions, 20 years

Denis Brodeur photo/ Scott Oates collection
Gary Carter, left, and Tim Raines in the Expos dugout

of catching and so on have never been a known reason for brain tumours. No one that I know of has alluded to those reasons. Doctors have no idea what causes brain tumours. I really don't think anyone knows what caused Gary's brain tumours."

Former NFL great Gale Sayers has said his rapidly worse Alzheimer's disease was caused mostly by repeated blows to his head during his football days with the Chicago Bears.

Messages left by me with a number of members of the Carter clan in Florida and California went unanswered. It's not surprising. Carter's wife Sandy remarried a few years ago and probably just wants to move away from any more commenting about her late husband.

Hansen's first boyhood hero was hockey great Bobby Orr but then Carter came along. When Carter died, Hansen was devastated.

"I knew the end was near so it kind of hit home about how fragile life is, that nobody is invincible," Hansen said. "Someone that young is not supposed to pass away, not a 57-year-old super hero. My childhood hero was gone."

The fullertoninformer.com website in Carter's home town in California even offered the theory that one of the theories leading to his death was Carter breathing the air, inhaling the metallic laden dust and the airborne organic compounds from the McCoy site, which was a dump for the petroleum industry.

Whatever, Carter's death was earth shattering.

In memory of Carter, Joe Forget of Montreal had a tattoo put on his left arm.

"Gary was passionate about the game. I admired his determination," Forget said. "When he was playing, it wasn't any half step with him. He was doing it all. You could see it in his eyes. It wasn't a job for him. That was Gary Carter on the baseball field.

"Every time the lights came on, he was there, if it was after a big loss, for charity events, for television commercials, with clutch hits in big games. He always rose to the occasion."

Indeed, he did.

26

Marriage for the flight home

During the 1983-84 off-season, the Expos thought they would take a flyer on a famous free agent by the name of Pete Rose, more out of nostalgia because he was long in the tooth at 42 years old and was coming off a lacklustre season with the Phillies.

Rose had hit an un-Rose like .245 in 1983 and the Phillies weren't interested in bringing him back for a sixth season so the Expos snapped him up for $700,000.

While with the Expos, Rose collected his 4,000th career hit off of another antiquated relic, 41-year-old Phillies pitcher Jerry Koosman, at the Expos home opener April 13 before 48,060 fans.

Rose had hoped to reach this plateau in Cincinnati in his hometown in the final game of the Expos eight-game road trip to start the season. Rose had played for the Reds from 1963-1978 so it would have been fitting for Rose to accomplish his feat at Riverfront but Reds pitchers walked him four times in the April 11th game. Hrmmph.

"I remember Bruce Berenyi of the Reds walked Rose that first series in 1984 and the fans booed Berenyi – their own guy," recalled Bob Elliott, an Expos beat writer in those days for the Ottawa Citizen.

So in Montreal in the fourth inning in Game 9 of the season, pitcher Charlie Lea was the batter up before Rose. Koosman had Lea 0-2 before throwing four consecutive balls. Up came Rose. On a 1-1 count, Rose drilled a ball on the outside part of the plate into the right-field corner for a double for No. 4,000. Rose clapped his hands a few times before Phillies shortstop Ivan DeJesus gave him the ball.

The longtime great then bounced the ball several times on the turf and walked the ball over to hand it to Expos hitting coach Billy DeMars, who had come out on the field. In doing so, Rose walked by first base coach Felipe Alou, who also had walked toward second base, figuring Rose would give him the ball. Check the video. Rose wanted to give the ball to DeMars because he admired DeMars so much going back to their days with the Phillies in the late 1970s and early 1980s. DeMars also became a coach under Rose with the Reds following his coaching stint with the Expos.

It's ironic that the Expos were also involved when Rose recorded his

3,000th hit. He did it on May 5, 1978 in Cincinnati against his future Expos teammate Steve Rogers. A five-minute standing ovation ensued.

While with the Expos, Rose committed to his second marriage by engaging in a union with long-time girlfriend Carol Woliung the opening month of the 1984 season in Cincinnati.

"They got married before a justice of peace in Cincy as (Expos president) John McHale had a rule that only wives were allowed on the charter," said Elliott, the founder of the Canadian Baseball Network and a member of the media wings at the National Baseball Hall of Fame in Cooperstown and the Canadian Baseball Hall of Fame in St. Marys, Ont.

"A guy from LA asked Pete rather awkwardly 'What do you call her?' Rose said, 'I call her Carol, but if you saw her you'd probably just say wow.' (Andre) Dawson was right behind me putting on his dress pants and was on one leg. He laughed so hard he lost his balance and nearly fell into the locker."

I contacted Ohio's Hamilton County marriage-licence department and I found out Rose and Woliung applied for a marriage licence on April 10 and got married on April 11 before Judge Melvin Rueger and minister David Miller, although they had been dating for six years or so.

They wed that day so they could make the Expos flight back to Montreal that night after their final game of the road trip at Riverfront Stadium. The courts waived a traditional delay period in order for the marriage to proceed in a hurry, according to the Certificate of Marriage.

According to the marriage certificate, Woliung is listed as having been divorced from Wilson Irvin Foerster on Oct. 7, 1977 and that Rose's divorce from his first wife Karolyn Engelhardt took place Dec. 29, 1980.

"Pete couldn't take his girlfriend on the buses or planes so he just married her and that was within the rules," Expos trainer Ron McClain said, noting that until manager Bill Virdon came along, no wives were allowed on buses or planes. "After Virdon came as manager, it was okay because he wanted to bring his wife. So wives were then allowed."

Woliung was a Philadelphia Eagles cheerleader whom Rose had actually met about 1978 when he was 36 and when she was a 22–year-old bartender at the popular Cincinnati haunt Sleep Out Louie's. Weird moniker but that was the name. Rose years ago told a reporter that Woliung boasted the "best bottom in the whole state" of Ohio.

Rose was seeing Woliung on the side in Cincinnati while still married to Engelhardt, whom he had married in 1964. Former Canadian junior hockey star Dennis Sobchuk told me last year for a Canadian Baseball Network story that he wanted to go on a date with Woliung in 1978 when he was playing for the WHA's Cincinnati Stingers.

Sobchuk would often see Woliung mixing drinks at Sleep Out Louie's near an old firehall on Cincinnati's riverfront. When Sobchuk asked Woliung out on a date, she demurred, saying she was dating someone

MELVIN G. RUEGER
Judge of the Court of Common Pleas
Probate Division
of Hamilton County, Cincinnati, Ohio

Court of Common Pleas
Probate Division
Hamilton County

State File

ML 341705

CERTIFIED ABSTRACT OF MARRIAGE

GROOM	BRIDE
1. Full Name Pete Rose	10. Full Name Carol J. Woliung
2. Birth Number (Do not write in this space)	11. Birth Number (Do not write in this space)
3. Age Last Birthday 4/14/41 age 42	12. Age Last Birthday 5/7/54 age 29
4. Residence County and State Hamilton Co., Ohio	13. Residence County and State Hamilton Co., Ohio
5. Birthplace (State or Country) Ohio	14. Birthplace (State or Country) Indiana
6. Occupation Prof. Baseball Player	15. Occupation None
7. Name of Father Harry F. Rose	16. Name of Father John Woliung
8. Maiden Name of Mother	17. Maiden Name of Mother
9. Previously Married (Number of Times) Once	18. Previously Married (Number of Times) Once

Previously Married to Carol Engelhardt
Divorced Date 12/29/80 Case No. A7907917
Court Hamilton Co., Ohio
Minor Children Pete
Previously Married to
Divorced Date Case No.
Court
Minor Children

Previously Married to Wilson I. Poerster
Divorced Date 10/7/1977 Case No. 20555
Court Dearborn Co., Indiana
Minor Children none
Previously Married to
Divorced Date Case No.
Court
Minor Children

The undersigned upon their oath state that the facts set forth in this application are to the best of their knowledge true, and they hereby consent to the marriage.

FATHER

MOTHER

The undersigned upon their oath state that the facts set forth in this application are to the best of their knowledge true, and they hereby FOR GOOD CAUSE SHOWN THE DELAY PERIOD AS DIRECTED IN SECTION 3101.05 REVISED CODE OF OHIO IS HEREBY WAIVED
MELVIN G. RUEGER, JUDGE
COURT COMMON PLEAS, PROBATE DIVISION
HAMILTON COUNTY, OHIO

FATHER

MOTHER

That neither of said parties is an habitual drunkard, imbecile or insane person, and is not under the influence of any intoxicating liquor or controlled substance that said parties are not nearer of kin than second cousins; that there is no legal impediment to their marriage; that is expected to perform the marriage, and that all of the above statements are true.

Sworn to before me and signed in my presence, APR 10 19 84

Patricia Miller Deputy Clerk

MARRIAGE CERTIFICATE

State of Ohio Hamilton County ss:

I do hereby certify that on the 11th day of April A.D. 19 84, I performed the marriage of Mr. Pete Rose with Carol J. Woliung

Filed and Recorded April 12 19 84 David L. Miller- Minister Clergyman

MELVIN G. RUEGER, Judge

Court of Common Pleas, Probate Division, Hamilton County, Ohio, April 10, 19 84

MELVIN G. RUEGER, Judge

Marriage license was this day granted to above applicants. By Patricia Miller Deputy Clerk

Hamilton County, Ohio marriage records

Copy of Pete Rose's marriage to Carol Woliung

else. In due time, Sobchuk found out that "someone else" was Rose.

Some online reports say Rose met Woliung in Philadelphia when she was an Eagles cheerleader but they had been fooling around in Cincinnati long before then and many years before he divorced Engelhardt.

Rose continued his relationship with Woliung in Philadelphia from 1979-83 when Rose left the Reds after 16 seasons to go and play for the Phillies. Woliung quit her bartending job at Sleep Out Louie's and followed Rose to Philly.

As a compromise when Woliung said no to Sobchuk, Woliung instead recommended that Sobchuk go on a blind date with her friend and roommate Julia Huffmann, a Delta Air Lines employee, who worked the 3 p.m-midnight shift. That worked out conveniently for Sobchuk because by the time he left Riverfront Coliseum after a game, it was around 11 at night.

Sobchuk got married to Huffmann several years later and they celebrated their 40th wedding anniversary in 2019.

Woliung and Rose sought a divorce in 2011 but apparently they are still technically married and still separated. Woliung is officially known as Carol Rose but sometimes is listed as Carol J. Woliung and lives in California.

In the early stages of the couple's separation, media reports say Rose began an open relationship with buxom Korean/American Kiana Kim and they are still together.

When the Expos decided to trade Rose in mid-August of 1984 while the team was in San Francisco, they helped the cause by shipping him to his former team, the Reds, in exchange for Tom Lawless. Although Baseball-Reference and other sites indicate the trade was made Aug. 16, Elliott believes it might have been a day earlier.

Elliott surmised that then

Canadian Baseball Hall of Fame
Pete Rose

Reds owner Bob Howsam felt that the Rose brand would stimulate ticket sales.

"We heard that Rose might have been traded on Aug. 15," Elliott said. "We were in San Fran. In those days, they gave you a rooming list upon check-in. I was supposed to go out but stayed in the room and called Rose's room every 15-20 minutes. I never got an answer. I am not sure if he went from Candlestick Park to the airport or an airport hotel.

"We were staying at the St. Francis. I ordered room service and stayed in all night. The St. Francis was where the Owl and Pussycat with Barbara Streisand was filmed. I had seen the movie and recognized the lobby as soon as we walked in."

Following the trade, Rose and Woliung apparently left together through a back door at the hotel to avoid the media.

Danny Gallagher photo
Pete Rose poses with a fan at an autograph session in Cooperstown, N.Y.

"Pete was the funniest guy we ever had," McClain said. "I knew him from my Reds days. We always got along good. One day, I told some players about how it took Pete seven years in Cincy just to make $100,000. He came into the training room and could remember every contract for his first 15 years or so. He was only making $500,000 in 1978."

Said 1984 teammate Jeff Reardon, "Pete was the ultimate gamer, rooting on our team the whole game even if he wasn't in the lineup."

Just like all of us, Rose has warts and detractors along with good qualities. Bob James, another mate from 1984, didn't take too kindly to Rose and some of his antics. James has no positive memories of Rose, just negative ones. "He picked a feud I thought was petty with Kid (Gary Carter)," James said. "Since everyone was more or less on the same talent level, I tended to judge guys on their integrity. Pete had none. Kid was pretty much the team leader and fan favourite. Pete tried to usurp that with snide remarks behind Kid's back. It was constant ridicule."

After our first print run for this book went to press, I wrote a story that was published in the Montreal Gazette May, 2020, revealing that Rose had his bats corked during the 1984 season with the Expos. This startling revelation was made by long-time Expos groundskeeper Joe Jammer, whose real name is Joseph Wright.

Jammer revealed that stadium employee Bryan Greenberg corked the bats for Rose. Greenberg even showed him the machine. Although Greenberg hemmed and hawed about whether he did cork the bats, he told me, "I really can't answer those questions. I really can't talk about it."

My story was confirmed several weeks later when Joe Capozzi of the Palm Beach Post went to Greenberg's residence in south Florida to ask him about my story. Greenberg said he corked a number of bats for Rose at his house on a lathe in suburban Montreal.

Jammer, currently a musician in Great Britain, was initially asked by me in our chat if he had an all-time favourite Expos player, he replied: "I had so many friends." Then he volunteered — out of the blue — to talk about "too many assholes."

"Pete Rose was the biggest dickhead," Jammer said before bringing up the scenario of corked bats. "That's why I'm coming out and telling you about him corking bats because he was a No. 1 asshole.

"On Pete Rose's birthday in 1984 (April 14), we made up a giant cake, four feet by three feet for him. He gave us shit. He said: 'What am I supposed to do with that?' We felt like telling him to stick it up his ass. And he was mad that none of the players came out of the dugout to shake his hand (at the cutting of the cake)."

Jammer is credited with recording the Expos' tribute song titled Let's Go Expos. He served as the Jam Master band leader at the owners' gala as part of the MLB All-Star Game festivities in Cleveland in 1997. In his younger days, Jammer was a roadie for Jimi Hendrix, The Who and Led Zeppelin.

Stadium model smashed

Many years ago, a young kid, maybe 15, broke into the storage room at the Canadian Baseball Hall of Fame in St. Marys, Ontario and smashed to smithereens a beautiful, full-scale model of the proposed new ballpark for the Expos in downtown Montreal.

"When I got there, and saw the model smashed into a pile of wooden splinters, I remember just standing there and crying," said Tom Valcke, the hall's former executive director. "He used a bat. Some people put a ton of thought and TLC to build that. To smash what was obviously a one-of-a-kind work of art like the stadium-to-be-in-Montreal, I just don't get why a person does those things."

27

Frobel's time in the majors

In what was an eye-catching experience as he began his major-league career, Doug Frobel of Nepean, Ont. shone against his home-country team, the Expos, in early October of 1982.

Doug Frobel was projected as the heir apparent to Pirates' right-fielder Dave Parker and this is what he did in the dying days of the 1982 season: he homered against Charlie Lea of the Expos at Three Rivers Stadium on Oct. 1 and then he homered again the next day, Oct. 2, against Bill Gullickson. Two days of grandeur, two days of showing the Pirates that he might fill Parker's shoes.

In 1984 in the first season the Pirates gave him a chance, Frobel would hit 12 homers and drive in 28 runs in 376 at-bats. He could never match that kind of production again in the majors.

Too often in 1984, Frobel would go days and days without getting a starting role in the lineup. The strategy would drive him crazy. For years, the Pirates had a policy of bringing in players at the end of their careers.

"Pittsburgh went through a transition in 1984," Frobel told me. "Teams like the Dodgers and Mets were bringing up seven or eight young guys from the minors but Pittsburgh went in the opposite direction. I was a young fellow on a team filled with 35-year-old players. It was like 'you gotta win now.' The Pirates would take a flyer on a guy for two years hoping he would produce like he did 15 years ago. It's not always the best thing for an organization. Bottom line is to stick with us young players.'

On Aug. 12, 1985, the Pittsburgh experiment ended. Frobel would never pan out, even with a tryout with the Expos in 1985. Expos manager Buck Rodgers did give Frobel a solid chance midway through September of 1985 when he gave him four consecutive starts in right field from Sept. 16-19. Frobel went 1-for-14 and struck out once in each game, according to my scrolls through game logs on retrosheet.org.

He was a September callup that year and would go 3-for-23 with the Expos, his most notable contribution being a two-run homer, a pinch-hit job.

"You look at patience and you look at who you are," Frobel told me about being acquired by the Expos. "I tried to be what the Expos were looking for. The confusion was what kind of hitter do you want to be? It's like the star hockey player, who scores a lot of goals and then he becomes a defensive player and not scoring a lot of goals and the team is wondering where that player went.

"It's like that Yogi Berra expression: 'Baseball is 90 mental and other half is physical.' The biggest mistake I made was to remake myself.

Canadians with Expos
Bill Atkinson
Derek Aucoin
Denis Boucher
Rob Ducey
Doug Frobel
Mike Gardiner
Shawn Hill
Mike Johnson
Larry Landreth
Matt Maysey
Claude Raymond
Joe Siddall
Matt Stairs
Larry Walker
Compiled by
Danny Gallagher
Scott Crawford

I was a power hitter with a fair number of strikeouts and then I was trying to hit for average, to put the ball in play more. Once you try to remarket yourself, it doesn't always work. You lose faith in yourself. You question yourself on how to play the game. It's knowing who you are.

"Once you lose confidence, it's hard to get it back. It's not an excuse. You have to learn to deal with it. You have to try and do things but in retrospect, it caused more confusion, when you start changing things. If you're facing a 102 m.p.h. fastball and you're thinking of the type of swing you want, it's confusing.

"You don't always get what you want. I am so very happy with the opportunity to do the best I could. It was never from lack of trying. I was quite proud of my time with Pittsburgh and playing right field as a guy who could throw guys out. A lot of teams, for example, like to go with guys who take the liberty of stealing bases but they can't throw."

Give Frobel due credit. At least he made it to the majors and had some success.

As we chatted on the phone, Frobel was sitting in a small booth on a street in downtown Ottawa, collecting money and arranging for cars to be parked. His father Frank once owned four lucrative parking lots in Ottawa, beginning in the 1950s and now there are two and they are gold mines operated by Frank's sons.

"I'm sitting in what was my father's chair. Even when I was in the major leagues, I was helping out with the parking lots," Frobel said. "I chit-chat with all of the customers. I gab too much.

"My brothers and I work together. We have a great relationship. We're proud of what we are doing. It's in our blood. I remember coming down here when I was nine years old and making 50 cents on a Saturday to make money. I can't tell you where the parking lots are located because people would want to come here and talk."

Ironically, Frobel never did get a baseball card made up by Topps, Upper Deck or any other company. Same thing happened years earlier when Elroy Face pitched for the Expos in 1969.

A few notes about the Expos over the years

* Dick Radatz, Elroy Face, Lee Smith, Claude Raymond, Howie Reed, Rocky Biddle, John Strohmayer, Graeme Lloyd, Anthony Telford and Steve Kline are among a group of pitchers, who collected their last saves in an Expos uniform.

* Tim Foli was the first Expo to hit for the cycle. He did it April 21, 1976. Brad Wilkerson was the last, doing it June 24, 2004. Tim Raines was a cycle guy on Aug. 16, 1987, Chris Speier turned the trick July 20, 1978 and June 11, 1995 was Rondell White's special night. Vlad Guerrero did it in 2003 on Sept. 14.

* Jose Morales was some pinch hitter for the Expos in 1976. He set a MLB record with 25 pinch hits that season. He held that record until John Vanderwal collected 28 with Colorado in 1995.

* Expos Up, Up and Away author Jonah Keri's fall from grace has been dramatic. The Montreal native and writer/commentator for Sportsnet and other publications was charged in 2019 regarding an alleged assault and death threats on his second wife Amy Kaufman but also for an alleged incident several years earlier. Keri deleted his Twitter account not long after he was charged. He's innocent until proven guilty.

* Larry Parrish is the only Expo to hit three-homer games on three separate occasions: May 29, 1977, July 30, 1978 and April 25, 1980. In the 1977 game, LP went 5-for-5, drove in five runs and scored five runs in St. Louis. "I think I was the only guy that hit three home runs in Old Busch Stadium," Parrish said. And believe this: the 1977 performance of 5s earned Parrish a nod in Ripley's Believe It Or Not.

* Chris Speier was Waxo, Tony Perez earned the Doggie moniker, Tim Raines was Rock, Rodney Scott was Cool Breeze, Bill Lee was Spaceman, Andre Dawson was known as Hawk, Gary Carter was Kid.

* Darryl Strawberry of the Mets, Henry Rodriquez of the Expos and Dave Kingman of the Mets (ruled a foul ball) hit balls that hit the rim of the roof at Olympic Stadium over the years. 525 feet from home plate.

* They were Expos who died way too young – murdered. Ivan Calderon, execution style, and Pascual Perez, hit repeatedly with a hammer and stabbed. Calderon, 42, died Dec. 27, 2003 and Prancin' Pascual, 55, died Nov. 1, 2012. Carl Morton was one of the youngest Expos to have died when he succumbed at 39 of a heart attack April 12, 1983.

* Rusty Staub's Second Coming with the Expos was something else. July 27, 1979, his first game in Montreal following his acquisition from the Tigers attracted 59,260 for a doubleheader. When he came in as a pinch hitter in Game 1, the stadium rocked as he got standing ovation after standing ovation. This author was at the game and it's the Expos' highlight of all highlights for me.

* Mike Lansing was humbled after his playing days were over. When he played, he was fiery and productive as an infielder. Off the field, he was a fiery, very assertive and in-your-face kind of guy, who turned Expos management off. He has matured apparently. He was a good friend of Larry Walker.

* Jeff Fassero was the Expos winningest left-handed pitcher with 51 wins. He was magnificent in 1996 with a 15-11 record and a 3.31 ERA.

* Who can forget Ross Grimsley? He's the only Expos pitcher to win 20 games in a season. That was in 1978.

* "It was my second home from 1969-76. I might have been in every section of the ballpark. I lived a five-minute walk from the ballpark." – Montrealer Guy Bourque talking about Jarry Park.

* "Alas, far too many were not done when they graduated from the Universal Expo Development College and took up residence in those rich American markets." – Expos fan John Duval talking about players leaving the Expos because management found them too expensive.

28

Remembering Scott Sanderson

John Sanderson worked in advertising for Sears Roebuck and it often meant relocating to other towns and cities in America.

One of those stops was Dearborn, Michigan where his son Scott was born. Over the course of time, John's last stop with the department store chain was Chicago. That's how Scott ended up in nearby Northbrook, Illinois for the rest of his life.

"Scott settled in Northbrook from sixth grade on through high school. And that move was my good fortune," said Cathleen Cavanaugh, who eventually became his wife.

They met through mutual friends more than 30 years ago

"His really good friend was a friend of mine," Mrs. Sanderson told me. "We met at Thanksgiving in 1978 and we were married in 1979 at the end of the season.

"What I noticed immediately was that he was different from anyone I had met. He was very good and mannerly and very focused. And he was a gentleman. He was 22- years-old and he knew what he was doing with his life."

When they met, he had been growing a beard and when he shaved it off to adhere to the Expos policy of no facial hair, she realized how impossibly handsome he was, moreso than when he had his beard.

"Scott was very respectful to the Expos and he loved John McHale," Mrs. Sanderson said. "For the team, he thought he would shave." But in the off-season, he let his beard grow and then when he went to spring training, he shaved again.

Sanderson, Bill Gullickson and Tim Raines all made the Expos roster out of the 1977 free-agent amateur draft. Sanderson was taken out of Vanderbilt and reached the majors at age 21 after making only 28 minor-league appearances. Big Scotty, 6-foot-5, was called up by the Expos in August of 1978 and his wife told me the team told him to go home at one point because he had "too many innings in his arm." He had pitched that season in Denver, Colorado, Memphis, Tenn. and Montreal.

Sanderson pitched for the Expos from 1978-83 and his best sea-

Dariush Ramezani Illustration
Scott Sanderson pitched for the Expos from 1978-83

son was 1980 when he posted a 16-11 record with a 3.11 ERA. In the strike-shortened 1981 season, he was 9-7 with a 2.95 ERA. He had a curveball that fell off the table.

One of the highlights of Sanderson's career was a grand slam he hit against the Cubs at Wrigley Field on Sept. 11, 1982. With Tim Wallach on third, Chris Speier on second and Doug Flynn on first, Sanderson hit the first pitch he saw for a homer to right off of Randy Martz in the third inning.

"When he came back to the dugout, it was really funny," Mrs. Sanderson said. Yes, Sanderson's teammates had initially given him the silent treatment before swarming him.

Sanderson later pitched for the Cubs, the Oakland Athletics, the New York Yankees, the California Angels, the San Francisco Giants and the Chicago White Sox. He made two appearances in the 1990 World Series when Oakland was swept by the Reds.

"Scott would say one of the highlights of his career was pitching in the World Series. He really loved that year," Cathleen said. "He just

Photo submitted by Cathleen Sanderson
Scott and Cathleen Sanderson made a great couple

really felt very fortunate to play so long for 19 seasons. He always felt so privileged to have had the opportunity to live out a boyhood dream.

"When he was traded to Chicago, he just cried. Montreal was a great city. Regarding being traded, that's just baseball. They don't tell you why, and we don't ask. But it turned out good because he got to play in his hometown with the Cubs."

Following his career, Sanderson became a player agent, representing the likes of Frank Thomas, Lance Berkman and Josh Beckett.

Sanderson died April 12, 2018 of esophageal cancer which his wife told me stemmed from throat-cancer radiation he endured 10 years earlier. He had his voice box removed and he suffered a stroke but we won't get into anymore details.

"He was one of my best friends," Wallach said. "As good of a person and friend you would ever know."

Sanderson was also very close with Larry Parrish, Terry Francona, Brad Mills, Tommy Hutton and many more. As former teammate David Palmer said, "Pitchers are always close, teammates for life. Scott and I were teammates in A ball, Double-A and the major leagues. We were teammates for a long time. He was just a great guy, a great person."

Parrish said that although him and Sanderson "came from different backgrounds", they jelled as friends.

"He was a good friend," Parrish said. "He was godfather of my son Josh. He was a tough competitor in baseball and he showed the same makeup in his battle with cancer. Scott is out of pain and in a better place now."

29

The extraordinary Dawson

If Andre Dawson had not panned out as a baseball player, what would he have done after graduating from Florida Agricultural and Mechanical University in Tallahassee, Florida?

As a physical education major, who wasn't inclined agriculturally or mechanically but took biology and math, he figured he would become a baseball coach.

But Dawson's magic as an athlete, mostly as a baseball player, won out because he went on to fashion a 21-season career in the big leagues despite a multitude of knee problems.

Dawson was a walk on at Florida A& M, an all-black university, and made the baseball team's starting lineup as a freshman after being turned down for scholarship offers because universities were reluctant to take a chance on someone following a knee injury. Undeterred, he made up with his talent on the field and sure enough, the Expos came along to sign him. He decided to forego his senior year to sign with Montreal.

Before he even got to Florida A& M, Dawson had to cope with knee problems. It all happened while he was playing football for Southwest Miami high school.

"It was just before the end of the first half," Dawson recollected with ease. "It was a kind of like a Hail Mary pass and the ball was overthrown. I was the free safety and the closest one to the ball. The cornerback Carrell Johnson jumped in for the interception. He was pushed by the wide receiver and the cornerback's helmet ended up hitting my left knee."

Since then, Dawson has been one courageous, brave man, who has undergone 15 knee operations, including three replacements, the left knee twice, the right knee once. Before the replacements, he had surgery six times on each knee.

Dawson rarely complained over the years and with help from Expos trainers Ron McClain and Mike Kozak, he was able to get on the field often and excel. As Dawson's good Canadian friend Russ Hansen said, Dawson provided his own therapy with extra-extra discipline and work-

Russ Hansen photo
Andre Dawson at Olympic Stadium in September, 1996

outs that he continues to this day. For years, he could bench press 400 pounds.

"Never in my life have I met an athlete with the discipline and commitment Andre had in caring for their body," Hansen said. "He would go to the gym every day when he was playing. Discipline is a big word. He looked after his body. That's why he survived 22 seasons. His upper legs above the knees to his waist, he's got a lot of muscle. When he played, he had a 30-inch waist, a 46-inch chest and a 37-inch inseam.

"Every winter, he would be rehabbing his knees. It was an annual right of passage for him. I can remember in the early 1980s after a game, I'd drive him back to his apartment in Montreal and he could barely get in and out of the car. He could barely move. He'd take anti-inflammatory stuff and fall asleep. Then the next day, he'd be on the field. It was totally amazing the pain threshold that man had."

Dawson's ascent into the majors came quick. After a short summer stint in 1975 with the Expos' Canadian rookie-league team in Lethbridge, Alberta where he batted .330, hit 13 homers and drove in 50 runs, Dawson spent time in 1976 with the Double-A Quebec Carnavals and the Triple-A Denver Bears before being called up by the parent club in September, 1976.

By 1977, the centre-fielder was ready to show the Expos and the opposition that he was for real as the Expos transferred to Olympic Stadium from Jarry Park.

"I played the entire month of September in 1976 and I thought I'd won the job outright," Dawson said. "I thought I had accomplished that. But in 1977 I was platooned at the outset with Del Unser. I played against left-handed pitchers, he played against right-handers."

Soon, though, Dawson was handed the CF job full time after he hit his first home run in Atlanta on May 18. He got into a rhythm, got more playing time and he went on to capture rookie-of-the-year honours with 19 homers and 65 RBI in 525 at-bats. And he just got better and better.

One day the following season at Olympic Stadium before a game, Hansen walked from the

Photo submitted by Paul Newsome
Greg Newsome with Andre Dawson in a photo taken at Olympic Stadium

Expos dugout up the tunnel, turned the corner to the right toward the clubhouse and ran into Dawson, who was rubbing the handle of his bat, taking away the smoothness of the handle by roughing it up on the concrete blocks on each side of the mortar joints. That way, he would be able to grip the handle better. It was one of Dawson's idiosyncrasies.

Hansen and Dawson struck up a conversation and Dawson was very accommodating. It was the beginning of a friendship that has lasted more than 40 years. Years later when Hansen's marriage was failing, Dawson brought Hansen to his Miami home for two weeks to help get his life back together during his grieving process.

"My 20th birthday was on the day Andre and his wife Vanessa were married Dec. 16, 1978," Hansen said. "Andre has been like a big brother to me more than my own brother.

"What solidified my relationship with Andre came in 1979 before a game at Olympic Stadium. His mother Mattie and his sister were there and we were outside the clubhouse and this security guy grabbed me and pinned my arms. I guess he thought I shouldn't be there. Andre's mother saw this happen and she let out about 30 f-bombs and told the guy, 'Leave him alone, he's part of us.' I was just a kid so I was surprised to hear this woman letting out all of these f-bombs."

Hansen also remembers the time he got together with the Dawsons in a room at the Inn at Indigo in Daytona Beach, Florida in 1979 during spring training. The Dawsons gave Hansen a bag full of clippings and photos so he took it and put the contents in scrapbooks for them.

Dawson was part of those wonderful Expos teams from 1979-82. He won't forget Willie Stargell hitting that big home run on Sept. 18, 1979, he doesn't forget the hurt of Mike Schmidt hitting a bomb against Stan Bahnsen Oct. 4, 1980 and he doesn't forget the extreme hurt and pain caused by Rick Monday's gigantic home run off of Steve Rogers on Oct. 19, 1981.

Dawson remembers the joy and elation at playing in the all-star game in Montreal in 1982 along with teammates Tim Raines, Al Oliver, Steve Rogers and Gary Carter.

"That was an historic moment, the first time the all-star game was played outside the United States. It was exciting to have it in our own ballpark. It was a sellout," Dawson said.

And how about the hurt, disappointment and soul searching that took place in the off-season of 1986-87 when there was a stalemate in contract talks involving Dawson and the Expos? After earning $1.2-million in 1986 when he hit 20 homers and drove in 78 runs, the Expos insulted him in the winter of collusion by offering him a slash in salary.

To add insult to injury, Dawson was being told by the Expos that he was washed up as a player, that he was no good anymore, according to Hansen. Dawson was very open to Hansen about what he was going through. Hansen was a bit of a sounding board for Dawson, who was concerned about his future, what with all of the knee operations as he contemplated free agency.

"They did make an offer but the offer was $200,000 less than the previous season," Dawson told me in late 2019 of the Expos' final approach. "Coming up as a free agent, that wasn't fair market value. My last meeting with the Expos was in West Palm Beach. I thanked them for the 10 years I was there but I told them I couldn't accept that offer and that it was time to move on."

Dawson decided to take his chances with the Cubs and told general manager Dallas Green in what became known as a famous declaration: "Fill in the amount you want to pay me and I will take it."

So Green jotted down $600,000 and Dawson, a man of integrity, signed the contract and went on to enjoy a career season of 49 homers and 137 RBI.

"Andre was the talk of the town in Chicago that season. It was pretty amazing," Hansen said. "What was really cool about Andre is that he evolved from being the quiet kind of person to become a guy that when he spoke, people listened.

"When he was in Montreal, Gary Carter was the spokesman and Andre was kind of shyer than Gary was. Andre has really evolved into a person who can speak so good. You are empowered when you watch and listen to his (Cooperstown) induction speech."

Dawson played six seasons with the Cubs before he left for free agency after new GM Larry Himes didn't offer him a contract for the 1993 season. Himes even had the nerve to chastise Dawson once because he wore cowboy boots and jeans with a sports jacket that had no lapels.

"Himes got on Andre's case because he thought he wasn't dressed properly," Hansen said. "Andre was an impeccable dresser. He was second to nobody. Him and Ozzie Smith were GQ kind of guys. Andre, when he was in Montreal, had all of his suits custom made by Alex Villani and Raffi Agnerian."

Dawson would go on to play for the Red Sox and Marlins. He made his final all-star game appearance in Toronto in 1991. It was there in a hotel room, the Crowne Plaza, that Hansen egged Dawson on by noting that he had never hit a home run in an all-star game.

"It might be your last all-star game," Hansen told Dawson. So what did Dawson do? He hit a home run to lead off the fourth inning off of Roger Clemens, a shot that bounced off the glass of a restaurant façade in centre field.

Hansen got Dawson to autograph a ball from that game and then Dawson got Clemens to sign the ball when he joined the Red Sox in 1994. Hansen still has that memento.

Dawson collected 438 career homers and 1,591 RBI but it took awhile for the Baseball Writers Association of America to vote him into Cooperstown in 2010.

"It was bittersweet," Dawson said of his induction. "It had taken nine years. I was numb, excited, emotional. I thanked my mother (Mattie) and grandmother (Eunice) both for how they raised me. I wanted them to be looking down on me."

For more than 15 years, Dawson was a goodwill ambassador for the Marlins but his salary was reduced drastically a few years ago by new CEO Derek Jeter so he decided to move on. Dawson had no plans to attend Jeter's induction ceremony in Cooperstown in July, 2020.

For many years, too, Dawson has played a major role in an unusual occupation: he's an undertaker. With help from family members, he runs the Grace Funeral Home in North Miami. He has been known to mop floors, clean washrooms, do general errands and occasionally counsels people through the grieving process. His wife, whom he met growing up, is the office manager.

"It kinda fell into my lap. I started out as an investor in one funeral home," he said. "I secured a loan on the property and got some financing. It was shut down by the state because of some violations. At that point, I made the determination to open it up under a different name (Grace)."

Dawson has always been a somewhat stoic guy but he admits he has shed a few tears while on the job at the funeral home, especially when he deals with the family of friends, who have departed.

"When you have people you know, it effects you to a degree. It was like how I felt with my mom when she died," Dawson said.

When I asked him if he had shed tears during his days in baseball, he immediately thought of the heartbreak experienced when the Expos fell short of the World Series in 1981.

"When we lost to the Dodgers, it was hard. I was sitting on the bench and was one of the last ones to go to the clubhouse. That's an instance I remember, a bitter memory."

Dawson has been very charitable over the years with most of his philanthropic work earmarked for Alzheimer's causes because his grandmother died of Alzheimer's. Dawson donated an autographed ball that I auctioned off at the Douglas Expos 50th anniversary reunion and fund-raiser Sept. 1, 2019 when we raised $605 for Hospice Renfrew near Ottawa, Ont.

Just don't get too demanding of Dawson. I remember being in the VIP room at the Warren Cromartie-organized 1981 Expos reunion in 2012 in Montreal when a woman kept hounding Dawson a few times for extra autographs. At one point, Dawson, deservedly so, got upset at the lady.

Here's another story: when Dawson drove from Miami to see the very ill Carter in Palm Beach Gardens shortly before he died, one of Carter's main autograph managers, Mead Chatsky, also showed up. Dawson lit into Chatsky big time and called him out, to say in no un-

Photo supplied by Dustin Puckett
Dustin Puckett poses with two of Andre Dawson's uniforms

certain terms that it was quite galling for Chatsky to appear at Carter's deathbed seeking autographs.

"If you got on Andre's bad side, you certainly knew about it," Hansen said, in referencing Chatsky.

And talking of autographed memorabilia, how about we mention this collector in Louisiana by the name of Dustin Puckett, who has delivered bread for decades and who is a serious, serious hoarder of Dawson stuff.

Puckett has gone crazy over Dawson. Puckett has collected over 200,000 of his cards, over 3,600 of them different. He has 1,093 Dawson cards autographed. There are 1,292 memorabilia cards and 170 rookie cards.

"I also collect other Andre Dawson memorabilia such as 8x10s, magazines, postcards, bats, balls, caps, cleats, jerseys, baseball boxes, cups, mugs, plates, buttons, coins, pins, plaques, statues and tickets," Puckett said in an interview. "I have 40 autographed balls. The number of Dawson Expos' cards I wouldn't know but it would be in the tens of thousands. I don't have my cards separated by team. I also collect cards of other players that Dawson happens to show up in the picture. I call these cards cameo cards and I have 28 of them. "

Puckett, 39, figures his collection of Dawson memorabilia is the largest not only of Dawson but likely of any sports athlete, period, in terms of size.

"Some of my online friends think I'm weird and crazy because of this collection but at the same time, they think it's fabulous," Duckett said.

Just don't ask Puckett what he has spent on his collection.

"In 1990, Dawson, Mark Grace and Jose Canseco came to Alexandria (Louisiana) for a baseball card show," Puckett related. "I got Dawson's autograph and I was so nervous when I went up on the stage to get his autograph that I couldn't even speak to him and I smudged one of the autographs because I didn't let it dry."

To help Puckett out, I asked Dawson a few years ago if he would talk with Puckett and they soon had a chat on the phone.

Dawson, the man, like Dawson the athlete, is extraordinary.

30

Cinderella team in 1987

This was a team that wasn't supposed to do much of anything in 1987.

The Expos were a measly 78-86 in 1986 and there was little hope for 1987 when iconic outfielder Andre Dawson left the team in the midst of free agency to sign a contract with the Chicago Cubs in what was deemed a collusion off-season.

Closer Jeff Reardon was dealt to the Minnesota Twins in the off-season, leaving the bullpen high and dry with no clear-cut man to close out the ninth inning.

All of a sudden, the Expos no longer had their reputable RBI star in Dawson. And his bosom buddy Tim Raines was not with the team to start the season because of free-agency rules. But not long after the season started, the team started to jell.

"I remember just the way we came together," starting pitcher Bob Sebra recalled. "We started 0-5."

At that point, Sebra started chuckling.

"Murray Cook, the general manager, came into the clubhouse and said, 'I want you guys to give it your best effort, blah, blah, blah. I was particularly offended when he said that," Sebra said. "For somebody at that level to give up on you after five games in a 162-game season and he wanted to kick you in the ass? People thought we weren't going to be worth a damn.

"We had a good team. We hit, ran bases good, the starters were going deep, the bullpen was great. Dennis Martinez (11-4) came up and was throwing great. Pascual Perez (7-0), he was doing the same."

So what happened? The Expos clearly became a Cinderella team that almost made the playoffs, winning 91 games. The Expos went down near the end of the season, only to place third in the NL East behind the first-place Cardinals and the second-place Mets.

The Cardinals swept a doubleheader in St. Louis on Sept. 29 by 1-0 and 3-0 scores and took the four-game series 3-1. That was a killer for Montreal.

The Expos sure made believers out of many people, including Cook, who wasn't around at the end of the season, because he was fired in August after it was discovered he was having an affair with Pamela Brochu, wife of Expos president Claude Brochu.

"Nobody thought we would be any good at all. We lost Hawk and Reardon and we weren't expected to be good at all," reliever Tim Burke said. "I definitely didn't think we'd be as good."

Burke formed part of a bullpen-by-committee that worked so handsomely under the guidance of manager Buck Rodgers. Burke said the manager's greatest forté was handling a pitching staff.

"He communicated great with players. You don't see a lot of that in sports, communicating, just letting guys know what their roles were," Burke said.

Burke was merely brilliant in what was his best season of all in his big-league career. Burke was 7-0 with an almost-unheard-of ERA of 1.19 with 18 saves, all of this coming after he started the season on the DL with an injury to his right elbow.

From July 1 until the end of the season, Burke posted 11 saves and an ERA of 0.54.

"I loved being a closer, the more pressure I felt, the more fun it was. It was the most fun year I've ever had, for sure," Burke said. "I was really locked in the whole year. I felt so good all year long. I felt unbeatable, absolutely unbeatable. I was just not going to give up a hit."

Andy McGaffigan was another solid ace out of the bullpen, going 5-2 with a neat 2.39 ERA and lefty specialist Bob McClure went 6-1 with an ERA of 3.44

"We came from nowhere," Burke said. "We had guys who believed in themselves, who worked really good. That was the year we were bullpen of the year, winning the Rolaids award. We were close out there. We had a lot of fun and laughed a lot and that helped translated in pulling for each other. What also helped was Mike Fitzgerald being our catcher. He was the best, I mean the best, in handling pitchers and hitters' weaknesses."

Fitzgerald played the entire season with a bashed up right-index finger which he hurt Aug. 1, 1986. That finger still looks ugly today. Think of an unsung hero, it was Fitzgerald.

Said McClure: "I'm not surprised we did so good. I believed we could win a playoff spot. If I remember anything from that year is that it was a pretty competitive year. It was a disappointment we didn't win. We had some bad luck. It was 25 guys on that team that helped us get as far as we got. That '87 team, if you could pitch at all, the offence would take care of itself.

"Oh my gosh, there were some great players. It was a pretty close knit group. There was great camaraderie in the clubhouse. It might have been a Cinderella team but we weren't surprised. I was lucky to be along for the ride."

Canadian Baseball Hall of Fame
Bryn Smith pitched for the 1987 Expos

Sebra was a tough-luck pitcher most of the season, losing 15 games while only winning six. Yet, his teammates appreciated what he did as a contributor in the starting rotation. His curveball that season was almost lights-out. He would often get little run support, thus the lopsided won-loss record. He lost five games by shutouts. The Expos scored just 88 runs in his 27 starts.

In his first start, Sebra allowed one run in seven innings but lost 1-0. Then consider that on July 1 at Olympic Stadium, Sebra lost 1-0 to the Cubs on a ninth-inning homer by Jerry Mumphrey in a game where he struck out a career-high 14 batters. The winning pitcher was someone who would go on to win 355 games in the big leagues.

"That was Greg Maddux. That was his first major-league shutout," Sebra said. "It kind of summed up my whole season (little run support). It was the first time I ever threw a cutter in a major-league game. It's like half a slider, you want it to be a hard cut in on the left handed batter, away from the right-handed batter. It spins like a fastball.

"I gave up one walk that game. I gave up two hits and Mumphrey had two of them.

"I had the best curveball I ever had that season. It was pretty much my pitch. Everyone knew I had a pretty good curveball," Sebra said. "I was consistent with that all year. I probably pitched better in '86 but I had no run support then either.

"I felt even though I was 6-15, I was a key part of the team most of that year. I was the No. 5 starter but I was the No. 1 starter because of rainouts.

"I pitched in two shutout games against the Cubs. I had 10 strikeouts in another game against Maddux. He was a rookie that year. I believe he was 6-14. He had a record like mine. You could tell he was going to be good. He learned how to become a pitcher. God, you're talking, as far as I am concerned, about one of the greatest pitchers of all times, for so many years."

One guy Sebra was very grateful to was McClure, an unsung hero who was a teacher, mentor and everything else wrapped in one.

"I learned a lot from him. He had balls, oh yeah," Sebra said. "I can remember the bases were loaded against the Mets and he went 3-0 to Keith Hernandez and threw three curveballs with the bases loaded. It was amazing. That sticks in my mind.

"McClure probably had the biggest influence on me. Some of the things he said to me stuck to me through my whole career. He said to pitch in early, pitch away later. It made a lot of sense to me.

"One game I was pitching against Steve Garvey. We were leading 4-2 and I had two strikes on him. I was trying to go back inside. It was a good pitch but he took me deep to tie it 4-4. On the plane that night, McClure said to me, 'Hey, rook? Do you think you pitched good today? You sucked. You're an idiot.'"

Yeah, Sebra had gone against McClure's wisdom by not going away against Garvey later in the count and went back inside.

If Sebra, for example, was 10-10 instead of 6-15 and if Neal Heaton went 14-9 instead of 13-10, the Expos probably would have won the division. Heaton started the season 10-3 and then finished 13-10. Maybe that lapse prompted Heaton not to talk with me for the book. I texted him and when I told him I wanted to talk to him for the book, he never replied.

Tim Wallach was outstanding, so was Andres Galarraga, Hubie Brooks and a host of others.

"The third baseman and the first baseman," Expos hitting coach Bobby Winkles said, when I asked him who his favourite players were during his tenure handling hitters.

As he struggled to glean their names because of dementia, I helped Winkles out by mentioning Wallach and Galarraga.

"I picked those two guys because they had their best years in Montreal," Winkles said. "I was lucky. Both had great years."

They sure did. Wallach batted .298 with 26 homers and 123 RBI, while Big Cat hit .305 with 40 doubles, 13 homers and 90 RBI. Many others fared handsomely under Winkles, including switch-hitter Mitch Webster, who hit 15 homers, scored 101 runs and drove in 63 runs out of the No. 2 hole. I wanted to talk with Webster, an underdog type of player, so badly but I never heard back from him through an email. He has chosen to be anonymous as his hometown of Larned, Kansas. He enjoyed one tremendous season. He merely took over in right field from Dawson with aplomb.

Webster never came close to enjoying the season he put together in 1987.

"Some of the Expos' players said I was the best hitting coach they ever had," Winkles said. "I'm not bragging about it because I don't think I was. I didn't mess around with what they did at the plate."

Brooks was superlative down the stretch in September even though he was bothered by a wrist injury. Despite a spate of injuries, including an annoying left-foot infection, Brooks stayed in the lineup. He led the team down the stretch with 29 RBI in September, a club record. He was some Mr. Clutch.

Brooksie is another guy I really wanted to talk with but he has disappeared, not interesting in talking with anyone, although I sent an email to someone who was supposedly his agent. On June 6, he went 5-for-5 and drove in six runs. Talk about a wonderful, special person to deal with from a media standpoint. A fun guy.

Raines? He was merely outstanding after he joined the Expos May 2. On that very day, he enjoyed one of his finest days in the majors: he went 4-for-5, including a grand slam to win the game against the Mets in the 10th inning. Heading into this at-bat with nobody out, Raines was 3-for-20 lifetime against Jesse Orosco. On base were the unlikely tandem of underdogs Reid Nichols, Casey Candaele and Herm Winningham.

Yes, unlikely heroes were the order of the day most of the season to go along with the big-name stars. Winningham posted career highs of 29 stolen bases, 347 at-bats, 83 hits, 20 doubles and 41 RBI. Talk about a terrific backup, a terrific part-time maestro. Add in 1981 hero Wallace Johnson, who collected 17 pinch hits and 12 RBI in 1987.

The Expos finished the season with the NL's top record in extra-inning games. Just think they were 12-1, which at the time was the highest extra-inning winning percentage in MLB history. The Expos were also 28-14 in one-run decisions.

Dawson? He had the Season of all Seasons in his career with the Cubs: 49 homers and 137 RBI, good enough for writers to vote him the NL's MVP.

Reardon? All he did was help the Twins to the World Series.

As you can imagine, Expos teammates can bond for a long time. Consider Cliff Floyd and Rondell White.

Terry Francona and Brad Mills. Andre Dawson and Tim Raines. Mike Fitzgerald and Tim Wallach. Bill Lee and Rodney Scott. Jeff Fassero and Sean Berry.

Floyd and White are this-close, even to the point of living on the same street in Davie, Florida near Miami. Now, that is close.

Did you know there is a special bond between Bryn Smith and McClure, who got acquainted with each other as Expos teammates from 1986-88 and then with the Cardinals in 1991-92.

"We're pretty tight," Smith told me.

How close? Every year for close to 20 years, Smith and McClure have been travelling to the Bahamas for a week of fly fishing. That's how close they are. They even make an effort to try and get to the Bahamas at least twice a year to improve their lot as saltwater anglers.

Fly fishing? Smith had always been a fisherman but had never engaged in fly fishing until McClure convinced in 1993 to give it a shot. At the time, Smith was pitching for the Colorado Rockies, McClure for the Marlins.

"I was in Miami and Bob asked me if I had ever caught a bonefish. 'I said no.' Bob said he had a gentleman at a fishing lodge in the Bahamas and they invited me down for the experience," Smith was saying. "I went the first time and I've been scooped ever since. We can't wait to hook up again in October, sit around a barbecue pit after fishing and watch the World Series."

With the Expos, Smith and McClure began their friendship over regular fishing and baseball, swapping tales and strategies about both sports but mostly about baseball.

"We wanted to find an edge somewhere and we became very close friends," Smith said. "We're both pitchers and we both liked to fish. We talk a lot. We'd always be talking baseball and pitching. Even during spring training, we'd go fishing at night on the golf course or we'd go fish during the season before we went to the ballpark.

"In Montreal, we'd be on the St. Lawrence River a lot fishing for small bass. Coach Jackie Moore and a few of the guys would come along."

Smith lives in California and McClure in Florida so what they do is fly to Miami and then take a plane to a very remote archipelago called the Exumas, a barely known metropolis originally settled by slaves from the plantations. If you know the Bahamas, you're more apt to recognize the mega-resort names of Freeport and Nassau.

It's in the Exumas where fishermen and baseball legends Mickey Mantle and Ted Williams would often seek adventure. Smith said Dusty Baker has been known to go there for fund-raising projects. There is little in the way of commercialism in the Exumas but the district boasts the most renowned fishing flats or marls in the world with miles and miles of shallows off the shoreline or amongst mangroves.

"You can walk in three feet of water the same depth for three miles," Smith was saying. "You're self-taught. I think I learned so much from Bob and he learned so much from me."

But Smitty is quick to tell you that fly-fishing takes a certain sense of patience because bonefish, tarpon and permit are not exactly easy prey. Patience, patience, patience, not to mention that fly fishing is merely a thrill because the fish are not edible. Bonefish are huge suckers, too, who put up a fierce battle.

"Even with slow vibration, the fish will swim away," Smith said. "It's a hard game. It's like deer hunting in water. You have to be quiet. You have to sight the fish and see them before they see you. It's like looking for a needle in a haystack. The fish can also become transparent and very spooky. It's very mind boggling but it's such a beautiful atmosphere."

Smith and McClure don't necessarily stand side by side in the water casting their lines because sometimes curiosity gets the best of them. You may go days without catching a fish. If you catch three in a day, Smith said it's tabbed a "grand slam."

"We split up on the flats," Smith said, laughing. "Everybody has their own idea where the fish are."

Unbeknownst to many is that McClure carved out a pretty neat career as a pitching coach in the big leagues, doing it with the Phillies, Red Sox and Royals. At last word, he was senior pitching advisor with the Minnesota Twins.

As we went to press on a second printing of this book, we were saddened to learn that Sebra died July 22, 2020 after spending almost a full year in ICU at Jackson Memorial Hospital in Miami.

A brave, courageous Sebra had been cooped up in hospital since July 24, 2019, suffering from various organ problems.

Sebra, 58, underwent two multi-visceral transplants in 2019 and both failed.

"He's a fighter," Sebra's son Ryan said in an interview a few days before his father died. "He's not doing good at the moment. He's on very high ventilator settings and needs a kidney transplant now.

"The first multi-visceral transplant did not go good and the pancreas failed. So he had to have another multi-visceral transplant. He's been fighting infections and has had dozens and dozens of surgeries since then."

It sounds very ugly but a multi-visceral transplant involves the liver, pancreas, spleen, stomach and the small and large intestines.

As he prepared to go under the knife for his first of two multi-visceral trans-

Sgt. Johanie Maheu, Rideau Hall ©OSGG, 2019

Long-time Expos fan and actor Donald Sutherland is shown here in the fall of 2019 receiving the Order of Canada from Governor-General Julie Payette. J.P. Allard of Ottawa recalls the time he and friend Fred Frenette running into Sutherland in the underground parking lot at Olympic Stadium years ago in between games of a doubleheader. "Imagine our surprise when he addressed us first, inquiring nervously on whether the Expos had won the first game and thus gain ground," Allard said. "At the time, they were embroiled in the middle of a tight pennant race with the Cards and Phillies and he'd been listening to the game in his car radio when Dave and Duke's signal went off the air as he entered the underground lot, with the good guys losing and risking falling another game back of the leaders. So it was with great pleasure, if not sheer reverence, that we told him that Montreal had pulled another ninth inning comeback victory. Donald seemed visibly relieved and then proceeded toward the gate, but not before I told him what a great honour it had been for me to meet him."

plants, Sebra said in an interview that the operation would be a 16-hour procedure.

"It's the most complicated surgery known to man," Sebra said.

Sebra had a liver transplant in 2012 when he contracted Hepatitis C, which he blamed on sharing razors with teammates and anti-inflammatory medications which destroyed his liver. Shortly before he had the liver transplant, he had to be revived twice by medical officials.

Although Sebra was never an alcoholic and hadn't drank for many years, a doctor told him when the pitcher was 26 that his liver looked like he was an alcoholic.

Sebra's ICU hospital bill would have been sky-high, although his son says his mother's insurance covered part of the expenses. Ryan Sebra, who called himself his father's "proxy", said he asked the Bat Assistance Team (B.A.T.) "many months ago" for financial help but he was turned down. B.A.T. said there would be no help rendered "until he is more stable."

B.A.T. was formed in 1986 by a group of former MLB players to help members of the "baseball family who were in need of assistance with nowhere else to turn."

Many of Sebra's teammates were saddened to learn of his passing.

"He threw a yellow hammer," Bryn Smith said a few days prior to Sebra's death. "That's what we called a wicked curveball. Not sure where the term yellow hammer originated.

"I remember throwing bullpens side by side in spring training. He had all these different pitches and I had to stop and ask, 'How many pitches do you have?' He said seven. I said the catcher doesn't have enough fingers to call all seven. You need to find three that you can throw for strikes."

31

The 1989 collapse

It wasn't a red carpet but it was the next best thing. Something thoughtful.

Mark Langston arrived in the Expos clubhouse on May 26, 1989 to find a line of bats that marked the route to his stall in the clubhouse at Jack Murphy Stadium in San Diego.

Langston was stunned at the trade the night before from the Seattle Mariners, moreso because it was to Montreal. He hadn't expected to be traded to the Expos but the set of bats arranged by pitcher Bryn Smith was something to behold. The gesture made Langston stand up and take notice.

"I didn't know whether it was a ritual they do before the game or what," Langston told us reporters. "What they did was special. It made me feel wanted right away."

Langston had arrived about 80 minutes late for the game, 30 minutes before the game, but nobody was going to blame him for the tardiness. He was the ace pitcher expected to get the team to the post-season.

"I'm still in shock over the trade and I'm tired after a long flight from Boston," Langston said. "And trying to say goodbye to your teammates after being with them for six years is extremely difficult."

Langston, one of the premiere pitchers in the game back in 1989, said he was happy the trade talk had ended but added Montreal wasn't on the list of teams to whom he wished to be traded.

"Most of the talk had me going to Boston, New York or Los Angeles," he said. "When I heard it was Montreal, it was a shock."

It was obvious Langston had not heard about my previous stories, one of which appeared in the Montreal Daily News about a month prior to the trade. In a pre-game chat with Expos manager Buck Rodgers at Olympic Stadium, the skipper had laid out what turned out to be the final trade: Langston in exchange for young studs Randy Johnson, Brian Holman and Gene Harris.

Langston said he was upset that the Mariners tried to sign him to a new deal in the middle of a game against the Red Sox, one day prior to the trade to the Expos. Seattle offered Langston a three-year deal for

Canadian Baseball Hall of Fame
Mark Langston spent part of the 1989 season with the Expos

$7.1-million but he felt it wasn't a sincere effort.

"They tried to sign me in the middle of a game in the locker room," said a bewildered Langston. "I'm very disappointed in the way they handled it. I don't think that's the right way to negotiate with one of the team's top players. I had to make a decision in about three minutes. I didn't even have time to talk to my wife about it."

Expos players were tickled pink with the trade and catcher Mike Fitzgerald remembered Langston for something unusual.

"The only thing I know about him is his moondance," Fitzy said.

Moondance?

"During rain delays, he perfectly imitates Michael Jackson's moondance in his spikes," Fitzy explained. "During the delays, Major League Baseball shows a tape of all the funny plays in baseball and he's part of it."

Prior to getting to the ballpark that day, I got a hold of Johnson and Holman. Johnson was in no mood to talk but Holman was.

"I was happy to be in the Expos organization for as long as I was but that's all I've got to say," Johnson told me from his hotel room in Milwaukee.

Was Johnson surprised with the trade?

"Sure." Was he disappointed?

"As I said, that's all I've got to say."

Holman said his wife was "scared and nervous" about going to live in Seattle because the family "really loved" Montreal.

"The Expos are trying to build a strong team and Langston is a big commodity," Holman told reporters. "I knew something was going to happen in the way of a trade. I know the Expos would have to give up young pitching prospects. But what they gave up is quite a bit. I was surprised."

On the night of the trade, I remember some of us beat writers sidling up to Expos pitching coach Larry Bearnarth in the visitors clubhouse at Candlestick Park for any information about what was coming down. Although he was usually full of nuggets and information off the record, Bearnarth said he wasn't at liberty to say anything, out of respect for general manager Dave Dombrowski.

"We've been told not to say anything," Bearnarth said.

At the time the trade was made at about midnight EST, the Expos were floundering at 23-23 and majority owner Charles Bronfman had given Dombrowski the green light to pull the trigger on this blockbuster transaction. Known as Dealer Dave, Dombrowski did just that: he pulled the trigger.

And for weeks, the trade worked. The results in the standings were gratifying. The Expos moved to the head of the pack in the NL East where they stayed for a long time. On June 28, they had climbed to nine games over .500 at 43-34. By July 7, they were 48-37. On July 14, they were 51-38. On July 17, the team had blossomed to 53-39.

Around that time, Dombrowski had pulled off another trade, acquiring southpaw pitcher Zane Smith from the Braves in exchange for Sergio Valdez, Nate Minchey and Kevin Dean.

Langston even pulled his weight and even stepped up to purchase a medical contraption to help his arm and the arms of teammates.

"It was a new device that I was familiar with," Expos trainer Ron McClain told me in 2019. "It's a pneumatic sleeve that fills with air from the finger area and gradually fills as it goes up the arm. Then it releases the air and starts again.

"This creates a milking situation in the upper arm. This helps milk the fluid, swelling, blood from the arm. We used it on swollen knees and post surgical swelling in the elbows, knees and ankles. It had minimal effect but psychologically, it seemed to help the players. It find of fell out of favour after five years or so.

"It cost around $2,000 in 1989. I don't think it's in use anymore. Langston helped us get some free weights and that piece of equipment that (Expos vice-president) Bill Stoneman never would buy."

The Expos were rolling along so fine that the Expos offered Langston a three-year contract for about $9-million to keep him beyond the 1989 season. At one point in early August, the Expos were 19 games over .500 at 63-44. That was Aug. 2. That's how good the sailing was. Remember when they were 23-23 at the time of the Langston trade?

That impressive 63-44 record was impressive until the bats started to go silent. It was a terrible August and September. They fell arse over teakettle. From Aug. 2-7, they lost seven in a row. On a road swing to California, Bob Nightengale sidled up to Langston in San Diego Aug. 19 to see what he would think of playing for the Padres as a free agent. Langston said he would be interested.

"I like it here, it's a nice city and everything," Langston said to Nightengale about Montreal, "but it's different. I don't know how to explain it, it's just different. I'm from California, and everyone knows I'd like to play on the west coast one day. We'll just have to wait and see whether it's next year."

On Aug. 29, Dombrowski, in one of those last-resort deals to try and help out the team, acquired long-in-the-tooth lefty John Candelaria from the Yankees.

"He wore the largest diamond ring and would frequently say, 'a man of my stature'," Expos reliever Rich Thompson said of the Candy Man.

The Expos finished at 81-81, all but ruining the team's chances of signing Langston to a free-agent contract. They lost their last five games and finished in fourth place behind the first-place Cubs, the second-place Mets and the third-place Cardinals.

Remember the 22-inning game that ended in the wee hours of Aug. 23? The Expos could not even score one run in 22 innings in a 1-0 loss to the Dodgers.

Talk about other turning points. How about Sept. 10 at Veterans Stadium in Philadelphia? Prancing Pascual Perez got royally pissed with Rodgers and Fitzgerald for forcing him to issue an intentional walk to Von Hayes in the fifth inning with the score tied 1-1 with a runner on second. Pitcher Pat Combs had reached base and stole second. So with first base open, Rodgers wanted Hayes walked. We don't know if this story has ever been told but Thompson was laughing when he told me about it.

"Pascual got two strikes on Von Hayes and he goes to strike him out but Fitzgerald stands up and puts four fingers up to indicate to Pascual to walk him," Thompson related. "Pascual shakes his head and points to get Fitzgerald to sit back down. Buck goes to the mound, scolding Pascual, like the teacher does to the school boy for resisting the catcher's direction from Buck in the dugout to intentionally walk Hayes with a 1-2 count.

"After an 0-2 breaking ball got past the catcher (Fitzgerald), the runner on first advanced to second base. Pascual stood on the mound with his head down as Buck made his point to Pascual. When Buck had finished speaking to Pascual and he turned toward the dugout, Pascual lifted his head and then made a gesture with his arms raised and feigned a kick in Buck's direction.

"When Buck finishes yelling at him, Pascual mimics a kiss in the ass. Oh, my God, this is a circus. So Pascual walks Von Hayes and the next batter (Tom Barrett) gets a hit to put Philadelphia ahead. Pascual comes off the field, he's mad. It was hilarious.

"After the inning had ended, Pascual ran off the field into the dugout as he typically did. Immediately after entering the dugout in front of me, Pascual turned to his left and began making negative comments that were intended I believe for only the players seated toward the first base side of the dugout to hear as he walked in the dugout in the direction of the right-field foul pole. He said something like you dumb son of a bitch, I'm gonna kick your ass.

"After taking a few steps in that direction, Pascual turned and walked toward the home plate side of the dugout, past me toward Buck and the other coaches seated to my left, and he said aloud something like it's ok we'll get it back, don't worry, let's go. At the time, I sat with Rex Hudler in the center of the dugout halfway between Buck and the coaches seated to our left toward home plate, and the players who were seated to our right toward the RF foul pole. Rex was laughing the entire time and said something to me like, 'this is great.'"

It was a turning point in the season because the Phillies went on to win 4-2 and it was the first of five consecutive losses, leaving the Expos with a 76-71 record. And then two days later, there was another turning point Sept. 12 at Wrigley when pinch runner Jeff Huson was picked off of first by veteran closer Mitch Williams, sealing the Cubs 4-3 victory.

To this day, it's one of the most embarrassing moments of Huson's career and another symbol of Montreal's collapse. The Cubs won the game but even then, the Expos were still in the hunt for the division title. Weird.

The Expos had men on first and second with two out when Williams took advantage of an inexperienced rookie in a flat-footed Huson leaning toward second and not paying sufficient attention, especially with Williams a lefty. Huson would tell me years later that first-base coach Rafael Landestoy made no attempt to help him out, although Huson was taking most of the blame himself. Talk about a rally killer.

Thirty years later, many people still commend Dombrowski for the Langston trade. He deserved a bouquet of flowers for the trade. To this day, it was a good move on his part, even though Johnson embarked on a Hall of Fame career. With Perez off to a 0-6 start early in the season, DD needed to do something to please Bronfman.

Langston was a shiny Cadillac in an automobile showroom so Dombrowski went after him. The Expos gambled but they wanted to win it all so DD shifted into high gear.

Years later, Dombrowski was dumbfounded at the Expos collapse.

"The 1989 team was the best team we had while I was there," Dombrowski told me in 2017. "I thought we had the capabilities to win, especially after we made the trade for Mark Langston. There were so many good players. It was such a good club.

"We led the division by a long time and then in August and September, for whatever reason, we just didn't swing the bats down the stretch. It was tough. We lost a lot of veteran players after that season and we brought in a lot of younger players."

It will go down as the worst collapse in Expos history.

"When I joined the team, I said, 'Wow, we're going to the World Series.' It was an extremely talented team. I'd put that team up against anybody. Then they stopped hitting," Thompson recalled.

"1989, oh, goodness, we just couldn't score any runs," recalled bench coach Ken Macha. "We had the pitching. The advertising was that we had five aces. The feeling was that Charles Bronfman was willing to give up some young players and go for it. Charles went out and spent the money. The guys who were clutch players didn't come through. It was awful at the end of the season."

Yes, the Expos had five aces: Martinez, Smith, Kevin Gross, Perez and Langston. Smith, the night he placed the bats down to Langston's locker, was the winning pitcher. But Smitty was an individual symbol of the Expos' collapse. He was sailing along with a 9-3 record but finished a disappointing 10-11. That's right. Langston fared poorly down the stretch, too. He was 9-3 at one point but finished at 12-9.

"Langston pitched good. People kind of blamed him and put too much heat on him," Macha said.

Those "clutch hitters" Macha was referring to? You could say Andres Galarraga, Tim Wallach, Raines, Hubie Brooks, they all slumped considerably down the stretch.

"What I remember is that we were making the run and trying to make the playoffs," catcher Nelson Santovenia said in 2019 . "Our main guys in August went a little silent. Hubie didn't have a good August or September. Rock, too. We didn't hit that great, myself included in there. We went into a little funk and we just couldn't pick it back up."

About halfway through the season, Dombrowski made every effort to try and trade Raines to the Red Sox for Mike Greenwell straight up. Dombrowski and a number of Expos scouts loved Greenwell. After a tremendous season in 1987, Raines' offence slipped in 1988 and the spiral continued in 1989. Dombrowski tried to trade Raines before he could attain 10-and-5 status, meaning 10 years in the majors and the last five with the same team.

But Red Sox general manager Lou Gorman wouldn't go for the 1-for-1 trade that would have brought Raines to Beantown and Greenwell to Montreal. It was hard to blame Gorman. In Greenwell's first full season with Boston, he hit 19 homers and drove in 89 runs. In 1988, he was even better with 22, 119. In 1989 when the trade talk took place, Greenwell finished with 14 homers and 89 RBI. In the end, he played his entire MLB career with the Red Sox.

At the time of the trade, Johnson was in Triple A after going a sporadic 0-4 with the Expos. Little did the Expos and Dombrowski think he would become a Hall of Fame pitcher. The one guy the Expos and scouting director Gary Hughes didn't want to lose was Harris, of all people.

"I thought that of the three players we moved, he was the one who would come back to haunt us most. I was obviously dead wrong,' Hughes said near the end of 2019. "He had a power arm. Very athletic."

Harris just never got untracked in the majors. His best season was 1993 when he went 6-6 with the Padres. By 1994, Harris had lost his closer's job to a fellow by the name of Trevor Hoffman, who went on to Cooperstown after posting 601 saves. By 1995, Harris was out of baseball at age 31.

Holman had a pretty solid career, mostly with the Mariners.

"I loved the Expos' organization," Holman told me a few years ago. "When I was traded, it was hard. I was a little hurt. I felt like I was part of the family. We had heard the Expos needed a big-league pitcher but we didn't think they'd trade three younger pitchers, who were kinda the future of the organization for a starter who might only be there for half a season. But David Dombrowski was under pressure to get something done.

"I was the only one of the three in the majors at the time. Gene and

Randy were in Indianapolis. I grew up as an Expo and I didn't think I would be traded so young. I was going off to an organization that I didn't know much about. I thought of myself more as an Expo but when I spent some time with Seattle I became more known as a Mariner."

Even though Dombrowski's gamble didn't pay off in a playoff appearance for his team, he made every effort to make up for lost ground with Langston. This is how clever Dombrowski was: he tried to trade Langston to the Padres after the season ended and before free agency started in the short period following the World Series won by the Oakland Athletics. Very few if any trades are ever made during that short, tight frame we just talked about.

Canadian Baseball Hall of Fame
Mark Langston

But sure enough, Dombrowski, only 32, was trying to get some compensation for possibly losing Langston to free agency by engineering a trade before he became a free agent. Padres GM Tony Siegle could have acquired Langston from Montreal following the season but opted not to give up the apparently high package of players Dombrowski sought.

Siegle told me in late 2019, 30 years later, that he indeed did chat with Dombrowski following the season about a possible transaction. He couldn't remember who Dombrowski wanted in return. Let's say it was two or three players: maybe pitcher Andy Benes, second baseman Roberto Alomar, catcher Benito Santiago? One or several of those players in return for Langston?

"David always starts high," said his then Expos scouting director Gary Hughes, referring to what DD wanted in return.

"We talked about it. It never got to first base," Siegle said, adding that "rumours" were being "circulated" about the trade that never went down. "I was not crazy about doing it. They (Expos) wanted the world for him (Langston). Back then, there was not a lot of pressure (to do a trade)."

Then Los Angeles Times baseball writer Bob Nightengale reported that fall that the Padres "botched" the Langston trade talks and Siegle admitted it to me it "might have" had something to do with his dismissal a few months later when field manager Jack McKeon took over as GM.

The deal would have made a lot of sense for the Padres because

Courtesy Houston, Texas police department Twitter account

Former Expos pitcher and Los Angeles Angels broadcaster Mark Langston poses with Houston police officers Paul Pollis, left, and Daryn Edwards, who helped save his life after he collapsed in the press box at the Houston Astros Minute Maid ballpark Sept. 20, 2019. Langston called it an "absolute miracle". Within in 90 seconds of Langston collapsing, Pollis and Edwards came from a nearby room to administer CPR and attach a defibrillator that shocked him back to life. Langston had been clinically dead for three and a half minutes. Langston was diagnosed with ventricular fibrillation that weakens the heart and inhibits the pumping of blood.

Langston is a San Diego native. The trade never materialized and the Angels won out in convincing Langston to join them as a free agent.

The 1989 collapse broke Bronfman's heart and he decided to sell the team, although the official switch to a consortium led by Claude Brochu didn't transpire until 1991.

"That was the straw that broke the backs of (co-owners) Lorne Webster and Hugh Hallward and mine. But the thought of selling had been brewing – pardon the expression– for a few years. It was very discouraging to go to the Big Owe to watch these terrific young players really busting their butts in front of 5,000 people," Bronfman told me a few months ago.

"I caught Langston quite a bit," Santovenia said. "He had a real good, hard slider down and in to the righties. He had a good changeup. He was a real good pitcher.

"At the time, I looked at the trade as us getting an established pitcher and I looked at it as Montreal wanted to win then. We gave up these three guys who were young with great arms. I wouldn't say I was surprised. We were just looking to give up something to get something.

"Langston was a rental. I remember he was a west coast guy and his wife was something into acting. He was looking to go out west. He was kind of quiet, always obviously a big free agent-to-be. He was already established. He was trying to help Montreal win."

Of further note about the Expos trying to keep Langston in 1989, late Expos scout Orrin Freeman told me that huge Expos fan and Canadian-born actor Donald Sutherland met with Langston at one point to try and implore him to stay.

"Langston's wife wanted to become an actress so Sutherland tried to convince them they could do it from Montreal," Freeman said. "Not sure if Dombrowski asked Sutherland to do it. It may have been face to face at one of our games."

Sticking with Freeman, he said that if he had been the Expos scouting director in 1992, he would have made a decision in the June draft that could have changed the fortunes of the Expos.

"I would have taken Derek Jeter," Freeman told me. "I told him that in our first meeting with the Marlins."

Jeter had become CEO of the Marlins in 2017 and Freeman had moved to the Marlins as a scout. So what was Jeter's reaction when Freeman told him that?

"He just smiled," Freeman said.

Image supplied by Rich Thompson

It was in August of 1989 and the Expos were in Chicago to play the Cubs. Expos players got off their bus at the team hotel and Rich Thompson saw a vendor on the street selling T-shirts. One said, "What the Hell's an Expo?" So Thompson decided to buy a few of the T-shirts as souvenirs.

32

22-inning game

The symbol of the Expos collapse in 1989 came on the night of Aug. 22 in a game that stretched into Aug. 23 for a total game time of six hours and 14 minutes.

Remember that one? The Expos could not even score one run in 22 innings in a 1-0 loss to the Dodgers. Veteran starter Dennis Martinez pitched the final two innings, allowing former Baltimore Orioles team-mate Rick Dempsey's homer to lead off the top of the 22nd.

Can you imagine, going 22 innings and not scoring a run? Hrrmph. This epitomized the drought of the Expos bats, even though they were still in the race for the NL East title.

There were some bizarre plays. In the seventh inning, Eddie Murray of the Dodgers hit a line drive that was trapped at first by Andres Galarraga. The Expos thought it was a triple play so they ran off the field, only to discover that the umpires ruled it a double play instead.

Centre fielder Dave Martinez, on a throw to third from centre, nailed cut-off man Spike Owen on the buttocks or the gluteus maximus, forcing the shortstop to remain standing much of the rest of the game.

Even Expos mascot Youppi! made his mark in team history. He donned a sleeping gown and banged on the top of the Dodgers dugout in the 11th inning. Dodgers manager Tommy Lasorda came out and gave Youppi! a puzzling look. Third-base umpire Bob Davidson came over and ejected the mascot.

The website retrosheet.org even made a boldface note of this ejection in its game log from that game. Youppi! did return to the game later but he was only allowed around the Expos dugout.

In what was a sign of things going eerily wrong, Larry Walker of the Expos could have won the game in the bottom of the 16th inning if he had not tagged up too early on a play that took a sacrifice fly away from Fitzgerald. Or had he tagged up okay? Walker had singled to right to start the inning and advanced to third on Galarraga's single.

Tim Wallach flied out to short centre, forcing Walker to stay at third. Still only one out.

Then Mike Fitzgerald flied to right with what appeared to be a play easy enough to get Walker home. He made it home okay and several umpires had already ran into the tunnel, believing the game was over. A sac fly in no time turned out to be a double play. Read on.

Walker took an RBI away from Fitzgerald and Fitzy's average went down because of the DP. A sac fly would have left Fitzgerald's average the way it was before the at-bat. Instead of going 1-for-7, he was 1-for-8. But conspiracy theorists abound.

Any indiscretion on Walker's part didn't bother Fitzgerald at all. First of all, as he got wound up, Fitzgerald said this as I was about to query him about his fly ball out involving Walker: "I missed two home runs to left field. They were warning track balls."

At that point, Fitzgerald continued his story by directing some umbrage toward Davidson.

"I hit a ball down the right-field line. The outfield was playing in," Fitzgerald remembered. "Mike Marshall catches the ball and Walker was sliding into home plate to win the game. Everybody is celebrating. We're walking into the dugout, the Dodgers are walking off the field and the umpires are walking across the field except for the guy at third. Bob Davidson was there with his arms crossed. He was telling everyone that he (Walker) left too soon. I think he wanted to make himself the story that night."

Murray, according to Fitzgerald, heard and saw what Davidson was doing so he ran into the umpires' room to get a ball from home-plate umpire Greg Bonin. Can you imagine? Murray ran to home plate as LA manager Tommy Lasorda officially appealed the play. To make the appeal official, Dempsey threw the ball to third baseman Jeff Hamilton, who stepped on third. Davidson promptly called Walker out in the days when there was no instant replay, no cameras and no discussion with officials up in the press box.

"That led to the extra-extra innings," Fitzgerald said. "It was a great game to remember in a bad way."

The official scorer's ruling was this: 9-2-5, a double play, Marshall to Dempsey to Hamilton. Oddly, Hamilton and Lasorda hadn't even argued that Walker had left early. The Dodgers dugout was on the third-base side and Lasorda had a clear view. So did Hamilton. They accepted that Walker tagged up correctly, leaving at about the same time that Marshall caught the ball.

Expos pitcher Rich Thompson went one step further than Fitzgerald as it pertained to the conspiracy theory, or revenge, on the part of Davidson, who was known to be very confrontational, even to the point of sometimes pissing off his MLB bosses. Back in 2011, Davidson was voted by MLB players and managers as one of the worst umps in the game in a Sports Illustrated poll.

Thompson, like Fitzgerald, surmised that Davidson was out to spite Walker and the Expos in this particular case. Thompson even made note of Walker's argument with Davidson in his 5,000-page diary of his time in the majors and minors.

"It was a quirky, funny game," Thompson told me. "I have some background stories. Larry Walker argued some calls with Davidson (a few days earlier in a game Aug. 18 against San Diego). There was a little back and forth with the umpire. They were fighting. It was heated. I surmise that Walker made a comment about a called strike and then Davidson overreacted.

"Walker struck out and he came back into the dugout and Rex Hudler told Walker, 'Don't argue with him. He'll hold a grudge.' A few nights later was pay back night. When Walker scored, the Dodgers had completely left the field. Everybody had left except Davidson. He had his arms folded.

"I told (manager) Buck Rodgers, 'They can't appeal. They've left the field. You have to protest, file a grievance.' I knew some stuff about the rules. You had to have a minimum number of players on the field. Buck looked at me like an idiot.

"The play was overturned. They called Walker out. Davidson had given it back to Walker. I told Buck, 'You have to protest the game.' He didn't. That was a mistake."

Thompson asked me if this game was Walker's debut game in the big leagues so I checked. He was close. Walker's first game was Aug. 16 against San Francisco and he got a hit. This all begs you to wonder why Walker was being so argumentative with umpires just days into his inauguration in the big leagues.

Thompson had studied in the off-season to be an attorney. It took him 11 years to get his degree to be a lawyer. And he was keen on studying up on some of the game's rules and regulations. He wasn't just some novice.

I did some research of the rule book to zero in on what Thompson was referring to. It states "appeals must be made before the next pitch or attempted play or before the entire defensive team has left fair territory if the play in question resulted in the end of a half inning." From what I gather, the Dodgers had crossed the white lines into foul territory before the appeal was made.

Although Thompson only enjoyed a short spin in the majors, one of his best games was his outstanding performance in that 22-inning game. Him and John Wetteland of the Dodgers both threw six scoreless innings in relief. How about that? Thompson allowed three hits, Wetteland gave up three.

"That was my best game in the National League," Thompson conceded. "I had a good game in the American League with the Indians in 1985 (May 21) in relief against the Brewers. I pitched $3^2/3$ innings. I got the save. I came in with two men on and one out in the sixth inning and I got Paul Molitor to hit into a double play."

Wetteland was the game's winner in the 22-inning game and his performance no doubt had an impact on Expos assistant general manager Dan Duquette, who was sitting in the press box. Duquette remembered and scooped Wetteland up in a trade with the Cincinnati Reds more than three years later.

"In the 17th inning, Wetteland walked me on four pitches," Thompson recollected. "I turned to coach Rafael Landestoy for signals and he said, 'No idea. Just watch the hitter.' Spike Owen tried to bunt and then he grounded to short. I already had a good jump and I took out Willie Randolph really hard at second. I whacked him with my leg. Randolph said, 'What are you doing?' I was laughing and I said, 'I'm trying to win.'"

As it turns out, Thompson was doubled up on the play.

I didn't reach out to Wetteland because he was awaiting trial on charges of allegedly sexually assaulting a minor several years ago in Texas where he lives. Serious allegations but he's innocent until proven guilty.

Thompson told another hilarious story, involving Lasorda. The situation was the 18th inning. Murray came to the plate to face Thompson. Murray almost immediately motioned for second base umpire Mark Hirschbeck to move because the ump was a distraction standing almost directly behind Thompson. Lasorda came out to yell at Hirschbeck.

"Lasorda was doing it to rile me up because I was just some rookie," Thompson said. "I turned to Lasorda, who was on some Ultra Slim Fast diet, and I said, 'Hey fatso, get off the field. Get off the field.' He turned and smiled at me."

So what did Murray do after these theatrics were finalized and his sightlines were improved? With Lenny Harris on first, he smacked a ball off the padding on the right-field wall into Walker's glove for what was perceived as a phantom catch and the third out. Many observers felt Walker had trapped the ball but it sure was some fantastic catch.

Just in case it might be ruled a hit, Walker did come off the fence in a hurry, firing the ball back into the infield as Harris slid into home. First-base umpire Frank Pulli ruled it a catch but Murray did come over and talk to Pulli and put up a mild protest. Weird play for sure, one of many in the game.

In the bottom of the 21st, Dave Martinez singled and was advanced to second on Walker's sacrifice bunt, Walker's second of the night. Very unusual. A budding slugger like Walker put down two sacrifice bunts in one game in the early days of his career. I bet he never did that again in his career.

So with Martinez on second, Harris robbed Galarraga of a game-winning hit with a spectacular catch off a line drive to left. Then Tim Raines was intentionally walked. Not long after, Dodgers gunslinger Dempsey picked Raines off first.

Then Dempsey, who had entered the game in the eighth inning, put the Dodgers ahead when he went yard off his old buddy from Baltimore days. Martinez told me that he had gone up to Rodgers and volunteered to pitch in relief.

"Why not?" Martinez said when I asked him about his volunteer stint. "I said (to Rodgers), 'Hey man, if you need somebody, I'm here.'"

In the bottom of the 22nd, Rex Hudler singled to get something going for the Expos with two out but star-of-the game Dempsey pulled the trigger again from behind the plate and threw Hudler out trying to steal second. Game over.

Dempsey had a wonderful night: he homered, he singled as part of a 2-for-5 stint, threw the ball back to third in case Walker left too early, picked Raines off of first and threw Hudler out at second. I emailed Dempsey to praise him and to see if he would talk but I got no reply.

When I emailed fabled Dodgers' announcer Vin Scully recently to see what he had remembered about the game, he said he wasn't there, that Ross Porter had handled the assignment all by himself.

Scully had worked the first two segments of the Dodgers road swing in Philadelphia and New York and then flew home for a break, missing the three contests at Olympic Stadium because none of the games were being televised.

That left Don Drysdale and Porter announcing the first two games against the Expos on radio. Shortly after the second game ended, Drysdale received a phone call, telling him that his wife Annie had gone into labour in California, expecting their second child.

"He rushed to the airport, leaving me alone to broadcast the final game of the series," Porter recalled.

Little did Porter know what lay ahead of him Aug. 22-23.

Porter's wife Lin was with him on the trip and since they were returning home after the game, she sat in the broadcast booth at the Big O alongside him, reading a book.

To his left were the French-speaking Expos announcers led by Jacques Doucet and to his right were the Spanish-speaking Dodgers announcers spearheaded by Jaime Jarrin.

"Someone asked me later, 'What would have happened had you not been able to continue?' My response was 'I guess Lin would have made her announcing debut,'" Porter said, joking.

Sandwiched around commercial breaks in between innings when he would scamper quickly to the washroom, Porter persevered. Round about the seventh inning, Lin asked her husband if he wanted a Coke and he said no because it would have meant that he would have to go to the washroom.

Talking about the 16th inning when Walker tagged up too soon, Porter thought at first the game was over and his marathon stint at the microphone would be over.

"Thinking they had won, the Expos celebrated," Porter was telling

Rich Thompson pitched six scoreless innings in the 22-inning game

me. "But the Dodgers appealed, claiming the runner had left the base early. They threw the ball to third and umpire Bob Davidson ruled in the Dodgers' favour."

As zeros continued to pile up on the scoreboard, the game went past midnight and then past 1 in the morning EST. Martinez came on to pitch, starting the 21st inning. He also threw the 22nd inning when finally a 1 was placed on the scoreboard.

"Rick Dempsey came to the plate on this the 23rd of August, having hit just one home run all season," Porter said.

And as Porter recollected so clearly, "Dempsey hit a low line drive that cleared the left-field fence by about a foot to put the Dodgers ahead 1-0. In the bottom of the 22nd, Rex Hudler of the Expos attempted to steal second base and Dempsey threw him out to end the game.

"Research found that I had set a major-league record for a broadcaster by doing 22 innings by myself. Shockingly, I did not have a sore throat. On the long return trip to Los Angeles, I heard on my transistor radio that Pete Rose had been banned from baseball."

164

**Highlights of 22-inning game:
Dodgers 1 Expos 0**

* Rick Dempsey star of the game, 2-for-5 with game-winning homer; picked Tim Raines off of first, started official appeal of Larry Walker leaving third too early; threw out Rex Hudler trying to steal second.

* Pascual Perez pitched 8 scoreless innings
* Orel Hershiser pitched 7 scoreless innings
* Rich Thompson pitched 6 scoreless innings
* John Wetteland pitched 6 scoreless innings

* Lenny Harris 5-for-9	* Andres Galarraga 1-for-9
* Eddie Murray 3-for-9	* Mike Fitzgerald 1-for-8
* Jeff Hamilton 3-for-9	* Larry Walker 1-for-7
* Tim Wallach 3-for-9	* Alfredo Griffin 0-for-9
* Willie Randolph 2-for-9	* Spike Owen 0-for-8

Assembled by author from game's boxscore at retrosheet.org

33

The Big Unit

When Bob Fontaine Jr. and Tom Hinkle drove into idyllic Grass Valley in northern California on a June day in 1985, they found themselves in an historic gold mining town in the Western Foothills of Sierra Nevada.

They were there for a specific reason. Knocking on the door of a house in the municipality, which dates to the California Gold Rush of the late 1800s, the two Expos' scouts, with much trepidation, found themselves face to face with a pitcher they had been scouting for several years on a regular basis. Someone very tall, 6-foot-10, that is, very intimidating.

Little did they know that young man would become an inductee into the National Baseball Hall of Fame in Cooperstown, N.Y. many years later. That man was Randy Johnson.

Not long prior to that visit to Grass Valley, the Expos had selected Johnson in the second round of the draft out of the L.A.-based University of Southern California which he decided to attend. Johnson had rejected a reported offer of $50,000 to sign with the Atlanta Braves, who took him in the first round in 1982 out of California's Livermore high school.

Johnson was born in Walnut Creek near Livermore but he and his parents relocated at some point to Grass Valley more than two and a half hours to the north. His father Bud was a policeman and also a security guard at Lawrence Livermore Labs and his mother Carol did odd jobs while raising Randy and five other siblings.

For many decades like in the 1980s, players did their own negotiating, not like today when high-powered agents spar with front-office personnel, most notably the general manager, president and maybe even the team owner. Back in the days when Johnson was drafted, players received five-figure or six-figure signing bonuses. For many years, though, the bonus has been in the millions. That's why players have left the contract talks in the hands of agents.

"I do remember the visit to Randy at his parents' house but it's been quite some time," Fontaine said in an interview. "Back in those days, scouts did the signing of players. In negotiations, Randy was tough, he was fair. Players negotiate like they play: tough but fair. He was very,

Canadian Baseball Hall of Fame
Randy Johnson

Seattle Mariners photo
Bob Fontaine Jr.

very active in negotiating his contract. He was very involved in negotiations along with his parents. He got a very fair signing bonus. The
Johnsons were wonderful people."

Although the late Cliff Ditto, a brother-in-law of Duke Snider, didn't
join Fontaine and Hinkle at the negotiating table that day in Grass Valley because he was signing players in southern California, he was instrumental in watching Johnson umpteen times along the way.

"Tom, Cliff and I handled the scouting for the Expos in southern California," said Fontaine, the son of the late Bob Fontaine Sr., who spent
decades as an executive and scout with the Brooklyn Dodgers, Pirates
and Padres. "Cliff and Tom saw him a lot. In Randy's junior year at USC,
either one of us always saw him every time he pitched.

"Randy, like so many power pitchers and power hitters, developed
one step at a time, from high school to college. We knew him from high
school on. The biggest thing I noticed earlier on about him was that he
was what we would call a thrower. Then he became a pitcher.

"When he started in college, he began to develop more extension
with a devastating breaking ball. With arm extension, when you're a
power pitcher or a power hitter, it takes longer to get consistency when
you are a bigger kid. It takes time to get a consistent release."

Johnson only got his feet barely wet with the Expos before moving on
to a stellar career in the uniforms of other teams but the Expos' tenure
was quite memorable for the late Jim Fanning, who was involved in
scouting with the Expos at the time Johnson was drafted.

"Bob Fontaine's father was a scout for years and years," Fanning said.
"I had Bob Jr. and Cliff go specifically to look at Randy. Rarely did I
move them out of southern California."

So Fontaine and Hinkle finally got Johnson to sign with the Expos' organization, although it wasn't easy. He didn't want to sign to play in the outpost of Jamestown, N.Y., which 12 years or so earlier met with much disdain from another California native and Expos great Gary Carter, who snickered/asked, "This is professional baseball?"

"Randy didn't want to sign a Jamestown contract," Fanning said. "He thought he was much better going to Double-A or Triple-A. He may have been right. He did not perform for us early at Jamestown. I brought him in to Montreal before a major-league game late in the afternoon. It was just a workout. Randy wouldn't throw the ball for us. He would throw hard but he wouldn't bare down like he should have."

So in no uncertain terms, Fanning went over to Johnson and gave him a scolding, saying, "Randy, you gotta throw harder than that. You never threw the ball."

As Fanning would reveal in the conversation with me, "I've never ever told anyone about my lecture to Randy Johnson on the pitching mound in the bullpen in Montreal."

Several days later in Jamestown after Fanning's sermon, Johnson threw harder in a performance that left Fanning fawning.

"He was absolutely dominate. Absolutely," Fanning said in the last interview he gave 10 days before he died April 25, 2015. "Randy said, 'I'm going to go down there and show these guys what I can do.' He showed it all. He showed big-league stuff. This guy is for the big leagues. You had to like him for his arm delivery."

Following his apprenticeship in Jamestown, Johnson would make minor-league stops for the Expos in the Florida venues of West Palm Beach and Jacksonville and then Indianapolis. With the Jax Expos, Johnson was 11-8 on a team that included Brian Holman, Larry Walker, Nelson Santovenia and Rangers castoff George Wright, who was trying to rebuild his career.

Holman, for one, is very close to Johnson.

"Randy is a true friend. We played together in the Expos' minor-league system, we played together with the Expos and we got traded together to Seattle," Holman said.

"Randy was a tall, lanky, slim kid, who always had trouble putting weight on," recalled Santovenia, a teammate of Johnson with Jacksonville, Indianapolis and then Montreal. "He threw hard. He had control issues. He'd load up the bases and come back and strike out the side."

It was during his time in Jacksonville that a mini brawl erupted during one game and Johnson would settle things down by throwing 97 mph heat to calm the opposing team down.

"That was Randy's way of saying, 'Don't mess with the family.' He took care of the family," recalled the late Tommy Thompson, Johnson's manager in Jacksonville. "It was not I. It was we. It was something we taught. I told him to not let umpires or the opposition get to him. He got better and better."

If Holman had to think of an anecdote about Johnson, it was June 15, 1988 in Indianapolis when Johnson's pitching hand was hit by a line drive.

"He walked off the mound, headed to the dugout and took his right hand and smashed it against a helmet/bat rack in disgust," Holman said.

When Expos minor-league pitching coordinator Joe Kerrigan heard about the incident, he would say, "Good thing it wasn't his pitching hand." Results from the line drive turned out negative and the front office was steamed at Johnson.

Whenever Johnson would show up in Montreal in between options to Indianapolis, veteran Expos pitcher Dennis Martinez would see things unfolding.

"What he was going through, I tried to help him. He had the talent but he was so wild. He was trying to do something with it," Martinez said. "He had the size and he had the power in his arm, something you don't see very often.

"He was frustrated, not being able to succeed in throwing a strike. He needed to have perseverance in going through the process in adjusting to his body. He was still getting uglier, too," Martinez said, laughing. "Every aspect of his life was changing. He was still growing."

By the spring of 1989, the Expos appeared they had the impetus for a playoff spot but GM Dave Dombrowski was still looking for a veteran starting pitcher and the binoculars focused on Mariners lefty Mark Langston. The trade came down in May, 1989: Johnson, Holman and reliever Gene Harris to the Mariners for Langston.

"Dave Dombrowski was on the phone with me a lot before that trade," Fanning said. "I told Dave that if acquiring this guy would win the pennant for us, you have to do it. It was giving away the farm. It was a hard deal for me to give Johnson up. Holman and Harris were also guys who were making contributions to the organization. No question it was a bad deal."

In the end, Johnson pitched until 2009, Holman was out of the game following the 1991 season due to shoulder problems and Harris never pitched in the bigs after 1995.

Johnson was the subject of a MLB Network documentary called The Big Picture: From Raw Talent to Dominant Force. The raw talent, of course, was exhibited in his Montreal days. The video is narrated by Mettalica band lead singer James Hetfield.

As Fontaine looked back to 1985 and looked ahead to Johnson's induction years ago, he couldn't help but be proud of the fact that Johnson was Cooperstown-bound.

"It's a thrill," Fontaine said.

Fontaine chuckled almost sheepishly when he told me he began scouting in 1973 at the very young age of 19. One would bet Johnson is his most prized signing and most prized player he brought into any organization. Fontaine was 28 at the time.

"It doesn't happen very often," Fontaine said of seeing someone he scouted and signed go to Cooperstown. "I was associated with him. I was a big part of him, scouting him and signing him."

Looking back at the Langston trade, then Expos catcher Mike Fitzgerald was blunt in his indirect way of critiquing what went down. He had been part of the reclamation project that was Randy Johnson.

"The team was good enough to win the pennant. We made a big trade that happens. It's to try to make a positive move and sometimes it doesn't work out," Fitzgerald told me. "Langston was a great athlete, a great guy, a great pitcher, a solid major leaguer with a solid track record. But we gave up a Hall of Famer. I caught Big Unit's first win (Sept. 15, 1988).

"I had been sent down to Triple-A by Buck Rodgers in 1988 to get my confidence back. The manager (Joe Sparks) with Indianapolis says to me, 'I'll make you a deal.'"

The deal was this: "Help that guy at the end of the clubhouse. He's struggling. His name is Randy Johnson."

One of the reasons Fitzgerald was sent down was that he could get Johnson back on track.

"I caught him for five consecutive wins," Fitzgerald said. "I'd catch him every start. In the sixth start of his comeback, there was a comebacker that hit him on the left forearm. The batter (Jeff Blauser) hit a 100 m.p.h. fastball straight back at him. The second baseman was given an error. He wasn't hurt but I guess they thought they didn't want to risk anything so they took him out of the game. He probably would have won his sixth in a row if he hadn't been hit by the line drive.

"He went back to the bench (livid at being taken out) and punched his right hand on the bat rack and fractured his wrist. He was just pissed off. He was mad."

The following day, the deal worked out between Sparks and Fitzgerald went like this: Fitzgerald was called back up by the Expos because he had done his job of straightening Johnson out. Tests on Johnson's left hand were positive but the tests on his right hand showed he had a broken wrist.

"Johnson was confused at the time. I don't think he knew how good he was. He probably never had a catcher like me," Fitzgerald said. "He took responsibility for what he was doing. I was trying as a catcher to slow him down, one pitch at a time. He finally realized how good he could be and once he did that, he just took off. When he was traded, I wasn't asked about him at all. It hurt."

When Pierre Arsenault was helping Expos bullpen coach Ken Macha in 1988, he saw the vast potential when he caught Johnson before his starts with the Expos. He threw some serious heat, the fastest Arsenault has ever caught, stuff that would often sting his catcher's decker.

"Randy Johnson, when he first came up, he was actually scary to warm up because you didn't know where he would go with the pitch," said Arsenault, who later was Expos bullpen coordinator from 1991-2001. "You had to be awake warming him up. You couldn't fall asleep with him. He was that hard rock young thrower who scared the crap out of everybody. When you're tall, it's hard to understand your body. But then once he got his consistency, his groove and his command, he was dominant for years. You could see the potential. Oh my God, those guys don't come around very often."

Palmer almost made comeback with Expos

We're going back down memory lane with this story.

Twenty-five years ago this month as we got close to spring training in West Palm Beach, Jim Palmer almost made his way to the Expos' camp as a non-roster player.

Palmer, who had entered the Baseball Hall of Fame just a year earlier, had wanted to come out of retirement at age 45. He had not pitched in the majors since May 12, 1984 when he was let go by his long-time team, the Baltimore Orioles.

At that time, I was an Expos' beat writer for the Ottawa Sun and someone told me that Palmer had accepted an invitation to spring training. He was a 268-game winner and won 20 games eight times over the course of a career that spanned 19 seasons.

Palmer won 186 games in the 1970s, the most of any major-league pitcher during that decade. He won the Cy Young Award three times.

"He'd bring a lot of class to the organization," said Expos scouting director Gary Hughes, who had been monitoring Palmer's workouts in Miami. "Those Jockey underwear photos aren't trick camera shots. He's really in excellent shape."

Two former Orioles' teammates in Dennis Martinez and Ken Singleton weighed in favourably in Palmer's favour at the time.

"He hasn't pitched in seven years but he's in great shape. It would be great to have him on the club," Martinez said.

"Jim had a lot of idiosyncrasies but he was the best pitcher I ever played behind," Singleton added.

In the end, the Palmer experiment never came to pass. After a number of his workouts, he told friends and baseball folks that he just didn't think he would be good enough to compete. He also apparently tore a hamstring in one of his workouts.

34

The fabulous Raines

When Tim Raines snuck into Arnprior, Ontario incognito to live for two winters not long ago, he never felt so cold.

"They were the coldest winters in my life," Raines was telling this writer recently in Montreal, while laughing one of those famous, contagious Raines laughs.

Arnprior is warm in the summer but can be a freezer-cold, snow-belt place during the winter. Yet, Raines, one of the best major-league baseball players to ever toil in Canada, didn't mind it so much, even though it does not compare to the sun-lathered Florida communities of Sanford and Lake Mary, where he was reared and lived for decades, and the decidedly hot Estrella Mountain Ranch district of Goodyear, Ariz., where he currently lives with his wife and two small children.

"Arnprior reminds me a lot of the area where I grew up in Florida," Raines said.

Meaning small. Arnprior, pop. 8,100, sits at the mouth of the Mississippi River which spills into the Ottawa River about 85 kilometres northwest of Canada's capital city of Ottawa in the Upper Ottawa Valley. Playtex, Pfizer and Boeing are among the brand names that set up manufacturing facilities in Arnprior. It was the birthplace of my lifelong friend Berk Keaney Sr., my coach with the Sudbury Shamrocks in Ontario's Nickel Region Senior Baseball League from 1976-78. It was the hometown of Sheila Paquette-Gallagher, my sister-in-law, who died of pancreatic cancer at the very young age of 60.

OK, so what was Raines doing spending winters in Arnprior? Well, he's married to Arnprior native Shannon Watson, a former volleyball player, who graduated from the University of Western Ontario in London before getting an internship with the Montreal Expos in Florida where Raines was managing the Class-A Advanced Brevard County Manatees.

When Raines' two sons, Tim and Andre, moved out of the Raines household in Florida, the two people left were their parents, Tim Sr. and his first wife Virginia, a high school mate at Seminole High, whom the former Expos player had married Oct. 16, 1979. It was a union that lasted more than 25 years.

"When my two sons were no longer in the house, it was just me and her and it was just wasn't working out," Raines explained. "It wasn't something that just happened. It was in the makings for a long time."

After they met in Florida, Raines and Watson never dated from the outset but down the road they would reconnect. At the end of the 2004 season, the last for the Expos in Montreal before they moved to Washington, Raines was promoted by the Expos as a coach under manager Frank Robinson from his job as hitting coach for the Expos' Double-A squad in Harrisburg, Pa. He would soon be leaving tickets for Expos' games for the Watson clan, including Shannon's parents, who would drive the estimated three hours from Arnprior.

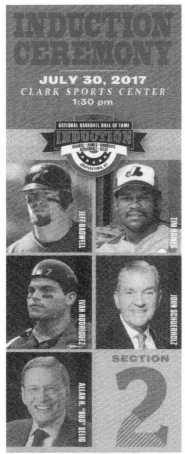

Author's pass for Cooperstown induction event in 2017

"I knew Shannon in passing. We weren't in any type of relationship," Raines would reveal.

That all changed when Raines arrived in Montreal in late 2004.

"We hit it off," Raines said.

What caught his attention about her?

"She's very smart, she has a great personality and she's tall," Raines said, as he started laughing again. "I'm 5-foot-8 and she's 5-foot-10. She's not skinny but thin. She's totally different from my first wife (5-foot-2)."

And Raines admired the fact that Shannon attended Western and it didn't hurt that Shannon's brother Tanner was a baseball player himself, who pitched in the minors for the Seattle Mariners and Chicago Cubs.

So when Raines' marriage ended, he made plans with Shannon to get married and that happened June 9, 2007. He was 43, she was 26. Then they decided to have a baby.

"It was planned. We wanted one baby but we got two," Raines said, referring to Amelie and Ava, who arrived in 2010 as stepsisters for Tim and Andre, both of whom are in their early 30s. "Having babies at my age is no problem, not really. I was no longer playing baseball so I have the time do this. I was ready."

So a new, young wife, more than 15 years his junior, two babies when he was close to 45. He's black, she's white. No sweat for the Cooperstown Hall of Famer and member of the Canadian Baseball Hall of Fame.

"I've been kidding him," said his long-time friend, former Expo teammate and Hall of Famer Andre Dawson. "He'll be 70 when he'll be a daddy and a granddaddy. But, hey, whatever he wants to do, I still love him to death. He's like a little brother to me."

Even moving to Arizona was a monumental change for Raines but

Danny Gallagher photo
Tim Raines has fun with a fan at the Big O in 2017

he's enjoying it. Why Arizona after decades in Sanford and Lake Mary?

"Hurricanes. In 2004, we had three hurricanes. There wasn't a lot of damage but I wanted to move. It's very warm in Arizona but there are no hurricanes," Raines said.

"Hurricanes? I have more hurricanes where I live in the Miami area than he did," joked Dawson, who longer can call Raines Homie, the nickname generated because they both had lived in the same state.

The 21st century has been good for Raines, even though he no longer plays and despite a multi-million dollar divorce settlement with his wife. He's free of the lupus disease he encountered while with the Oakland A's in 1999, an ailment he was told had no known cause, a disease that attacks the kidneys. He sat out the entire 2000 season to recover from the attack.

After retiring following the 2002 season, Raines managed and coached teams, topping out with a World Series championship as a coach with the Chicago White Sox in 2005. He currently holds down two MLB positions: he's a special assistant in the Blue Jays player-development department and he's a goodwill ambassador for the White Sox.

Raines collected 808 stolen bases, walked 1,330 times, had 2,605 hits, scored 1,571 runs and batted .294 over 23 big-league seasons with the Expos, White Sox, Yankees, Oakland, Baltimore Orioles and Florida Marlins.

When this reporter approached Yankees icon Derek Jeter in the visitors clubhouse at Rogers Centre in Toronto a few years ago for a chat,

I asked him among other things who his all-time favourite Expo was.

"Tim Raines," Jeter said without any hesitation about his Yankee teammate from 1996-98. "He could do everything. He could run, he could hit, he could steal bases, he played good defence."

Who knows how many bases Raines would have stolen in 1981 if the strike had not occurred. He snagged 71 bases in a mere 88 games. How many would he have stolen during a full season of 162 games? How many would he have stolen during the strike year of 1994 which shut down Aug. 12? Instead of 808 SB, could he have had 950? Of course, there were also times when Raines declined to steal bases, just for the sake of stealing bases. He admits it. There had to be a purpose in stealing a base. It was not laziness or indifference that he would decline the opportunity.

"There were teams that gave me bases to steal and I could have padded my stats," Raines said, "and not to downplay anyone who did that and stole bases, that was not how I played the game."

To many, it may have appeared Raines lacked interest in 1988, 1989 and 1990, his last three seasons in Montreal when he batted .270, .286 and .287 with 33, 41 and 49 stolen bases. Expos brass seemed perplexed with Raines and traded him to the White Sox in December, 1990. It appeared Raines had indeed worn out his welcome in Montreal.

"That was the misconception people had about Tim but it was not lack of interest," said former teammate Bryn Smith. "It was frustration. A good many of us had been together for a long time in Montreal in the 1980s to try and accomplish something and win something and it never happened.

"He never had a bad day and what I mean by that is that whether he had four hits a game or zero hits, he was always the same personality-wise," said Smith, ever the philosopher. "No matter what he did in a game, he brought the same approach to his game. There was no complaining.

"He just loved to play the game. He had a lot of love for the game and his teammates. Dawson would come into the clubhouse always serious but Tim was always smiling. He would be like a little mosquito onto Hawk and Hawk would be trying to swat him away. They were so close.

"I always saw Tim laughing. I never saw him on a bad day. That personality engulfed the clubhouse. He was a court jester."

Steve Moore Archives

Tim Raines poses here in 1984 for photographer Steve Moore, who has shot many athletes and celebrities over the years. Moore says each photo he took of Raines at his MLB debut at Wrigley Field in 1979 is worth in the five figures. Imagine.

35

Booze, sobriety and El Perfecto

In the three years following sobriety, Dennis Martinez was a changed man on the baseball field, not for the good, but for the worse. By 1986, the Orioles gave up on Martinez and traded him to the Expos on June 16, 1986.

By Martinez's token, the decision to quit drinking took a toll on his pitching, rather than improve it. In 1984, he was 6-9. In 1985, he was much better at 13-11 but in 1986 prior to the trade, he had slipped again.

"I dedicated myself to sobriety, I just focused my mind on not drinking, to change myself and to train myself not to drink," Martinez told me. "When I tried to play, it wasn't the same. I wasn't the same pitcher, not the same before I stopped drinking. And it's true, you can't concentrate on the game and on sobriety at the same time. You have to concentrate on one or the other."

Martinez was first introduced to booze when he was a teenager with Flor de Cano, a famous rum made from sugar cane and molasses and manufactured in his native Nicaragua at a distillery that sits at the base of the San Cristobal Volcano. On a road trip with an amateur team in Nicaragua, a teammate gave him drink after drink of Flor de Cano straight up on the bus after the game. He threw up after many gulps.

Later, it was beer for Martinez on the drinking circuit and then he switched to white wine, which over time got boring, too. What was odd about Martinez's binge drinking is that he didn't indulge at home in the company of his family.

"Beer? I was not a big beer drinker. Somebody told me that beer would get you fat and you would get a belly," Martinez said, chuckling. "I started drinking wine but it gave me a headache. I wouldn't feel good the next day. I changed to amaretto, just with ice. I liked it because it was fruity. Then I went to Grand Marnier, pretty much like amaretto. I liked its sweetness. It was less sugary than amaretto and it was something strong. I wasn't a serious drinker. I was just going with the flow."

One night in 1983 after a night of drinking white wine because the bar had no amaretto or Grand Marnier, he was pulled over by the cops

Sylvain Légaré photo

Dennis Martinez poses with Montreal mayor Valerie Plante at City Hall in 2019

and his family knew about it because they had heard about it on the radio and saw it on television. At that point, Martinez made one of the biggest decisions he has made in his life.

"I decided to do something about it. That's it, no more," he said of the alcohol. "I haven't drank for 36 years. I don't feel the urge anymore. I don't want it. I don't need it but you always have to be alert."

The Expos had been known for taking on exclamation projects. Drug addict Pascual Perez was one of them. So they decided to give Martinez a chance. The Orioles had become fed up with him.

"I was so grateful to be traded to the Expos, to a different country, to a different culture," Martinez said. "That was my second chance in baseball. They treated me so good in Montreal. I was so happy to play there. People took me under their wing."

And he proved them right, even though he was knocked around early on. During one particular game when he was being bashed by the Pirates, pitching coach Larry Bearnarth came to the mound to make him feel better.

"OK, kid.' Those were Larry's words," Martinez recalled. "He said, 'You are a veteran, kid, you have been successful, do what you love to do.' He helped turned my life around. That game against Pittsburgh, I got hit so bad. They were hitting the ball hard and I wanted to come out of the game. Larry came with the right things to say. At the end of the season, I started showing signs of pitching better. I won three games at the end, including a shutout."

After a rough 3-6 stint in 1986 with the Expos, Martinez made progress and more progress. By 1987, after a stint in the minors, he would emerge as the ace of the Expos' pitching staff. This is what he did during his tenure with the Expos: 11-4, 15-13, 16-7, 10-11, 14-11, 16-11 and 15-9.

The highlight of his career came July 28, 1991 on a scorching hot day in Chavez Ravine at Dodger Stadium when he threw a perfect game against the Dodgers. 27 up, 27 down, including shutting down former Orioles teammate Eddie Murray three times.

This piece of art by Martinez was something to behold in a terrible season experienced by the Expos after Tim Raines had been traded to the Chicago White Sox in the off-season and following the official take-over of the team from majority owner Charles Bronfman by a consortium led by Claude Brochu.

The Expos had a young manager, Tom Runnells, in over his head and trying to be an army general, much to the chagrin of the players, after long-time favourite Buck Rodgers was fired June 3, 1991. GM Dave Dombrowski wanted to fire Rodgers following the 1990 season but Bronfman ruled against him. Now that Bronfman was no longer the owner, Brochu gave DD the okay to can Rodgers.

To add sodium to the wounds, just a month before this no-hitter, a 55-ton beam at Olympic Stadium came crashing down, forcing the Expos to play a number of home games on the road. The Expos were also dealt a blow on May 23 when Tommy Greene of the Phillies fired a no-hitter at Olympic Stadium.

Martinez, with a huge wad of chewing tobacco in his right jaw, fashioned his no-hitter at age 36 in his 15th season as a major-leaguer. It was done in the midst of trade rumours that suggested he was going to the Toronto Blue Jays in exchange for Quebec native Denis Boucher.

As Martinez said about the moments heading into his no-hitter, "We were struggling. We weren't winning too many games."

When the 27th batter, pinch-hitter Chris Gwynn, hit a long fly to centre, Martinez turned around and saw right away that outfielder Marquis Grissom had lots of time to get under the ball.

"Fly ball ... centre field ... Grissom ... El Presidente, El Perfecto," Expos play-by-play man Dave Van Horne said after Grissom caught the ball. And there was nothing said in the broadcast booth for some time as Van Horne and partner Ken Singleton decided on The Sound of Silence as they let the cheering crowd take over the sound waves.

"When Gwynn hit it, I knew that he hit it good but I knew that he didn't hit it far enough. That ball is not going anywhere," Martinez said a few months ago. "He took up too much of the plate. He was all over the plate and on top of it. I didn't want to hit him. I tied him up real good. He had a pretty good swing but he didn't extend his arms the way he wanted to. He'd gotten it on the big barrel of the bat and the ball stayed up in the air so it gave Marquis a chance to get going after it."

In the Dodgers' radio booth, there was also magic from the lips of Vin Scully. I asked Scully what his best memory of that day was. So in an email exchange Oct. 21, 2019, the grand master of the microphone told me.

"When Dennis finished the job, he sat in the dugout and sobbed," Scully said.

When I told Martinez that about Scully, he replied, "That's what I did. That's the emotional part. I was feeling so grateful. I knew it was a gift from God, what I was going through, grateful for what was going in my life."

Yes, grateful that he had turned his career around, grateful that the Expos had given him another chance.

"The Orioles gave me the first chance," Martinez said. "The Expos gave me the second opportunity, the second life, not only in baseball but as a human being. I was able to stay focused and clear my mind."

As the ball landed in Grissom's glove, Martinez was whooping it up and turned toward third baseman Tim Wallach. They may have been teammates but they were adversaries, too. Wallach never cared much for Martinez's style of popping off to the media if he felt the team was playing poorly. That day, though, Wallach forget the past to hug Martinez.

"Eli was showing his emotions," Martinez said. "There was that bond between us despite the past. He hugged me and I hugged him, too. I was happy but my emotions took control of me. I started to cry."

Martinez said he threw 80% fastballs that day. Of the 96 pitches he threw, only 30 were balls. Prior to hitting to Grissom to end the game, Gwynn had hit a line drive foul past third, causing a few hearts to flutter.

"I made no bad pitches. I've watched every single pitch on the video. It was remarkable," Martinez said. "When I went out to the mound for the ninth, I was shaking. The crowd (more than 45,000) was clapping and giving me ovations. I said, 'Please, God, help me.'

"There were tears in my eyes because of the joy, what God allowed me to do. I thought of the people in Montreal who treated me so good," Martinez said of his time alone. "I was just praying to me. I was kind of numb. I was dreaming. I was biting my tongue."

Dodgers infielder Alfredo Griffin told me years ago that he recalled Martinez as having a "nasty slider."

The next day, Martinez appeared on NBC's Good Morning America at 4:45 a.m. with Bryant Gumbel, the same Gumbel, who 10 years earlier, had interviewed Rick Monday of the Dodgers after his Blue Monday homer beat the Expos Oct. 19, 1981.

A few days following his masterpiece, Martinez sent his uniform top, a ticket stub and an autographed ball from the game to the National Baseball of Fame and Museum in Cooperstown, N.Y. and he has kept many souvenirs: his uniform bottom, cleats and gloves, even the starting lineup posted by Runnells.

At the first game back in Montreal at Olympic Stadium, Expos' brass gave him a Chevrolet Blazer and a framed photo of himself. Three weeks later, accompanied by reporters from the Montreal Gazette, La Presse and Le Journal de Montréal, Martinez travelled to his birthplace in Granada to be feted by his countrymen. It was special because he was the first player from Nicaragua to play in the majors.

"I pitched that game in L.A. but to share it with my people in Nicaragua is something I will never really forget," Martinez told me. "It was an unbelievable feeling, a great day I will never forget. Everytime I look at the video of the game, I'm living a dream. It happened (29 years ago) but it feels like yesterday."

When he returned to Montreal from Nicaragua, Martinez arranged to spend over $7,000 with the Royal Canadian Mint in Ottawa to obtain Canadian Maple Leaf coins for his teammates, other uniformed personnel and Expos' staff members to commemorate his special day.

When we talked to Martinez in late 2019, he told me he runs three times a week, lifts weights and just in the last three years, at the behest of his children, he has been golfing three times a week. Golf is a relatively brand new adventure for him. He weighs about 185 pounds, down from his playing weight of 192.

And what is his favourite dish? "Rice and beans, man."

King of official scorers

Michel Spinelli was the longest reigning official scorer at Expos home games, doing about 1,000 contests during his 24-year run from 1980-2004.

"I did an average of 40 or 41 games per year plus a few playoff games in Philadelphia and L.A.," Spinelli said. "A few of the Expos games in the last two years were held in Puerto Rico and I personally went four times out of six homestands. I probably did about a dozen games in Puerto Rico."

Others who scored many games over the years were Pierre Ladouceur, J. P. Sarault, Bob Mann, Jacques Doucet, Ted Blackman, Bob Dunn, Ian MacDonald and Mitch Melnick. The author of this book even scored two games in the early 1990s.

"I did about 350 games," said Mann, who began working when beat writers and broadcasters were no longer permitted by MLB to do the job.

"A little footnote on the work of the official scorer: some players were regularly lobbying for their stats," Ladouceur said. "So when they say stats are not important, they are lying. Because when they were lobbying, they were lobbying against a teammate. Hit or error? Defensive average vs. ERA."

The lobbying would begin with a player picking up the dugout phone and talking to the scorer about a debatable call. Batters, of course, would want to be given a hit as opposed to an error for the fielder on a close play because an error would take their average down.

"It was a tougher job before replays. We had 24 hours to change the verdict," Ladouceur said.

36

A smashed helmet

Nikco Riesgo boasted a passion and intensity that some Expos team-mates didn't like. So much so that he got into a fight with the usually mild mannered veteran Tom Foley in April of 1991.

And the fight may have been the reason Riesgo was let go by the Expos the next day.

Foley had taken exception to Riesgo's over the-top enthusiasm while sitting on the dugout bench with a helmet on when he wasn't even in the starting lineup. Riesgo would shout and shout and Foley and some of the other players resented it. Foley had-had it.

So what did Foley do? He took a baseball bat and smashed Riesgo's helmet to smithereens in the clubhouse before a game and before Ries-go arrived at the ballpark. Riesgo didn't taken too kindly to what Foley did and they went at it and had to be restrained.

Riesgo was an underdog at Spring Training in West Palm Beach, Flor-ida in 1991 because he was a Rule V draft pick plucked from the Phillies in December of 1990. I, for one, was pulling for him to make the team. I like underdogs who don't get much ink or air time. I even went up to Canadian Press photographer Ryan Remiorz at spring training to see if he would take a shot of Riesgo and put it on the wire for newspapers across Canada to run it but I don't think he took any photos.

"I like to talk a lot. It was my ego," Riesgo said about his enthusiasm on the bench, trying to stimulate his teammates. "I had a ferocious pas-sion for the Expos. I was the only one on the team on the bench with a helmet on. I'm one of those players who can't shut up. My heart beats the game. I had a ferocious passion for the Expos. My football coach at San Diego State was Tony Gwynn's father Charlie.

"When I saw my helmet was shattered, it violated every sacred thing in my soul. The helmet was for me, a part of my strength. I became the man in the locker room. I challenged any man to step up. I didn't care who it was. It was Foley. They broke it up real quick. Foley said it was a joke that he shattered my helmet."

The next day, Riesgo was released. It was either Foley or Riesgo would be released because of the dustup. Riesgo was told by equipment manager John Silverman that GM Dave Dombrowski wanted to see him at his Olympic Stadium office. Riesgo said it boiled down to the Expos wanting to bring in pitcher Jeff Fassero so they had to create a roster spot for him.

"Dombrowski said, 'We needed pitching.' Go figure, doesn't everyone? You don't waste a young talent like myself over aging vets. Did it happen because of the fight? It was the wrong decision."

How Riesgo was kept around was interesting. They wanted to keep him on the roster to start the season so Riesgo said manager Buck Rodgers told him that they would pretend that Riesgo had a shoulder injury and he would be placed on the disabled list.

"It was a way for them to keep me," Riesgo said.

When he was activated from the DL, Riesgo made his MLB debut April 20 in right field and collected his sole hit in the big leagues the same day, a single off of Mets veteran southpaw Frank Viola, a fastball down the middle.

"What I remember very vividly is Frank Viola at the time, he apparently was one of the top dominant lefties in the game," Riesgo said. "I got my start in Montreal in the Game of the Week on television."

Technically, Riesgo wasn't released. The official wording is that he was returned to the Phillies as part of the Rule V draft terminology. Before he was actually returned to the Phillies, he had to pass through waivers with the Expos farm team in Ottawa.

37

Felipe gets his chance

You couldn't blame Felipe Alou if he felt neglected or bypassed or ignored. Was it the colour of his skin or his Dominican accent?

The people running the Expos for years felt Alou was excellent at developing young players in the minors or as a coach with the Expos. It was a subtle putdown of him and all those years he spent in the minors. Who could blame Alou if he was perceived to be a very remote figure so caught up in his personal journey? He was much like cranky Frank Robinson, bitter and resentful. Understandably so.

Patiently, Alou waited and waited for the Expos to offer him a big-league job as manager. The closest he got was his few seasons as a major-league coach.

Then Dan Duquette, GM of the Expos, decided to pull the plug on Tom Runnells on May 22, 1992 and offered the job to Alou. Duquette called Alou into his office that day and as they began talking, Alou tried to get Duquette to give Runnells more time. Duquette said no.

Duquette told Alou that if the didn't accept the job that he would offer the job to another coach, Kevin Kennedy. So Alou took the job at a time when the Expos were floundering under a manager in over his head and not liked by most of the players.

Under Runnells, the Expos were 17-20 and had even won their last game with TR at the helm. On May 20, the Expos had rallied from a 5-2 deficit to beat Cincinnati with four runs in the bottom of the ninth inning. But it wasn't a very satisfying win. When I looked down at Runnells from the press box after the winning run had scored, I saw a sour look on his face. I said to myself, 'I wonder if that is his last game.' I worked that sentiment into my game story for The Associated Press and Ron Blum on the AP desk in New York thought I shouldn't have written it.

The next day, an off-day, Duquette pondered what he was going to do and talked with managing general partner Claude Brochu and vice-president of baseball operations Bill Stoneman. Duquette decided to fire Runnells the next day. Duquette arranged to meet Runnells at his suburban Montreal home to deliver the news. Runnells cried and pleaded to keep his job. Duquette said no.

The Expos finished 70-55 under Alou and 87-75 overall that season. And just think, from May through October, Alou was deemed an "interim" manager by Duquette. But the interim tag was eliminated heading into the 1993 season.

The Expos just got better and better in 1993, becoming a powerhouse. It was the beginning of a two-year reign as one of baseball's top teams. At the end of June, they were 41-36 but the rest of the way, they turned it on.

June was also a month of upheaval in the front office but it was kept secret for a long time. Then the secret was let loose: the organization had reached a parting of the ways with long-time employee Jim Fanning, who was 66 years old. It was a difficult negotiation for Duquette, one that went on for months.

Fanning was a jack of all trades with the Expos, beginning in 1968 when he became general manager alongside buddy John McHale, who was team president. Fanning eventually ran the Expos farm system, was a scout and even tried his hand in the broadcast booth. As he approached his 65th birthday, Fanning wasn't do much of anything for the Expos, who didn't relish the fact he was more or less a figurehead goodwill ambassador making some good coin, working mostly out of his suburban home. He no longer was in a decision-making role he had enjoyed until the late 1980s.

But Fanning pushed and pushed in his demands, insisting on this and that in the final agreement. Even his wife Maria got involved to voice her displeasure. When all was said and done, Fanning left the Expos and made an appearance in the press box the night of the announcement. But a day or so later, his press-box and free-ticket privileges were taken away. Outfielder Larry Walker asked that Fanning put some tickets away for him one game but management balked. Walker called up to the press box to complain to Stoneman.

By the end of July, the Expos had pushed to 12 games over .500 at 56-48 but then another shocking move came along. The Expos placed veteran starter Dennis Martinez on the waiver wire and was claimed by the Atlanta Braves. The Expos contacted the Braves to work out a trade but in the end, Martinez vetoed the deal because of his rights as a 10-and-five player, 10 years in the majors, the last five with the same club.

Martinez would tell reporters on the day he quashed the trade that he wanted to continue pitching for the Expos. With the Braves, he felt he would become the fifth starter and wouldn't get many starts.

In the month of September, two events shook the Expos and their fans. On the 16th, outfielder Moises Alou suffered a gruesome injury in St. Louis when he rounded first base following a single. Going all out, he reversed field to come back to first base but one of his spikes got caught in the artificial turf and down he went in excruciating pain with a badly mangled right leg. Sheesh, it was awful if you were there in person or if you saw it on television. Not surprisingly, Alou was in tears with the pain and how the leg was bent out of shape.

The next night, when Alou chatted with reporters after being treated first in St. Louis and then by orthopedic surgeon Dr. Larry Coughlin in Montreal, he was upbeat.

"I'm surprised it doesn't hurt at all," Alou was quoted as saying in a story in the Montreal Gazette. "They gave me some codeine and I guess that did the job. The main thing is that I'm happy to see my foot straight. That was scary."

Without Alou the remainder of the season, the Expos forged on. That night, fireworks erupted in the seventh inning when unheralded rookie Curtis Pride was summoned as a pinch hitter against Bobby Thigpen of the Phillies. Pride was 95% deaf so his story was inspiring. What transpired was deafening. Pride cranked a two-run double into the gap and as he stood on second base, the crowd of 45,757 gave him a five-minute

Danny Gallagher photo
Felipe Alou and his wife Lucie in 2019

standing ovation. He couldn't hear the love but he could feel it.

In video of the scene, Pride is seen walking over to third-base coach Jerry Manuel. Pride asked Manuel if he had the green light to steal third. Manuel bypassed that question and replied, "Tip your cap." And Pride said, "What?" So Manuel said, "They're cheering you."

So Pride tipped his cap. Third-base umpire Gary Darling walked up to Pride and said, "Smile." Pride later told reporters, "I was trying to hold in my smile but he told me to go ahead."

It was one of the most treasured moments in Expos history: a disabled man getting special attention.

"Here," Pride said, pointing at this chest, when a reporter asked him about how he felt the crowd's support. "I could hear the vibrations. I was very, very excited. I never had a curtain call in my life. I could see them clapping and it looked like they wouldn't stop."

The Expos won the game 8-7 in 12 innings but it wasn't the main story. Pride was the story, a big sidebar.

"The ovation came rolling out of the seats, louder and louder, reaching out to a man who is deaf," wrote esteemed Gazette wordsmith Michael Farber. "Curtis Pride never knew he had this many friends. He

Sylvia Légaré photo

Felipe Alou captures the attention of Montreal mayor Valérie Plante

heard the loudest sound of his life in his gut."

After the game was over, Farber was able to chat with Pride's best friend Steve Grupe from their hometown of Laurel Springs, Maryland.

"People are amazed by Curtis," Grupe told Farber. "They don't see someone who has a disability. A lot of my friends who met Curtis don't understand how he could have gotten into a life of sports with what he has faced."

As Manuel would say, "It was an emotional moment for me. To see Alou (in better spirits than the night before) and then to see the Canadians or whatever they want to call themselves in the stands and cheering this kid, it was special."

The game lasted four and a half hours, a deadline monster for reporters, Farber included. In the 12th inning, Marquis Grissom doubled and on his own, stole third and scored on a sac fly by close buddy Delino Deshields to finish the barnburner of a game. Grissom apparently was under direct orders not to steal but he did anyway.

"We didn't give him a red light," the manager said afterward. But in the next breath, Alou added, "We trust his good judgment. He's one of the best."

The Expos took two out of three from the Phillies and showed the baseball world they meant business. But in the end, the Phillies ruled the roost in the NL East with a 97-65 record, three games better than the 94-68 Expos. The Phillies would go on to the World Series where they were beaten by the Blue Jays.

Grissom finished the season with some impressive stats: .298 average with 19 homers and 95 RBI. Larry Walker hit 22 homers and drove in 86 runs, although his BA was off-kilter at .265. Alou hit .286 with 18 homers and drove in 85 runs. On the pitching side, Martinez led the way with a 15-9 record and John Wetteland saved 43 games.

What was about to transpire in the off-season and the following season provided much fodder for years to come.

38

The good and bad of 1994

Larry Walker was on his way to hitting maybe 65 doubles. He had 44 at the time and he had driven in 86 runs. He was on a roll. Magical Walker.

Ken Hill was in striking distance of 20 wins. He was 16-5 at the time.

But their tidy figures of 1994 went down the drain when commissioner Bud Selig announced the cancellation of the strike-shortened season on Sept. 14. It was a bitter pill to swallow.

"If Major League Baseball understood that in preventing the Expos from possibly winning that it would be the beginning of the end of the team in Montreal?" Expos general manager Kevin Malone told me. "Did MLB not have enough vision and understand how damaging that decision was or did they care?

"The powers that be at the time didn't really care about baseball in Montreal to make that type of decision. I don't have any facts or data but baseball had enough intelligence not just that season but about the long-term ramifications.

"We had a great manager, great coaching staff and we had the players on the field and the fans were coming out in Montreal. I think it was creating a foundation that would have kept the Expos in Montreal. We were opening up people's eyes."

That's for sure, Kevin.

But the players, including the Expos, coached by MLBPA executive director Donald Fehr, are partly to blame for this travesty that ended the season. It wasn't just the owners, who tried to implement a salary cap but Fehr and his assistants drew the line. On Aug. 12, the players went on strike. Malone was in Pittsburgh with the team Aug. 11 and received a call from managing general partner Claude Brochu.

"We're going on strike," Brochu told Malone.

"We were playing so good," Malone said. "We had won 21 of 23 games. I remember being in the clubhouse and telling the players. It was like the air went out of the balloon. It was a punch in the stomach. The initial shock was a minor setback. We thought the strike would last just a few days, a week or so, maybe a pause, that put us on hold. I thought the season would continue at some point."

A month after the players went on strike, Selig made his dramatic announcement.

"It started to cause depression and blackness. This can't be happening," Malone was saying. "It was almost a nightmare, a really bad dream. It was extreme disappointment and a shock that the players union and MLB would allow this to happen.

Malone had taken over as Expos GM in the off-season of 1993-94 when Dan Duquette was finally permitted by Brochu to leave and take over his dream job as GM of the Red Sox. Duquette had laid the groundwork for Malone by assembling a wonderful team to take the field in 1994 but he had already put a great product on the field in 1993.

And just think, before Duquette left the Expos, he engineered a trade to acquire young pitcher Pedro Martinez from the Dodgers in exchange for infielder Delino Deshields. That was November 19, 1993. Some reporters and fans were upset with the trade because they had come to admire Deshields. But Duquette, Brochu and vice-president of baseball operations Bill Stoneman had wanted to cut salary and Deshields was getting expensive. DeShields' replacement at second, Mike Lansing, would cost a lot less money.

Duquette was thinking ahead of the game. He envisioned this Martinez to take over from the departed Martinez, Dennis, who was deemed too expensive as a free agent. Dennis signed with the Indians as a free agent and Pedro took over his spot in the rotation. Simple as that.

Of all the players Malone had at his disposal in 1994, the one he cherished the most was Marquis Grissom.

"Him and I started in Jamestown, N.Y.," Malone was telling me.

Grissom was a young whippersnapper, who had been selected by Expos scouting director Gary Hughes in the 1988 June amateur draft and Malone was the Jamestown field manager. Malone had come on board with the Expos after a stint as a scout in the Angels' organization from 1985-87.

Jamestown is one of baseball's outposts, a small metropolis that didn't turn on such great Expos alumni as Gary Carter and Randy Johnson. Jamestown Municipal Stadium and its clubhouse were hardly endearing. But hey, you have to start somewhere. Jamestown was a short-season rookie venue that Malone called a "field of dreams", a place where baseball people can start dreaming of a future in the game. Jamestown is located in Chautauqua County near Lake Erie and can't be that bad. It's the birthplace of NFL commissioner Roger Goodell and standout comedian Lucille Ball.

"Marquis had come out of Florida A& M (like Andre Dawson) and he struggled at the very beginning. He was something like 0-for-45 through the first 20 games or so," Malone said. "He could not get a hit but every day, we'd go out and we'd do soft toss and he'd hit off the tee.

He came out of the slump and hit .323 for the year. He went on a tear."

Grissom finished his summer stint in the New York-Penn league with eight homers and 39 RBI and proceeded to be a bonafide star with the Expos. Malone used his one-year stint in Jamestown as a springboard to a two-year gig with the Twins as a scout before Duquette called and asked him to get involved with him in scouting for 1992-93.

"It was culture that Jim Fanning, Dave Dombrowski and Gary Hughes started," Malone said. "It was an Expos culture of emphasis on scouting and player development. You promoted (people) from within. There are so many major league managers, coaches and scouts, who started with the Expos. I was blessed to come and take over. I was grateful. Dan knew what he was doing and had a plan. How do you build upon what Dan Duquette did?"

> "My first year with the Expos was 1981 and my last year was 2001. 21 years. Then I had 18 years with the Marlins: 2002-2019. One World Series in 2003 and two all star games: one as an Expo in Texas in 1995 and one as a Marlin in 2008, the last one at old Yankee Stadium in New York. One of my favorite accomplishments was rehabbing Moises Alou's ankle in 1993 for him to come back and make the all star team in 1994 before the season-ending strike."
> **– Mike Kozak, a Toronto native, who has spent 39 years in the majors as an assistant trainer. As we went to press, Mike was still looking for another job after his contract was not renewed by the Marlins following the 2019 season.**

39

How Tommy Brady became Tom Brady

Other than paying attention to Tom Brady, my interest in the NFL is minimal.

For a good part of the last 20 years, Brady has been the king of football except for his down season of 2019. Six Super Bowl wins. A boyish-looking, hunky, freakish force of nature, fitness aficionado and strict nutrition fiend.

And just think, the Expos drafted him June 2 in 1995, the hangover year they suffered from the awful aftermath of the strike-marred 1994 season when they were gunning for the playoffs and a possible berth in the World Series only to be dismissed by the cancellation of the season.

Brady was a 6-foot-3 catcher at Junipero Serra high school in San Mateo, Calif. and Expos scout John Hughes decided to draft him for scouting director Ed Creech and general manager Kevin Malone. Brady was 17, just shy of his 18th birthday.

One week after Brady was drafted, the Expos just so happened to be in San Francisco at Candlestick Park for a series against the Giants so they arranged for Brady to come from his nearby home and take BP, tour the clubhouse and meet the players and staff. That was June 9.

"I was travelling with the team and John Hughes said he was bringing in a young catching prospect," Malone recalled. "We thought very highly of him, his stature, his poise. He was very mature for his age and presence. He worked out for us. He had all the tools we were looking for, to project him as a major-leaguer. He had the arm strength, he was a left-handed hitter with power. He had a good swing. He was cerebral and analytical."

Something got in the way, though. Brady's father Tom Sr. wanted his son to go to college and get an education. So Jr. enrolled at the University of Michigan. The rest is history.

Just like Condredge Holloway and Matt Dunigan and a few other future quarterbacks in the CFL and NFL, Brady was much loved by the Expos. As it turned out, Holloway, Dunigan and Brady didn't suit up in a big-league uniform for the Expos. Like Brady, Holloway was 17 when he was selected by the Expos as their No. 1 pick in 1971 out of Lee high school in Hunstville, Ala. Like Brady, Holloway turned down the Expos to take a scholarship – at the University of Tennessee. Dunigan tried out for the Expos on a minor-league contract in the 1980s but he was let go.

"It was a great honour for Tommy to be drafted by the Expos but we had made it clear that he was going to go to Michigan to play football," his father told this writer. "At the time, he was a pretty good baseball player. He was more skilled in baseball than he was in football.

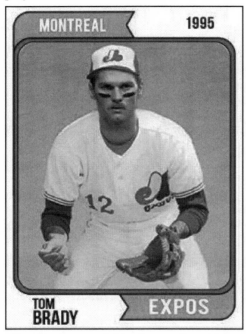

Tom Brady posted this photo online of how he would look in an Expos uniform

"He had a complete résumé in baseball. He had played 12 years of baseball when Montreal drafted him. He started playing at a young age, whereas he had a checkered résumé in football. He had only played four years of football including 7-on-7 when he went to Michigan. He loved baseball. Football, he wracked on it. He had the right tools for baseball. He had a terrific gun to second, he had some power in his bat. The Expos had said they would take care of him but that didn't sway him, even though he was told he was pretty highly rated."

And then came the kicker from Tom Sr.

"The background on all of this is that for one reason or another, Tommy hurt more after baseball games. His arms always hurt, his knees hurt, his elbows hurt. He didn't hurt so much in football," Papa Brady said. "And he'd been a 49ers fan for many years. Plus, he would get a great education at Michigan."

On that cold and windy day at Candlestick, Hughes approached Expos outfielder Rondell White, whom he had known for several years in California, to guide Brady through his day with the Expos. There was a moment in time in the clubhouse when a group of Expos' veterans and younger players crowded around Brady as he sat on someone's stool at a locker.

Brady was like a god, it seemed, as the players hovered around as if he was holding court. Somehow, White and the other players got it ingrained in Brady's head that he should indeed go to Michigan and play for the Wolverines and not pursue baseball.

The players were preaching and bemoaning to Brady that he would earn $800 or so per month in the minors and drive around on school buses for games before a few hundred fans, whereas at Michigan, he could have a lot of fun on and off the field and that there would be 100,000 fans at every game.

"Go to Michigan, go to Michigan. That's what Tom was told," his father said. "Tom didn't have the pedigree in football and he kinda chuckled when the players told him that he should go to Michigan. He had been to Candlestick so many times watching the Giants.

"Tom was a pretty good catcher and could have fit in under the optimum circumstances but we knew that coming up through baseball's minor-league system isn't easy, that you would struggle. In college, you cut your teeth right away. There is also more emotion in football than in baseball. It's 60 minutes a week."

The funny, ironic part of Brady and his short time with the Expos at Candlestick was that he was more or less a nobody at the time. As 1995 bench coach Luis Pujols told me last year, there were many unproven draft picks like Brady, who came to different ballparks to work out with the Expos. Pujols doesn't remember Brady that day at all.

In his 300-page, 11x14 coffee-table book The 12 Method: How to Achieve A Lifetime of Sustained Peak Performance, Brady talks on Page 7 about his decision not to go and play baseball with the Expos after he was drafted. Although football is a brutal sport, Brady thought baseball was just as gruelling in many ways.

"But by then I didn't want to play baseball anymore," Brady wrote in the book. "Ironically, the punishment it inflicted on my body, and my knees especially, was probably the biggest reason I ended up losing my love for the game.

"It was the pain I coped with day after day that led me to focus exclusively on football – though by that point, my love of the game had overtaken my love of baseball anyway."

And it seems, nobody took photos of Brady that day at Candelstick for keepsakes. That was in the days when there were no cell phones.

"We don't have anything on that part of Tommy's story," his father told me, when I asked him about photos. "It was so fleeting. We didn't hone in on it closely. I can't help you at all, my friend."

There is the mythical narrative going around that former Expos handyman F.P. Santangelo was one of those who stood around the cubicle as Brady held court in June of 1995. Santangelo even told former New York Times reporter Tim Rohan of Sports Illustrated's Monday Morning Quarterback platform. Santangelo told Rohan that he was among those egging Brady on to go to Michigan. Santangelo told me the same stuff.

But Santangelo wasn't there to chaperone Brady, to tell you the truth. It's all fiction. He has never met Brady. Wanna know where Santangelo

194

was that day? He was playing for the Ottawa Lynx, the Expos' triple-A affiliate. He was in his last days with the Lynx, who would eventually retire his No. 24 to honour his three-season stint in Ottawa.

Santangelo confirmed to me in an interview that he wasn't there at Candlestick.

"I wasn't with the Expos then," Santangelo said. "I was called up by the Expos on Aug. 2, 1995. That was my debut in the big leagues."

As I searched the prestigious Retrosheet database, I saw that the Expos also visited Candlestick in late August of 1995 following Santangelo's arrival but Santangelo said Brady was not there for any workouts. Brady's father said that by the time the Expos rolled into San Francisco the second time that season that his son had already gone to Ann Arbor to get ready for the coming football season.

Santangelo did say that it made sense for Brady to go to Michigan because Santangelo himself was a Michigan native and his mother attended the university. As he looks back, Santangelo said, "I never knew who Tommy Brady was. I never drew the parallel. Maybe he's the greatest quarterback ever."

When word got back to Hughes about the huddle Brady had with the Expos' players in the clubhouse, Hughes recounted, "They were saying to Tom, 'Wait a second, you have an university scholarship to Michigan. Go to school, for crying out loud.' I told scouting director Ed Creech this, that these guys were not going to help us much in signing him."

Brady's alma mater, Junipero Serra, an all-Catholic college preparatory school in the Roman Catholic archdiocese of San Francisco, was attended by alumni such as legendary baseball scout Gary Hughes, baseball players Jim Fregosi, Barry Bonds and Gregg Jefferies and NFL star Lynn Swann.

In the spring of 1995 and for several springs and falls prior to that, scouts had attended Junipero Serra Padres' games mainly to see another prospect, Greg Millichap. But Brady ended up higher on the depth chart than Millichap.

"Millichap was probably more recognizable than Tom because Tom spent part of his summer preparing for football but Tom really came into the radar in his senior year," said John Hughes, who has been a Marlins' scout for a number of years. "He was a left-handed hitting catcher, who could throw and had a little pop in his bat. You could tell he had leadership on the field.

"Anyway, I went in to see Tom this day and I had already seen him a few times. So I told my supervisor, Jim Fleming, that my first report on Tom was a little light. I needed to raise him. So the supervisor saw Tom and said my report was a little light. As the season went on, I knew he was going to be very, very difficult to sign or highly unlikely to sign. Signability was going to be difficult.

"After we drafted him, I went over to his parents' house. Tom Sr. was telling me along the lines that the family was thrilled and appreciative that the Expos drafted him but I remember him saying, 'Tom is the worst athlete in the family. My daughters are better athletes.' We didn't actually make an offer. I knew I had a rough idea of the money we had to offer."

When I asked Hughes if the Expos were prepared to offer Brady $1-million to sign, he replied, "No, half that."

Submitted photo
Tom Brady in authentic picture as confirmed by his dad

As we found out, that figure was $500,000, much more than the signing bonus for a typical 18th-round pick. Remember this was 25 years ago.

"We told his family that we wanted to offer him the equivalent of let's say a pick in the top half of the third round or the bottom of the second round," Hughes said. "Based on the type of money we were prepared to offer him, we were projecting him to be an everyday catcher in the majors. We thought he could play in the majors. Oh, yes. Personality-wise, the way he carried himself, his demeanour on the field, I thought he was like Joe Mauer. To this day, he's the mostly impressive high school kid I've dealt with in scouting."

For 36 years, Pete Jensen was Junipero Serra's baseball coach and when he and Brady weren't on the baseball diamond, they were in the classroom. Jensen taught Brady architectural design. To this day, Brady, a "great student," continues to design his own houses based on what Jensen taught him. Brady really got into the architectural design course and "loved it."

Brady had been a regular at first base most of his time at Junipero Serra but he also caught. It was only in his senior year there that Jensen saw a vastly improved product, compared to his earlier years.

"Tommy could hit and with power and he could really throw. His size, his ability to hit, he was a good receiver and thrower. I honestly thought he would choose baseball but I was wrong," Jensen said, laughing. "He was one of the best I've coached. He was one of the top prospects in the area. He also played football and basketball at our school. I've coached a number of big-league players and he was right up there with any of them. In his senior year, he really, really lit things up. All of the scouts saw Tommy and they were interested in Tommy. We probably had every scouting director out to see Tommy and Greg Millichap work out.

"Here's a funny story. In a playoff game that year, we took a school bus to a game against Bellarmine in San Jose. The school bus driver parked, hiding right behind the right-field fence. Tommy hit two home runs that game, including one off the top of the bus and woke up the driver. The driver was mad. The greatest thing about Tommy was that he was a great leader, mostly by example, extremely competitive, tough on himself. He wanted to win in the worst way. I was actually a part-time scout for the Mariners back then and I arranged to take Tommy to a pre-draft workout at the Kingdome. He hit and ran and threw. He put on a show with a couple of balls into the seats."

When the scouts got out their stopwatches, though, hmm, the speed was slow.

"He didn't run so good," Jensen said.

That's why you see Brady stay back in the pocket with the Patriots, rather than venture up the field for rushing yardage. If you look at his lifetime rushing totals, you will see he never ran much. At least one baseball scouting report alluded to that slow-of-foot deficiency.

"Good arm strength, slow feet, kind of gangly," Marlins scout Or-rin Freeman told this writer recently in a Facebook exchange. "Need-ed strength. Good swing. More hit than power. Prospect as a back-up catcher. I think he picked the right sport."

Sounds like a typical, point-form, no-sentence scouting report Free-man would have submitted to scouting director Gary Hughes.

"Pretty close," Freeman said.

"I didn't realize he would turn out to be Tom Brady," said Gary Hughes, who was the Expos scouting director before he headed to the Marlins. He was Freeman's boss when Freeman handed in his report on Brady.

So stop and think about that statement by Hughes. Put the word be in italics and then comprehend what Hughes said. A powerful state-ment coming from a gentleman, who attended the same high school as Brady.

"I'm not only proud of what Tom has done and how he has done it but he's been very kind to the school. He's a special young man and the whole area is proud of him. To this day, he's Tommy at Serra, not Tom," Hughes said.

Who knows, if he had signed with the Expos, he would have made it to the majors in the late 1990s and stayed a few seasons before he would have been traded because he would've been too expensive. We can only dream what Brady would have done with the Expos. Maybe he would have saved the franchise from moving to Washington.

Brady photoshopped a photo of himself in an Expos uniform a few years ago with this post, "21 years ago today, I was fortunate to be se-lected by the Expos in the 1995 ML Draft. But I'm so happy I stuck with football! What do you guys think?"

And so you ask me: did you make an attempt to get a hold of Brady? I sure did but nothing materialized. I'm not surprised. Brady has reached the echelons of stardom where one-on-one interviews are rare. It's akin to somebody trying to do a phoner with Tom Cruise or Tiger Woods.

I thought back to something else Freeman said, "Brady wasn't really a football star in high school and wasn't a high draft in football for a guy, who may go down as the best ever."

Long-time Expos coaches	
Name	Seasons
Pierre Arsenault	11
Tommy Harper	10
Larry Bearnarth	8
Luis Pujols	8
Joe Kerrigan	7
Jerry Zimmerman	7
Cal McLish	7

Arsenault was officially called bullpen coordinator, not a coach
Compiled by Danny Gallagher

Floyd's gruesome injury

If the April, 1995 departures of Larry Walker, John Wetteland, Marquis Grissom and Ken Hill weren't bad enough for the Expos franchise, then how awful was Cliff Floyd's gruesome injury suffered May 15, 1995?

Floyd was playing first base and collided near the bag with runner Todd Hundley of the New York Mets, doing frightful damage to his right wrist.

"It was a nightmare," Floyd remembered.

"Trainer Ron McClain came out and he was queasy and he asked, 'What happened?' Then I showed him the wrist and he tried to fix the dislocation. It was numb. There were no feelings for an hour."

Subsequent surgery by orthopaedic surgeon Dr. Larry Coughlin required eight screws to repair the damage. The injury was akin to what one might see of a motorcycle rider or downhill skier after crashing in a high-speed accident, according to Coughlin, when he was asked by a reporter shortly after the accident.

As for the long-term prognosis, Coughlin told Floyd he would probably be as good as he was. There were some reports that suggested Floyd would miss the remainder of the season but he made it back on Sept. 12 after frequent rehabilitation sessions.

So his first test came when Jim Eisenrich of the Phillies hit a ball that Floyd took after.

"The ball came under the lights and I dove on the turf and caught the ball," Floyd said. "The crowd went crazy. Funny thing, the wrist pops but it was just the scar tissue that popped up. It didn't hurt."

In the many years since the accident, Floyd said, "You have your moments," when he was asked if the wrist causes pain, especially in cool weather.

Floyd actually went on to enjoy four seasons where he collected at least 90 RBI, but none with the Expos. He finished his career with a .278 average with 233 homers and 865 RBI.

40

Celebration

July 1, 1997, SkyDome, Toronto. Canada's 130th anniversary.

What a day: Jeff Juden facing his idol Roger Clemens, the Blue Jays' stud. Sold out crowd of 50,436.

And what does Juden do? He outduels Rocket Roger as the Expos win 2-1. Pretty magical stuff for a kid, who grew up near Boston in Salem.

"That was a very special day absolutely, pitching against a guy I looked up to," Juden was saying more than 20 years later. "It was real special. The television crew came down and looked at me before the game. They kept playing the Rocket Man. I wanted to see Roger pitch. I was a fan for a second. I was kind of in awe with the whole thing. It was scary out there.

"What I can remember is that a few of the guys were saying, 'Hey guy, Roger Clemens. Roger Clemens is facing Jeff Juden. We got him, dude.' I was excited at the chance to beat him. If I could beat him, it would make me the best and put that notch in that belt.

"Thank God. God blessed me that day. He gave me all the ability. For me, it was a God moment. It was a crazy place. The roof was open."

Juden had never pitched a more glamorous game. His late father Frederick, who was born in nearby Kingston, Ont. was in the stands. He most assuredly was thinking of his mother Regina, who had passed away years earlier of cancer and his sister Kim, who died of cancer when he was only six.

It was Toronto, it was Ontario, the Battle of Canada in a rare game between the Expos and Jays.

You think of special moments in the Expos' 36 seasons of operation and you think of this day in Toronto like you think of Jerry White's play-off homer to win Game 3 of the 1981 NLCS on Oct. 16.

You think of the electric moment and the standing ovation upon Rusty Staub's return to the Big O July 26, 1979. You think of the earth and air vibrating as deaf Curtis Pride hit a double in September, 1993. You think of El Presidente's perfect no-hitter in July, 1991.

Juden had never come even close to the 14 strikeouts he had that day. The win gave him a pretty nifty 10-2 record on a team that was medio-

Photo by Dick Loek, ©Toronto Star

Jeff Juden looks up at the crowd at the Rogers Centre after his sterling performance on Canada Day, July 1, 1997, outduelling his growing-up hero Roger Clemens of the Blue Jays. A crowd of over 50,000 was on hand. At left sitting are assistant trainer Mike Kozak and infielder Andy Stankiewicz.

cre. He went into the ninth inning, getting home plate umpire to ring up Otis Nixon to start the inning. But Orlando Merced singled, prompting manager Felipe Alou to summon Ugueth Urbina, who notched his 15th save to preserve the win for Juden.

Poor Joe Carter. The Blue Jays outfielder just couldn't figure Juden out and struck out three times. The ball would be coming in straight on Carter and other batters and then "it fell out big time", according to Juden.

"I had a great curveball that day. I was letting it fly. The mound in Toronto is really high, one of the higher mounds in the league," Juden said. "Oh yeah, I could really get on top of the ball. I was trying to match Roger. It was a sword duel: he's striking out two, I was striking out three.

"My speed varied from 88-98. I threw a couple of two-seamers, a four-seamer, a good breaking ball, a good slider. I was in the zone. It was surreal. I was lucky that day. It was an evenly played game. The turning point in the game, it made the difference. A ball dropped in and that scored a run."

It was actually the first inning when Juden's 'turning point' took place. FP Santangelo singled to right and scored when David Segui doubled to centre, just out of the reach of the Blue Jays outfielders. Then Rondell White hit a solo home run in the second to put the Expos up 2-0.

And from there, Juden sailed until Shawn Green homered to right-centre in the eighth inning to make it 2-1. Green just smoked it.

"Curve ball," Juden said when he was asked what he threw Green.

"I got heckled at the very end. Some fan came down and heckled me," Juden said.

Following the game, reporters from Toronto and Montreal converged on Juden and other players. Segui had this to say about Juden: "There's cuckoo guys in baseball and he's one of them." Juden joked that he grew up in "witchcraft Salem".

Little did Juden know he wouldn't be with the Expos much longer. He was traded at the trade deadline July 31. He knows why he was traded, calling it a "Latin thing."

Juden figures teammate Pedro Martinez and manager Felipe Alou had something to do with getting Juden out of town.

The wheels set in motion for Juden's exit came one night a few weeks following his gem in Toronto. After a game in Colorado when the Expos lost to the Rockies, Alou called Juden out – in front of the assembled media in his office. The reason why?

"They felt I was celebrating a loss by playing my guitar," Juden said. "That was Felipe's approach, taking the lesser of the two evils. He did it through the media. He wasn't man enough to say it to my face. I didn't appreciate that. I never celebrated a loss. I was just playing my guitar playing blues and sipping on some wine."

So when the media left Alou's office, they headed straight to Juden's locker for an explanation.

"I didn't like that particular aloofness in that situation I described," Juden said about Alou. "It put me in a bad light for a long time. To be called out by Felipe was a fucking joke. I liked Felipe. He was fair to me other than that (situation)."

On another occasion July 27, Juden said he was goaded by Martinez when he sat down in his seat to hear Martinez, Carlos Perez and others getting a bit noisy with the help of music on a radio owned by Santangelo. The song was Celebration by Kool and The Gang, still a staple at weddings, parties and of course, in airplane cabins.

Celebration reached No. 1 on the Billboard Hot 100 chart on February 7, 1981, and held that position for two weeks before being ousted by Dolly Parton's '9 to 5' song.

Celebrate good times, come on!
(Let's celebrate)
Celebrate good times, come on!
(It's a celebration)
Celebrate good times, come on!
(Let's celebrate)
(Come on and celebrate tonight)
Celebrate good times, come on!
('Cause everything's gonna be alright, let's celebrate)
Celebrate good times, come on!
(Let's celebrate)
Celebrate good times, come on!

"On the plane from Houston, Pedro was jumping up and down like we had won the World Series," Juden said. "Where did he get that? Fuck that asshole. Who the fuck does he think he is? We had lost four games in Houston and Pedro never pitched in any of the games. He had no respect for the guys who had pitched."

So what does Juden do? He heads up to first class to see general manager Jim Beattie and tell him that he didn't appreciate the noise from Martinez and others further back in the plane.

"Beattie got out of first class. They did tone it down for a brief moment. He wasn't able to get it under control," Juden recalled.

Celebrate good times
Come On
Celebrate good times
Come On

Juden then said he "asked them nicely" to tone the music down. "They were doing it full blast. They were celebrating for what? They were celebrating, playing it not once, but playing it over and over. Give me a break.

Photo submitted by Jeff Juden
Jeff Juden with parents Frederick and Regina

"And they said, 'Fuck you,'" he related.

Then, as Juden said, Martinez got in his face. Martinez is 5-foot-9, Juden is 6-foot-7.

"It was provocative. It was like someone walking up to me and sticking a camera in my face," Juden said. "He's at fault there. He's up against me because I'm the big guy. He's a little guy, a little pussy, coming at me and saying, 'Hey, bully.' He was trying to provoke me. He runs his mouth. I'm not the guy you want to fight. I would have preferred to meet him in the parking lot. Pedro wanted to take it to the next level and smash the radio over my head. They tried to provoke me. I'm not the guy you wanted to fight."

Instead, Juden smashed Santangelo's radio to smithereens before Martinez did.

"I saw it on the chair, I punched it with my fist and that thing exploded," Juden said. "Santangelo, he understood it. He got it. He was okay with getting another radio."

There is a myth about Martinez, there's an air about him and people put him on a pedestal of goodness. But he can be confrontational. When he told the Canadian Baseball Hall of Fame in June of 2018 that he couldn't make it to his own induction because of a medical problem, there were many who thought he just didn't want to have to come and spend five days, Wednesday through Sunday, in smalltown Ontario in St. Marys, glad-handling and signing autographs for free.

Because of his size and personality, Juden was sometimes portrayed as a negative influence in some clubhouses. Juden said former Yankees manager Joe Torre called him a "cancer on the team".

"I was made out to be a bully. I was bullied as a kid," Juden said.

I reached out to Martinez and Santangelo through text messages for comment on this episode but they didn't reply.

Four days after the Celebration episode, Juden was traded. Beattie called him up at the Manhattan Condominiums complex on Lincoln Ave. in Montreal where he was staying to give him the news.

"I was surprised. It was at midnight, a last-minute deal," Juden said. "I didn't say much. I didn't argue."

Fassero glad he kept his dream alive

It was the highlight of the 1996 season for Jeff Fassero when the Expos threatened to win the NL East.

On June 29 in Philadelphia, Fassero had a perfect game going until the sixth inning when rival pitcher Curt Schilling singled to centre. Fassero finished with a two-hit complete game as the Expos won 1-0, one of the great memories of his tenure in Montreal.

Fassero finished the 1996 season with a 15-11 record and a 3.30 ERA.

"I was in the minors for six years and all of a sudden, the last 15 plus were in the majors. It's awesome. I can't complain."

Fassero came a long way after considering retirement in 1990, so much so that he lives in Paradise Valley, Arizona.

41

Felipe almost leaves

Near the end of the 1998 season, Felipe Alou was reported to have quit as Expos manager during a road trip to St. Louis. Then somehow, he was talked out of it.

But what followed was something out of a movie, a cloak and dagger affair because Alou had told Dodgers GM Kevin Malone, his close buddy, that he had accepted his offer verbally to become the new Los Angeles manager on a three-year deal to start with the 1999 season.

"Felipe and I were close personal friends," Malone told me. "His wife and my wife and their kids and our kids were really close, even after I left Montreal. Dodgers president Bob Graziano and I met Felipe in the Dominican and he said, 'Yes, I'm coming.'"

So Felipe, shortly after agreeing with Malone, took a plane to West Palm Beach and then drove to his house in nearby Boynton Beach. Who should be waiting for him but Expos GM Jim Beattie and Mark Routtenberg, a minority shareholder in the Expos consortium headed by managing general partner Claude Brochu.

"They offered him the moon and convinced him to stay," Malone said in an interview. "It was a shock. We had agreed. Felipe is a man of his word, it was a done deal. But the Expos had gone in and bought him off."

Malone recollects that the Dodgers' agreement was for about $1.5-million per season whereas Beattie and Routtenberg went higher at about $2-million per season.

"I think they went above what we offered," Malone said. "His wife Lucie is a French Canadian established in Montreal. Here's the thing: we are the Dodgers and we negotiated with him to be the Dodgers manager. I don't think it was a money issue but Felipe didn't give us a chance to counter. He's a close friend and professionally, he should have talked to me personally, not on a phone voice machine. That was disappointing."

That's right, Malone had flown from the Dominican to Los Angeles and then home to California and found out by a phone message that Alou had changed his mind.

"Bob Graziano and I went to both places. We went to the D.R. and followed him back to Florida and met at his home. We had a handshake agreement when we left Florida," Malone said.

When Brochu found out what happened, shit hit the fan. And commissioner Bud Selig was livid, too, because the salary structure for managers went all of whack apparently because of the Alou agreement.

So Alou would stay with the Expos and it was part of the continuity that Brochu used in an attempt to get funding for a new downtown stadium that never came to pass. Brochu sure gets kicked around a lot by Expos fans but I have to admit I'm in his corner.

In four previous books I've been affiliated with, including one printed in French, I have been in support of Brochu and this book is no exception.

"The saddest thing of all is the way Claude was treated," said one of Brochu's best friends, Bob Armand. "To this day, people who are very close friends of mine, ask me, "You're friends with Claude Brochu?'"

The question is posed to Armand in a negative way as a way of knocking Brochu but of course, Arrmand says yes all the time to that question.

"I don't think people know how hard Claude tried to make that situation survive," Armand said. "He comes out looking badly in all of this. We still talk about it. He's not the kind of guy who is going to blow off air. He got kicked around like a football.

"What people don't know is that Claude had put together a master plan with the province of Quebec to incorporate the Canadiens and the Expos in a downtown complex. Bernard Landry, the finance minister, was all for it but it got bogged down with premier Lucien Bouchard. It would have saved baseball in Montreal."

The premier botched the concept, saying something along the lines that "How can we do this when we're closing hospitals?"

Brochu was the managing general partner of a consortium that included numerous companies and businessmen in Quebec and other parts of Canada that put up $5-million to $7-million to be minority shareholders. These companies came in knowing that they had no power in decision-making but were willing to be partners with Brochu. In the end, a number of partners such Routtenberg of Guess Jeans and Pierre Michaud of the grocery-store chain Provigo grew to dislike Brochu very much because Brochu held all the power in decision-making.

"Pierre Michaud and Claude got into a pissing war," Armand said. "These people came on board as shareholders and they wanted to be president."

At one time, Routtenberg and Brochu were "very close" but they separated and apparently never spoke to each other for close to 12 years.

Then one day as he was organizing a reunion of the 1994 Expos in 2011 to raise money for the Cummings Jewish Centre for Seniors Foundation in Montreal, Routtenberg decided to end all hostility toward Brochu by inviting Brochu to the affair. Brochu agreed to come.

Another guy who got into a war with Brochu was the late Jacques Menard, who at one time was close to Brochu. He came on the Expos executive board as chairman from Burns Fry. For years, I've been trying to get a hold of Menard but no, he wouldn't talk. Menard wanted to lambaste Brochu inside the corporate walls but didn't want to talk outside.

"The power may have gone to Menard's head," Armand said.

Face it: Brochu had no money so-to-speak to put up any money to get a ballpark built downtown in the Peel Basin and his cash flow didn't allow him much leeway when it came to keeping star players around, especially following the debacle of the strike and the cancellation of the season in 1994. Brochu wasn't a wealthy owner like Charles Bronfman so he had little money to play with. So there.

Put the most of the blame on that shyster Jeffrey Loria, who followed in Brochu's footsteps as the managing general partner and then full partner after the minority shareholders decided not to put in any money to keep the club going. Brochu was given a going-away present of $18-million.

Loria had initially got involved with the Expos by forking over a paltry sum of what was believed to be close to $15-million to own a portion of the team. Loria made a quasi attempt at resurrecting the new ballpark deal downtown but as in the case of Brochu, it never came to pass.

Near the end of the 2001 season, the Felipe Alou era in Montreal ended when he found out via a New York Times story that he was fired by Loria, who some say fed the newspaper the news. If that wasn't bad news for the Expos and their fans, then what went down at baseball's ownership meetings on Nov. 6, 2001 was devastating. The ugly word contraction came up. Owners voted 28-2 to eliminate two teams. The dissenting votes came from the Expos and Twins, the two teams to be dropped.

"That (decision) really came from owners," Selig told me in an interview. "It would take hours to answer. It never really materialized. We never talked about clubs, we never got to specifics. The economics of the sport were bad."

At the time, Selig issued a statement to say, "the teams to be contracted had a long record of failing to generate enough revenues to operate a viable major-league franchise."

The Twins filed an injunction against the contraction and eventually MLB backed off its plan. But in the works was another bombshell deal.

In a sweetheart of a transaction, this clown Loria was able to sell the Expos to Major League Baseball while grabbing the Florida Marlins for a mere $158-million in a cheesy charade that saw Marlins owner John

Henry acquire his dream team, the Boston Red Sox, from the Yawkey Trust organization. It was all apparently done by commissioner Bud Selig as a favour to Loria and Henry.

Loria was allowed to drop the Expos in exchange for taking over the Marlins' franchise and Henry was somehow permitted to buy the Red Sox. I tried to get those notoriously media shy men to talk with me for this book. But I knew it was a hopeless task.

"I orchestrated the biggest triple play in baseball history," crowed Selig in his book For the Good of the Game, which was released in 2019.

Loria single handedly killed the Expos and then cried poverty as he convinced south Florida politicians to pay for a new stadium in Miami. What do you call that? Greed, stench. He was a millionaire but he cried that he was a pauper. Then he ended up selling the Marlins for $1.2-billion to a group that included Derek Jeter.

When I approached Loria at spring training in Jupiter, Florida before he sold the Marlins to ask him what he thought about the Expos possibly making a return to Montreal, he went ballistic and got mad at me. Later, he came over and apologized.

42

A team owned by MLB

Tony Siegle should have been called the general manager of the Expos from 2002-2004 because he did most of the work associated with the job.

His title, though, was assistant GM. Omar Minaya was the GM, a rookie at the job, when he was hired by MLB to run the vagabond Expos.

The Expos were Minaya's first crack as a GM so he made sure he had solid people surrounding him because his knowledge of some of the duties associated with the position was limited. Siegle was one of those handymen.

"My expertise was rules, waiver procedures, baseball administration and contract negotiation. Omar had never done that," Siegle told me.

Siegle was operating in an unique environment, the most unique environment there was in the history of MLB: A franchise seemingly in transition but nobody ever was sure if it would stay in Montreal or be transferred. It was a scenario never seen before in baseball at least not in the 20th or 21st century because MLB owned the team and Siegle did his darndest to try and make it work.

"We had a farm director, myself and Omar, when Omar was there," Siegle pointed out.

Yes, Minaya didn't spend a lot of time in Montreal. He spent a lot of time out of his office "somewhere in North Jersey," as Siegle put it. Specifically, it was Harrington Park, N.J. A rather peculiar arrangement for someone, who was a major man in the front office.

"I had an apartment near the old Forum. I loved it in Montreal. I loved the Bar B Bar (restaurant). I never went home (Denver at the time). On occasion, my family would come up. I spoke a little French and that helped," Siegle said.

Siegle went to spring training in Viera, Florida in February, 2002, not to the lush confines of Roger Dean Stadium in Jupiter because the Expos were kicked out of their base in Jupiter, thanks to a sweetheart deal given former Expos owner Jeffrey Loria, who had taken over the Marlins.

One of the first things on Siegle's agenda was to connect with long time Expos executive assistant Marcia Schnaar.

"Marcia said they (Marlins) took everything, including the computers," Siegle said. "I had to bring my own computer. I hit the ground running. There was very little ground to run on.

Siegle enjoyed his time with the Expos and had no ill feelings about the situation, although it was weird being employed not by an owner or owners but by MLB.

"We had Vlad Guerrero in 2002 and 2003," Siegle said. "We had a lot of good memories, a lot of good times. It was very satisfying for Omar and I to accomplish what we did. We won more games than we lost over the three years we were there.

"In 2003, we darn near pulled it off. We were tied for first place in August but MLB wouldn't let us bring in players. They conveyed the message that we couldn't expand the roster on Sept. 1 and we fell by the wayside. MLB owned the team and didn't want to spend a lot of money running it. We were in contention and we couldn't bring in three extra players. It was embarrassing for us and the rest of baseball.

"It was the middle of 2004 when it was apparent that we were going to Washington," Siegle said. "There were rumours about Portland, Ore., Charlotte, N.C., Washington but we were still trying to keep the team in Montreal."

Hats off to Siegle, Minaya, president Tony Tavares, manager Frank Robinson and vice-president of stadium operations Claude Delorme for helping to keep the franchise together during those three difficult seasons.

Vidro was one fine player

It was the type of move expected from Jeffrey Loria.

It was the off-season of 1999-2000 when Loria, the Expos majority shareholder, personally signed free-agent second baseman Mickey Morandini and invited him to spring training in Jupiter, Florida.

It was a move intended to give notice to and put pressure on the incumbent second sacker Jose Vidro, who enjoyed a pretty solid season in 1999 of 12 homers and 59 RBI with a .304 average. So Vidro was perplexed when he got a phone call from his agents, the Levinson Bros Sam and Seth, about a strange off-season move made by the Expos in signing Moradini.

"Felipe Alou called me into his office at spring training to talk about it. They had told me that I might have to go and play some other position. I told Felipe that he's not going to play over me," Vidro said.

An awkward situation was avoided when the good-field, no-power Morandini, 32, was released before the end of spring training. He ended up playing that season for both the Blue Jays and Phillies.

Vidro responded with a fantastic season in 2000.

"That was my best year," Vidro recalled. "I had 51 doubles, I played 153 games and had over 650 plate appearances."

Of course, the switch-hitter also started talking about what else he did. He hit .330 with 101 runs, 200 hits, 24 homers and 97 RBI, by far the best season by an Expos' second baseman in franchise history. Wheew. He was also pretty slick with the glove, committing only 10 errors.

Vidro went on to record another stupendous season in 2002. He hit .315 with 19 homers, 96 RBI, 190 hits and 103 runs in 681 plate appearances.

43

Big Sexy was trivia item in 2002

Bartolo Colon enjoyed one of his best seasons as a major-leaguer in 2002, half a season with the Expos, half a season with the Indians.

He was 10-4 with the Expos, 10-4 with the Indians, the only time in MLB history that a pitcher recorded a 10-4 record on two teams totalling a 20-8 record for the entire season. This was confirmed to me by both the MLB's Dominic Colliani and publicist Craig Muder of the National Baseball Hall of Fame in Cooperstown.

How about that for trivia? Here's more: he threw 116.1 innings for the Indians that season, 117 for the Expos. Almost identical. Cool.

Colon was relatively slim that season but during the latter stages of his fine career he was accorded the moniker of Big Bart or Big Sexy because he became a huge man of what 285 pounds. His girth still makes a popular dude as the winningest Latin American pitcher of all time with 247 wins.

"He spoke fair English. He was a very good guy. Fairly quiet," recalled Expos trainer Ron McClain. "He loved to show off his strength skills and velocity. He was a delight to have. I enjoyed him. He had a sore elbow for half the year."

Here was a team, the Expos, in the throes of possibly facing contraction by MLB but going all out to improve the roster by acquiring Colon from the Indians on June 27, 2002, even though he was earning $4.925-million that season. President Tony Tavares and GM Omar Minaya decided to go for the moon but they gave up the moon, much to the chagrin of assistant GM Tony Siegle.

Going to the Indians with Colon was Tim Drew and heading to the Indians were Lee Stevens, Brandon Phillips, Cliff Lee and Brady Sizemore.

"I do remember being livid with rage for losing our three best prospects to get him and I expressed that to both Tavares and Omar. Too much," Siegle said in an interview.

And before you even knew it, Colon was dealt to the White Sox prior to the following season on Jan. 15, 2003 in another trade where the Expos swapped him and Jorge Nunez for Rocky Biddle, Orlando Hernandez, Jeff Liefer and cash. Obviously, Colon was going to be too expensive to keep in Montreal.

"As I recall we got Rock Biddle, a decent reliever and a couple of players for him," Siegle said in early 2020. "We dumped his salary and we didn't need his services."

When we checked Baseball Almanac for his 2003 salary, his stipend had jumped to $8.25-million.

Now here's an interesting story about Colon as it is told by Gary Davidson of Toronto, who has collected over 40,000 autographs over the years. Yes, over 40,000.

So Davidson is out to get Colon's autograph at the Rogers Centre in Toronto a few years ago because he didn't have his autograph. He sees Colon walking from the team's hotel to the ball park on the Friday of a weekend series. Davidson and a few others fans approach Colon and he says, "Not today."

So the fans try the same strategy on the Saturday and Colon's reply was, "Sunday."

"So on Sunday, he came in a different way into the ball park by coming up the ramp beside the stairs," Davidson explained. "I was the only one waiting for him that morning as he walked up. He was wearing his sunglasses and pulling a small luggage case. I asked him if he could sign for me.

"He stopped in front of me, took off his sunglasses and reached for my board for cards to be signed. I had a Mets' photo of him on top of the cards. He signed the photo and left it on the board for me to take off. He then took my board back and also signed five cards for me. Then he handed me the board back, smiled and started walking to the ball park. It was nice to see he was a man of his word."

44

Selig comes out swinging at Expos fans

Bud Selig is a poster boy for criticism, a polarizing figure in the late-stages history of the Expos. He's considered a scoundrel, a villain, the dartboard of vitriol directed by Expos fans.

All too often fans from Montreal and elsewhere direct their hatred on social media platforms toward the man now known as Commissioner Emeritus Selig.

"The misinformation is really incredible," an angry Selig told me. "Either there is misinformation, too much information or no information. It's an age-old story."

Selig wants everyone to know he tried his darndest to keep the Expos in Montreal. He comes out punching his fists at Expos fans.

Despite what many Expos fans think of him, Selig went to bat in an attempt to keep baseball alive in Montreal.

The vitriol directed against Selig is very much unwarranted but he faces the music head on. The dislike for Selig by Montreal fans began in 1994 when the season was cancelled. And the dislike continued in the 2000s over other issues that rankled fans in Montreal. The departure of the Expos to Washington for the 2005 season only fuelled the dislike for the former commissioner.

Yet, he doesn't take the criticism lying down. I got him wound up in defence of himself and Major League Baseball.

"They're mad about what?" Selig asked me emphatically as we chatted in late 2019. "I understand that whole situation was somewhat controversial. I'm not sure why. Danny, I worked hard to get local ownership in Montreal. I wanted to keep the team there. I led the fight. Why don't you blame the right people (lack of owners some 15 years ago)?

"I kept trying but nothing was happening. We didn't get anywhere. We worked on things. By the way, I can say to the people that I was aggressively looking for people in Montreal to be owners. I bent over backward. What frustrates me is that I was trying to be helpful. Nobody really wants to move a team but we had no options."

Selig's work on behalf of the Expos began in the late 1990s when he attempted to help Expos managing general partner Claude Brochu to get a new stadium to replace the spaceship Olympic Stadium.

Selig even went to a meeting in Quebec City with provincial premier Lucien Bouchard to see what participation the provincial government could render in support of a new stadium.

"We didn't get anywhere. Claude and I went up there. Claude was great. He tried everything and so did I," Selig said about the meeting with Bouchard.

The feisty premier later told reporters that he couldn't see the province putting money into a new stadium when hospitals were being closed but Selig retort to me was this: "Every city, they all usually found a way to get it done to get a new stadium. It was disappointing. It's easy to blame somebody. I know there is criticism. Attendance underscored that. There was no owner and no stadium. What was baseball fucking supposed to do? We kept the team in Montreal three years longer than people (owners) wanted me. People were asking, 'Where was the ownership group?'"

Selig said MLB experimented with Expos' games in Puerto Rico "because we were trying to boost that franchise up."

So in the end, after a few years of threatening to move the Expos, MLB finally did just that by agreeing to move the team to Washington in time for the 2005 season.

"We were going nowhere in Montreal. There were no plans for a ballpark," Selig told me. "It broke my heart to see the Braves leave Milwaukee. That's why I helped Milwaukee get the Brewers. Nobody really wants to lose a team. The ballpark (Big O) was a disaster. We couldn't find anybody (an owner) so what are the fans mad at? "We were criticized for not moving fast enough (to relocate the team). Understand the points I'm trying to make? We kept trying and nothing was happening. We didn't get anywhere. Moving Montreal was difficult, frustrating and disappointing but left us with no alternative. There was no future when you can't find local money. With all of the anger and so on and so forth, they (fans) don't know what they're talking about."

When Selig ran into some Expos at a party in Cooperstown for 2017 inductees, including himself and Expos legend Tim Raines, there was no confrontation. Instead, he convened for intelligent conversation and selfies.

"Those fans I met in Cooperstown shrugged. When I talked to them directly, they talked differently," Selig recalled. "Charles Bronfman and I are very, very close friends. He was one of the great owners I've known. He was tremendous. When he sold that team and left, it was not a good thing for Montreal. I'm telling you that he was one of the great owners of my generation."

Bronfman's son Stephen and other partners are gung-ho for the return of baseball in Montreal and Selig feels the city will get a team at some point.

"I do. Montreal is a great area," he said. "I talk to Charles a lot. You need a new stadium, no question. You have a lot of work ahead of you. It's been many years (since the team moved to Washington) and you don't have a ballpark."

Irabu and Urbina

Little known fact: MLB players are all required to travel to spring training at their own expense.

The late Hideki Irabu raised a stink in February, 1999 as he began his travel route to West Palm Beach, Florida from his native Japan to attend spring training with the Expos.

"Outside the season, all travel was to be in economy only except when Hideki Irabu's agent raised holy shit," said Stephen Pickford, an Expos travel consultant back in the late 1990s. "He was booked into business from Tokyo via Chicago, Japan Air Lines to American Airlines.

"And getting back to the 1998 all-star game in Denver, Ugueth Urbina was booked on Northwest via Minneapolis. I was monitoring the situation and noticed the flight was cancelled so I rebooked him around the same time via Detroit.

"I called up Sean Cunningham, who was my team contact for player travel. They were playing a home game that afternoon. My call was patched through direct to the dugout and while I was on hold, watching the game at home, the TSN camera panned the dugout, and I saw Sean walking down to pick up my call." Urbina was known to be a prick. He would rarely if ever talk to the media and he later spent many years in prison in his native Venezuela for attacking some people with a machete. Bad dude. He was the antithesis of fellow Venezuelan and Expos alumnus Andres Galarraga. Too bad Urbina couldn't be a great fellow like Big Cat. The media could never get Urbina to talk. Former Expos beat writer Stephanie Myles tried many times to get UU to talk with no success.

"As long as he got his own way, and nothing went wrong, he was no different than any other corporate traveller," Pickford said about Urbina. "Corporate travel policy was that only Sean Cunningham, Marcia Schnaar, or Bill Stoneman/Jim Beattie/Larry Beinfest could make arrangements. Not a player directly, unless he was going to pay for family members to accompany him."

45

The last home game

On Sept. 27, 2000 at Sydney Baseball Stadium in Sydney, Australia, Brad Wilkerson got very emotional after a special game.

Almost four years to the day later at Olympic Stadium in Montreal, the tears flowed again for Wilkerson after another special game.

The scenarios were different. In Sydney, the tears were ones of joy. In Montreal, the tears were ones of sadness.

Wilkerson had helped the U.S. men's baseball team to the Summer Olympic Games championship in a 4-0 win over the heavily favoured Cubans. It was an unexpected turn of events, considering Cuba was mighty on the field in any baseball competition.

To beat the Cubs was akin to a huge upset. Some call it the Miracle On Grass like the Miracle On Ice moniker bestowed upon the U.S. hockey team that won Olympic gold in 1980 in Lake Placid, N.Y., in a rousing upset of the Goliath-like Soviet Union at the height of the Cold War and the backdrop to the Iranian hostage crisis and the Russians' invasion of Afghanistan.

"We won the gold medal. We were on the podium with the national anthem being played. It was emotional," Wilkerson told me in an interview.

Those were the only two times Wilkerson can recall shedding a bunch of tears on a ball field, the first time in a joyful atmosphere, the other in a tidal wave of sadness.

That sadness at the end of September in 2004 was the end of the Expos, the official end at home. This indeed was "the last home game." You look at video of that scene and you could see Wilkerson with his lips just twitching and shaking in emotion. It was the symbol that epitomized the cruel demise of the Expos franchise, that indeed, the Expos were moving to Washington for the 2005 season.

Think of the photo of Expos sage, confidante, former player, broadcaster and coach Claude Raymond using his left arm and comforting the right shoulder of Wilkerson, who was in tears. Wilkerson knew that the transfer of the team to Washington would mean many Expos employees and stadium tradespeople would lose their jobs.

Photos courtesy USA Baseball

Brad Wilkerson celebrates Team USA's gold-medal win at the 2000 Summer Olympics in Sydney, Australia

"It's not something you think will happen. It just happens," Wilkerson said of shedding tears after the final Expos home game. "I'm not ashamed of it. The Expos gave me my first opportunity.

"They employed a lot of people. It's basically not fair in a lot of ways. When you look at someone (employees) who gave their heart and soul to the organization, it was the culmination of all those emotions coming out at once. It was emotional at the Summer Olympics and I felt that way in Montreal. At the Olympics, it was happiness but with the last Expos home game, it was definitely more negative stuff that came out."

The game between the Expos and Miami Marlins had ended and speeches were being made as most or all of those in attendance looked on in disbelief. Yes, after 36 seasons of operation, the Expos had played their last home game.

"I was a very close friend with Brad. Before every game, I'd go give him a high-five, maybe two," Raymond said.

For a few years, Raymond was asked by Expos executive Claude Delorme to say a few words to the crowd following the team's last home game. Because the Expos were owned by Major League Baseball, there was no knowing when the plug would be finally pulled on the franchise. MLB had taken over the Expos in time for the 2002 season.

"It might have been the last year. It was the last year, the last year – they'd been saying that for two years. I didn't know it would be the real last game. Every year, I was prepared to talk in French and English," Raymond said.

But this time, it was "the last year."

Like he had done often, Raymond had drove to Olympic Stadium from his long-time home in St-Jean-sur-Richelieu, Quebec located some 25 miles away. Because he was still an important part of the Expos enclave at age 67, Raymond would meet often with manager Frank Robinson, fellow coaches Randy St. Claire, Bob Natal, Tommy McCraw, Jerry Morales and Manny Acta and some of the scouts to discuss 40-man roster players.

"Our meeting started at 9 in the morning and when we got out of the meeting, they came and told us Washington was going to get the team," Raymond.

"They" meaning team president Tony Tavares.

"I had a lot of interviews on the field afterward with television guys, radio guys, newspaper guys," Raymond said.

Knowing what was coming down the pike, Raymond changed his game routine for this game.

"Normally, I'm in the press box as a spotter in the sky," he said. "But I decided to do it from the dugout. In the seventh inning, I realized my time to talk was coming. I had to tell something different to the fans. All of a sudden, I had to go on the field to the pitcher's mound and they

Photo by Phil Carpenter ©Montreal Gazette

Brad Wilkerson gets emotional following the Expos' final home game Sept. 29, 2004 with Claude Raymond looking on behind. This photo symbolized the sad ending of the Expos' franchise.

gave me the microphone and I had to talk."

What he told the fans was that there was no tomorrow, no chance of another season and that "it has been 36 beautiful seasons."

Raymond looked around and saw a very emotional Wilkerson close to him on the mound.

"I put my arm around Brad Wilkerson's shoulder. I was crying. I was all my myself. Brad was crying," Raymond said. "I passed the mike to Joey Eischen and then Tim Raines and they gave me the mike back. I ended up saying this was our last game and I hope one day a miracle happens and the Expos will be back. Everybody stayed on the mound."

Raymond saw that Natal had come in from the bullpen so Raymond decided to spontaneously do something out of the ordinary. Natal stepped in behind the plate.

"I took the ball and there were photographers and writers around and I decided to throw the last pitch," Raymond remembered.

The photo of Raymond and Wilkerson has gone viral since then, a symbol that represented the true, emotional feeling everyone felt about the end of the Expos.

Denis Brodeur photo/Lesley Taylor collection
Claude Raymond as an Expos pitcher

"I left the field and I went to the clubhouse and then I went to see my wife and kids in the family room. I was going to drive home with my uniform on. My wife thought I was crazy," Frenchie said. "I drove home with my uniform on, took a shower and had some cognac.

"When you are a player and get attached to the team you play for .... I was released (by the Expos) in 1970 but this hurt more. This was my living for 50 years in ball as a player, broadcaster, ambassador and then I knew that was it. That was the end of the line. It really hurt more than when I was released by the Expos."

Wilkerson had a sense all through the 2004 season that the franchise

Danny Gallagher photo

Claude Raymond, right, Brad Wilkerson and rapper Annakin Slayd are pictured here at an Exposfest autograph table in Cooperstown in 2018

might move and as the Expos player representative, he would often call meetings in the clubhouse to let his teammates know anything he could pass on.

"We knew that would kind of happen," Wilkerson said about a possible move to Washington. "I don't think we knew 100%. We had meetings with the players throughout the year to keep them up to date. We were still a bit in the dark. It was a tough time dealing with the players."

Wilkerson had enjoyed a terrific season in 2004 and it all made his departure that much more sad. Wilkerson played 160 games, amassed 688 plate appearances, scored 112 runs, hit 32 homers, drove in 67 runs and drew 106 bases on balls. It sure was something to write home about.

"We'd lost Vladdy after the 2003 season. Everybody was writing us off. We had a lot to prove. I had a lot to prove, to keep improving and get better in baseball. I had my best power numbers, scored a lot of runs. I got on base a lot," Wilkerson said.

After the Expos finished the 2004 season on the road in New York, most players, including Wilkerson, returned to Montreal to pick up their belongings and head home. It was so surreal.

"It didn't seem right. It was an eery feeling," Wilkerson said. "I didn't see any Expos billboards around the city. It was a weird feeling. I remember talking to some fans and drove out of Montreal in my car and saying, 'What really just happened?' I was driving home to Kentucky. I love driving home after the season. I was thinking of the good and the bad, thinking of all the memories I had in Montreal."

When he looks back at the special friendship he has enjoyed with Raymond, Wilkerson talks this way: "Claude was a great ambassador for the Expos and the city of Montreal. I was very fortunate to have gotten to know him. We were not super close but he did an excellent job of teaching and reaching out to every player. He took the time to talk to the guys. I was fortunate to have him to mentally get me through the seasons. The chance to learn from a veteran like that is unbelievable. He's been awesome. When I saw him in Cooperstown (in 2018), it was the first time I'd seen him in awhile. He hadn't aged a bit. I asked him what his secret was and he said, 'A glass of wine and a margarita.'"

46

Sledge hammer in team history

Like Brad Wilkerson, Terrmel Sledge enjoyed a banner season with the Expos in their swan-song season in 2004. It was nothing short of inspiring.

With a name like his, is there a better baseball name around?

"To be honest, it was my first big-league season and I had a very good year," Sledge said. "I was a very good rookie breaking into the big leagues. We played about 75 games in Puerto Rico so it wasn't easy, especially breaking into my first big-league season."

Sledge can only thank manager Frank Robinson for being patient with him, mentoring him, guiding him, coaching him, accepting him when maybe the hard-nosed skipper could have just abandoned him and had him dispatched to the minors.

"Frank was a big mentor me. Sometimes, I almost never got a hit but this man, this hall of famer, my biggest mentor, stuck with me," Sledge said. "He didn't have to do it. I had a pretty good year. Yes, I did."

Sledge batted .269 with 15 homers and 62 RBI after he had enjoyed a banner season in 2003 at Edmonton Triple A, where he turned more than a few heads in the Expos organization with 22 homers, 92 RBI and a .324 average. It was a sensational campaign.

Near the end of the 2004 season, Sledge was prominent as the Expos dug in for their final days in big-league ball. At the Expos final home game Sept. 29, he was the last out of the game in a 9-1 rout by the Marlins on what he called "a weak flare to the third baseman" Mike Mordecai off a fastball thrown by Rudy Seanez.

A wonderful crowd of 31,395 showed up to send the Expos off. Sledge may have been the final out but he saw the whole picture of how why very few fans would come to support the team during most of the regular season, especially from 2002-2004 when Major League Baseball owned the team.

Just prior to the final home game, Expos players were told the franchise was being moved to Washington for the 2005 season.

"I thought 'I can't believe there is no baseball in Montreal anymore,'" Sledge said. "The last home game was a sellout (close to it). It was pretty loud, very loud, the loudest I've heard at a game. I could barely hear myself thinking. It was an old school dome. It was an echoing sound. It reminded me of the noise a few years later at the Tokyo Dome, where I played, the same scenario. It was heart-breaking to see the last game being played.

"We really never thought it was a big deal (team leaving) until that last day. We wondered why the fans didn't come out beforehand. I was breaking into the big leagues as a rookie and there were no fans. We didn't understand the business part of that, how hard it was to get the fans into the stadium. I had played in Edmonton on the west side of Canada and I played for Ottawa on the east side of Toronto. I loved Edmonton, Ottawa and Montreal.

"I tried to get a better understanding of a team not having an owner, not having a competitive team and how that all played a big role in fans not coming out. We didn't have an owner. It was a tough situation. We were just staying almost stagnant. Playing in Puerto Rico, it was pretty weird. We didn't have a home. We kinda felt we left a city behind. We almost felt they would regret it but not the people. You still see Expos gear and hats. I'm flabbergasted."

In the Expos final game at Shea Stadium, Sledge was prominent, this time, more in a positive way, going 2-for-3. Ironically, the first-ever Expos regular-season game was at Shea Stadium in 1969 and the team's last regular-season game was at Shea. Hall of Famer Ralph Kiner was a Mets broadcaster at the first Expo game in 1969 and he was on hand for the Expos final game 35 years later.

"Shea Stadium was a perfect situation," Sledge said. "I grew up a Mets fan. I grew up in California but I was a Mets fan for some reason. I hit my 15th home run in the last game."

When the players came back to Olympic Stadium to collect their belongings, Sledge made an effort to take home some other souvenirs.

"To tell you the truth, I wanted to keep both home and away jerseys because of how sentimental they were so I asked the clubhouse manager," Sledge said. "He said no. I got into an argument with him. He did give me our home white pinstripe jersey. I have it, No. 48, framed in my home in Arlington, Texas. I think MLB wanted the away jerseys."

Sledge never did enjoy another season like 2004 in the majors, although he does go down in history as the first player to hit a home run for the Nationals in 2005 with a shot off of Jon Lieber. He said that ball is in the National Baseball Hall of Fame in Cooperstown. He would later spend five seasons playing in Japan. Why did he not succeed in the majors after his solid rookie season?

If pitchers were nibbling him on the corners of the plate often and throwing other pitches to throw him out of whack, he admitted he didn't adjust properly. He was too hard-headed.

"I have no excuses. I wasn't mature enough to comprehend what was going on," Sledge said. "Most people have a screw loose. I was looking for the approval of my father to get to the highest level. Happiness doesn't get fulfilled because of emptiness inside. The mental aspect, the physical aspect aside, I didn't make adjustments. I was too stubborn to make adjustments. I'm not saying he was the best father. We didn't have a good relationship. He just wasn't around.

"It was the last era before the millennial era. Parents just weren't around. My father died in 2018. He was a retired sergeant major in the army. My mother Song and my father were divorced."

In recent years, Sledge has been a coach, most recently with the Cubs as an assistant hitting coach. Eventually, of course, he would love to be the head hitting coach with a MLB club. Good luck, Terrmel.

"I was a GM of a nightclub one and a half hours from my home, so I listened to a lot of music on the way up. It was the Saturday night before the final game and I was lucky that I could watch the broadcast on WPIX, the Mets station for the final game. One of the songs that came on was "You're the Best Thing That Ever Happened To Me" by Gladys Knight and the Pips. I broke into tears and I kept repeating the song over and over. It really hit home to me. My Expos were about to be gone forever. By the time I reached Scranton, my head bartender asked me, "Have you been crying?" **– David Ziegenfuss of rural Pennsylvania talking about how emotional he got regarding the Expos last game Oct. 3, 2004.**

47

The great Steve Rogers

It was mid-January of 1986 and Steve Rogers was looking to see if his ailing right shoulder had any more gas in it after he was released by the Expos and what followed with failed tryouts with the California Angels and White Sox organizations.

Rogers arranged for a young catcher to take his throws in a warmup session at Oral Roberts University in Tulsa, Oklahoma, where Rogers grew up. Rogers let it all hang out in one last ditch effort to see how the shoulder would respond.

"The throwing mounds were under the third-base side in the base-ball stadium," Rogers recollected. "I was throwing really, really hard. My throws had some life but the mechanics were out of whack. And the pain, it felt like someone had taken a pick to the back of my shoulder. I went to one knee and I looked up at the kid and said, 'You just saw me retire.'"

At age 36.

Yet, this dramatic turn of events in the life of the winningest pitcher in Expos history didn't sink in until two months later as he looked out the window of his oil-company office in Tulsa. It hit him, that his career was over. It was another kind of pain.

"It was a beautiful spring day, the second week of spring training," Rogers recalled close to 35 years later.

"The season was about to start and I'm sitting there and I'm aching all over. It was something clinical because I wasn't playing baseball. I was not feeling what I had done for 15 years. That hit me hard. It's like I can't even describe it. It overwhelmed me. Most definitely, it was some-thing that manifested itself physically. It was not a chest pain. Rather, it was an overwhelming numbness, sense of emptiness."

It's what some people would call withdrawal symptoms, a feeling of anxiety, nervousness, quasi-depression. There is a huge void in your life after you had enjoyed something positive for so long. Something good you had enjoyed has disappeared and you are trying to get over the sense of loss and feeling. From mid-February to Oct. 1 of most years, Rogers was in a baseball environment with Expos teammates, going to the clubhouse every day, make all those road trips and then all of a sudden, that time was gone. He was trying to get used to a new environment of the oil business after the lights went out on his career.

That feeling of emptiness didn't last too long that day but it also prompted Rogers to call his agent Dick Moss and set up an appointment. He wanted Moss to call the Expos at spring training in West Palm Beach, Florida and make arrangements for him to have a chat with president John McHale and majority owner Charles Bronfman. Apparently, it was a meeting that the media didn't know about.

"I wanted to have a conversation with them. My time with the team had really ended on a really, really bad note," Rogers told me in early 2020. "The message I wanted to send was, 'Look, I harbour no feelings toward the Expos. To my knowledge, it was a private meeting.

"I told them I was profoundly sorry that I had not been able to give them a better 1984-85. I felt I needed it to happen (a meeting). I had to be honest. It was about 30 minutes long. The reason I was there was nothing but positive feelings about the Expos. There was nothing adversarial."

And did he mention to McHale and Bronfman about his feelings regarding his awkward departure the previous May? He can't remember. He thinks he may have brought it up but emphasized the meeting was really about the "large point" of saying he held no negative feelings toward the organization.

Back on May 21, 1985, Cy Rogers had been given the pink slip. Nobody with the seniority he had spent his entire career with the Expos. And now he was gone.

Expos with seniority	
Player	Seasons
Steve Rogers	12 1/4
Tim Wallach	12 1/4
Gary Carter	11 1/4
Tim Raines	10 1/2
Andre Dawson	10 1/2
Bryn Smith	8 1/4
Steve Renko	7 1/2
Mel Rojas	7 1/4
Larry Parrish	7 1/4
Warren Cromartie	7 1/4
Chris Speier	7 1/4
Woodie Fryman	7 1/4
Orlando Cabrera	7 1/4
Dennis Martinez	7 1/4
Vlad Guerrero	7 1/4
Jose Vidro	7 1/4

Compiled by the author with help from Baseball Reference website

The 1984 season was terrible for Rogers. He struggled through a 6-15 season. He suffered through right-shoulder problems and he was advised that there was no surgery, "no correctable" operation possible really to fix him up.

His rotator cuff and the tissue around it had worn out and stretched out. After throwing more than 3,000 career innings (including the minors), Rogers' rotator cuff was acting up big time. So in the off-season of 1984-85, he went through an extensive therapy program to try and get his shoulder up to sync by spring training in 1985.

"The season before was a very difficult year and the shoulder news was bad. I didn't have a surgical procedure so I did my rehab, worked hard all winter with all kinds of exercises and came back," Rogers was saying. "It was the last year of my contract. I wanted to try and pitch as best as I could.

"When I got to spring training, I was clearly like 1984, that I was not really capable of pitching at the major-league level. I knew it. I wasn't pitching that good. I was also on the (union's) negotiating committee. We were headed toward some type of labour strife."

What didn't help in this attempt at a comeback was that neither McHale nor Jim Fanning was no longer the GM. It was Murray Cook, who McHale, as president, brought in to be the new GM. Cook had been the GM of the Reds. Not only that, Rogers had a new manager in Buck Rodgers, brought in by Cook.

"So they had a new manager and a whole new coaching staff and they had a new front office," Rogers said. "All the decision makers in

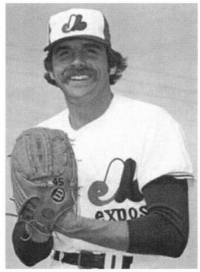

Canadian Baseball Hall of Fame
Steve Rogers

the front office were new and all the decision makers on the field were new. I hadn't built respect for them because they were new.

"I knew Buck knew there was another Rogers on the field. It was frustrating to the new manager that he was being mistaken for me. That played a role."

"I was coming in, knowing at best I was a marginal asset. You know, I didn't know to pitch anymore better than that – marginally. I was being may be stubborn. I needed to process everything that spring training and that year to make a determination. I had to change whatever it was, to try and be a positive for the team. I became absolutely convinced I had to do something different or get out of the way of the team and the younger players."

On May 19, Rogers had survived only 4.2 innings and was rocked for 11 hits and 6 runs as the Expos lost. On May 20, an off-day, Cook and Rodgers discussed Rogers' situation and felt they would release him the following day. He was in the final year of a contract that paid him over $1-million in 1985. He said he was the 12th MLB player to make over $1-million a season.

So on May 21, Rogers showed up in the clubhouse and the first thing he wanted to do was approach new pitching coach Larry Bearnarth to try and buy time, not knowing he was about to be released. Bearnarth knew what was going to go down.

"I had talked to Larry when I got into the locker-room that day, a Saturday or a day game," Rogers said. "I went over to Bear and asked if there was time to figure out any way to use a reduced effectiveness or develop a new pitch so I could still be a plus because I wasn't doing the job now.

"It was interesting the coincidence was the fact I had comes to grips with it (release) that day. I voiced that to Larry that day as to what that 'else' was. I was an open book, whatever Larry wanted. But that never had a chance to be implemented or discussed. I was willing to go on the disabled list and try to be a positive influence on the team and that younger players."

So Rogers walked back to his locker and someone told him that he was wanted in the office. He knew what was coming. Waiting for him were Cook and vice-president of baseball administration Bill Stoneman, as he was known at the time. Rodgers wasn't present. Neither was McHale.

"It was no more than five or 10 minutes," Rogers said of the meeting. "My guess is that Murray didn't say a word. He was the new guy on the block, he was building his authority. I had no history with Murray Cook, whereas I did with Stoney. Stoney was my first roommate in the big leagues. He genuinely said good luck.

"They made a business decision all predicated on the fact I wasn't an effective pitcher, that I was damaged goods. There was a whole lot of dynamic involved, that the continuity of the decade prior had gone and it allowed them to make that decision to cut ties."

In the next breath, Rogers said that "if there had been continuity like in the past, they might not have just said goodbye."

In other words, Rogers thought that his departure was awkward and he felt he deserved more respect and more love. After all, he had spent his entire career with the Expos.

"To be honest with you, I feel it could have been done differently. It was anger probably and disappointment that it wasn't done differently. Terminology wise, you could say that," Rogers said. "I said goodbyes to people, friends, teammates in the next 2-3 days."

What was really interesting and alarming was to sift through Rogers' earlier performances that season. I looked it up on Retrosheet and saw that Rogers had thrown a complete-game 7-1 win on April 18 over the Cardinals in St. Louis and had contributed a run-scoring single. It was vintage Rogers, the 73rd and last complete game of his fantastic career.

Then just over a month later, he was gone. He asked Moss to check around to see if other teams were interested. Moss discovered that the Angels were interested. So he had a brief stint with the club's Triple-A affiliate in Edmonton before being released.

"I had limited skills. It was pretty evident. It started hitting my psyche that maybe this was it," Rogers said.

He then caught on with the White Sox organization after a throwing session in front of manager Tony La Russa, pitching coach Dave Duncan and former Expos teammate/catcher Bobby Ramos. Rogers knew his stuff wasn't of major-league quality but him and Moss were able to convince La Russa and Duncan to get a one-month trial in Triple-A with Buffalo. That didn't work out either.

"My last professional pitch was against Indianapolis, the Expos farm team. It was a struggle," Rogers said.

Holding a chemical engineering degree from the University of Tulsa, Rogers formed a small oil company with three other individuals to keep himself busy in the absence of baseball at a time when the price of oil hovered in the not-so-good range of $10-20 per barrel.

That company, Rogers said, "didn't do good." He also obtained his real estate licence and did some work in that field but even that wasn't lucrative. When oil is really down, house sales are really down, he quickly found out.

His big break came with some outside consulting work he began doing on collusion cases for the Major League Baseball Players Association in 1986-87. Soon, he was working full-time for the MLBPA and he has been doing that for the last 31 years. Many of those years has been spent as a pension specialist, either in New York City or in Tulsa, where he has worked for the last six years.

Rogers is 70 and plans to work for the PA another two years before retiring. He was open with me about a difficult divorce he endured years ago and his entanglement with the ultra-tough Internal Revenue Service over limited partnerships he was connected with.

"I had financial advisors do investments in land and partnerships. Income-tax situations hit partnerships. It became a very difficult financial situation, very deep," Rogers said. "Two partnerships were voided. Ultimately, you are personally responsible for anything you do.

"I wasn't trying to do anything unseemingly. It was all above board. It was basically a 30-year process to get closure. It's been taken care of (paying off taxes)."

For years, Rogers has been a physical fitness nut, mostly through light running and consuming some supplements. He gets a kick out of his use of the elliptical machine, which gives him a solid workout in aerobics and strength exercises.

"It's a low impact machine. It's like a little running action," Rogers said. He left the game with a playing weight of 193 and he's staying close in the 195-200 range.

And how is that shoulder after all of these years?

"It doesn't hurt as long as I don't throw a ball or propel it," he said.

So there, you have a follow-up story on one great Expos pitcher. His legacy isn't the Blue Monday homer. His legacy is that he was a work-horse with 158 wins, 129 complete games, 37 shutouts, a 3.17 ERA, his appearance in five all-star games and some great performances in the 1981 playoffs, good enough for induction into the Canadian Baseball Hall of Fame in 2005.

Loving the Expos

Submitted photo
Joe Sarkees, Jr is a big Expos fan

Joe Sarkees, Jr., a physical education teacher at Niagara Falls High School in Niagara Falls, N.Y., figures he might be the only Expos fan in his town.

"You had asked me, what drew me to the Montreal Expos. Well, as a fourth-grade, nine-year-old kid, that's easy – the logo," Sarkees said. "The Expos logo is one of the most unique, in all of sports. Every other boring logo seems to align logically with the city they represent or their mascot – but the Expos didn't and that's what made it so great.

"It was mysterious and it baffled people. But mostly, it just looks cool. The best part was most people couldn't recognize it, so as a kid, it was always a great feeling, when teachers or classmates would have to ask you, 'What team is that?' You'd stump them. It made you feel proud to tell them the 'Montreal Expos'.

"So as an added bonus, in Niagara Falls, New York, there are no other Expos fans. So whether it was 1990 or 2020, I was and still am the only guy in the city donning Expos gear," Sarkees said.

"Jerseys, jackets, baseball hats, winter hats – heck my three licence plates on my vehicles are: 1EXPOS, 2EXPOS and 3EXPOS. To most people, I'm the only Expos fan they've ever met. The uniqueness of being a life-long Expos fan, as a kid and now, never gets old."

48

Vladdy had a great Expos career

Vladimir Guerrero officially announced Jan. 25, 2018 that he wanted to enter the National Baseball Hall of Fame in Cooperstown with an Angels' halo instead of an Expos' logo on his plaque but the seeds for this decision were planted prior to that.

On Aug. 26, 2017, Guerrero was leaning toward the Angels when they inducted Guerrero into their own hall of fame.

Lobbying by the Angels for him to use their logo began in earnest back then but it kicked up a lot when it became apparent that Guerrero would garner the sufficient numbers of votes to enter Cooperstown on his second try.

On Jan. 23, a day before the Cooperstown inductees were announced, Angels owner Arte Moreno and vice-president Tim Mead had flown to New York in anticipation of the announcement.

"If you would have asked me, I would have guaranteed he was going in as an Angel. The deal was done between Arte Moreno and hall of fame before the ballots were counted," said Russ Hansen, an Expos/Angels fan and photo historian, who befriended Guerrero over the years, both during the slugger's time in Anaheim with the Angels and in Montreal with the Expos.

Hansen doesn't think the hall nixed any attempt by Guerrero to go in as an Angel.

"No, not at all. "I think it was an agreed upon deal made when he was inducted into the Angels' hall of fame. I'm 99% certain," Hansen said.

"It made sense. A Hispanic player in southern California, I get it. This will improve the Latin-Major League Baseball connection. Montreal could not help this agenda. Arte will sell thousands of shirts, jerseys, bobbleheads, hats, etc."

Moreno, like Guerrero, is Hispanic with his Mexican background so there was a bond between Moreno and Guerrero. And don't forget: Guerrero has a home in Anaheim. He has no home in Montreal.

Expos fan Sheldon Miller of Ottawa wondered if any desire by Guerrero to take the Expos' logo was "nixed."

"I have been surprised, dismayed and disappointed about Vlad Guer-

Russ Hansen photo
Vladimir Guerrero played more than seven seasons with the Expos

rero's induction as an Angel," Miller said. "I was overjoyed when he did get inducted, not surprised obviously, but the turn of events made no sense to me. We do feel honoured that Montreal was part of Vladimir's career. It would be nice to have the cherry on top that is deserving."

Todd Hosler, another Expos' fan in Chazy, N.Y., was equally disappointed with Guerrero's decision.

"I feel that Vladimir turned his back on an organization that recognized his talents in 1993," Hosler said. "He was recognized from poverty and made his Montreal debut in 1996. His Expos' career was longer and more productive than with any other hat on. The Angels adopted an Expo. It's really perplexing."

Somebody close to the Angels said it's "99 percent certain" that Guerrero has been signed to a lifetime personal services contract by Moreno and the Angels. From a financial standpoint, taking the Angels' logo means more because it will mean more marketing opportunities and endorsements for Guerrero down the road. In Montreal, with no team there, what endorsements could he get there?

Hansen saw Guerrero play hundreds of times for both the Expos and the Angels. So when the Saint John, New Brunswick resident found out Guerrero had chosen the Angels' halo over the Expos' logo for his Cooperstown plaque, he wasn't upset.

After all, Hansen figures he probably saw Guerrero play at least 300 times at Anaheim Stadium and got to admire the Expos' homebrew up front and centre when he lived in southern California for more than a decade.

"I saw Vlad hit over 80 homers in Anaheim," Hansen said, proudly.

Hansen admired Guerrero so much that he had a licence plate made up that said Vlad 2B in California Expos Halo Heaven. Guerrero somehow found out about the plate so Hansen did something nice and sent him a framed edition.

Let's not forget what Guerrero did with the Expos. He was an extraordinary player. With that awkward hitting style which saw him swing at pitches over his head, way outside or at his ankles, Guerrero hit .323 lifetime for Montreal with 234 homers and 709 RBI.

Remember when he nearly had a 40-40 season in 2002 when he collected a career-high 206 hits? He finished with 39 homers and 40 steals because an umpire ruled in a late-season game that an apparent home run was a ground-rule double.

49

No CB initials on Expos logo

Charles Bronfman discounts long-standing conspiracy theories that his initials CB are on the Expos logo. There was no intention of a vanity logo or a quasi-eponymous hint. There was no snuggling up to graphic designer Clair Stewart to have Bronfman's initials placed discreetly on the logo. What looks like a C on the logo is really a small e as in the e for Expos.

"Definitely false," Bronfman told me. "The design had an overall M for Montreal, a B for Baseball and the E for Expos. I loved it all as soon as I saw it. I never thought of it in any other manner than what I described. When the first person suggested that it was my initials, I was shocked. And remained so all these years."

In another breath, Bronfman said, "Some people have good intentions."

Meaning they probably wouldn't mind if CB was actually on the logo.

Whatever, that Expos' logo is still killing it and rocking it and corporate branding pioneer Stewart is part of the reason why manufacturers and retailers around North America, but especially Canada, are reaping the benefits of a symbol still resonating and ubiquitous with fans even though the Expos left Montreal for Washington, DC following the 2004 season.

Stewart designed the logo in 1968 and how he came to be hired by Bronfman and his ownership team is unknown.

"I have no idea what Clair's firm was paid and I don't even recall how we knew him," Bronfman told me in an interview. "I recall that we wanted to have a Canadian do the design and he was great. And don't forget that we originated the tri-coloured cap. He designed the uniforms, did the logo and the cap."

Stewart had worked primarily for the Toronto-based Stewart and Morrison firm, which was considered Canada's first truly modern graphic-design company. He helped produced logos for CTV, Laura Secord, Air Canada, Catelli Pasta, Salada Tea, Canadian National Railways, Canada Packers, the major banks, many wine companies and many other companies. He died in 2008 at the young age of 98.

The Expos logo was considered a take-off on the Montreal Canadiens

Perry Giannias, top left, is the founder of Exposfest, a terrific fund-raiser and mega-collector of Expos memorabilia. Guy Soucy was so thrilled with the Expos logo that he had someone make a bowtie for him from scratch. Ron Grossman proudly wears this uniform top with a nod to No. 8 Gary Carter. Frank Michaelis proudly displays his fancy beige top.

colour scheme and it sure has worked wonders, even though the Expos no longer exist.

"The logo is a simple, stylish mark born during the all-time greatest period of design, the late 1960s," said Chris Creamer, founder and editor of sportslogos.net, which he operates out of Port Perry, Ont.

"The Expos still have a place in people's hearts. People love to wear Expos stuff," said Abe Rotenberg, co-owner of Gertex, which operates a studio and factory on Densley Ave. in west-end Toronto. "Scarves are a popular item, a great item."

Ironically, it was following the demise of the Expos that saw Gertex experience a growth in Expos' merchandise sales. Fans can obtain Expos stuff online at gertex.com but the company's products are also available in retail stores such as The Beer Store, an Ontario conglomerate that has been selling suds for over 60 years.

"We don't carry clothing but we have all kinds of wares, socks, toques, gloves, scarves, blankets, all proved by Major League Baseball. We have a MLB licensed store," Rotenberg said. "We have a market out there that loves to wear Expos merchandise.

"I do wish the Expos were still around and that there was a National League team in Montreal. I've always been a Yankees' fan. I was devastated by the 1994 strike. I was born in New York and grew up there. I was a big Don Mattingly fan and it would have been nice to see the Yankees and Expos in the World Series but the baseball gods had other plans," Rotenberg added.

"Expos caps continue to be in the top 10 selling teams in Canada each year and we also see sales in the United States due to the iconic logo and style," said Rick Baetz, New Era Cap's Managing Director of Canada. "The New Era Cooperstown Montreal Expos Pinwheel cap is the most iconic and popular Expos item.

"We see fans buying these in multiple silhouettes including the 59FIFTY, 39THIRTY and 9FORT. Fans can find a number of Expos caps, including the original New Era Montreal Expos Authentic Collection 59FIFTY as well as New Era Cooperstown Collection Expos caps in multiple colourways."

Fans can find Expos caps manufactured by New Era Cap at Lids, Sports Experts, Champs and Footlocker along with boutique fashion retailers in Canada.

Even a Philadelphia company called Mitchell and Ness Nostalgia Co. has been getting in on the must-have Expos action.

"We can tell that in Canada and the United States, there is still a lot of interest in the Expos apparel," said Lynn Bloom, Mitchell and Ness' director of authentics and archives. "The Expos' logo remains one of the most popular logos out there. We find that people respond to the red, white and blue logo.

"Without a team being there, we do pretty good. People still respond to the vintage logo. I still think there's just something about the logo that really captivates people."

Bloom revealed that batting-practice jerseys for three Expos legends in particular are very popular: Tim Raines, Gary Carter and Vladimir Guerrero. The 1984 Expos jacket also draws a lot of interest along with T-shirts, hoodies and authentic jerseys, Bloom said.

"The Guerrero jersey, definitely, did phenomenally well when it was brought in for his hall of fame induction in 2018," Bloom said. "Upcoming, we're going to bring in jerseys for Larry Walker and Randy Johnson in April, 2020."

MLB's senior manager of business communications David Hochman said MLB doesn't reveal figures for Expos sales and doesn't identify what teams are the top revenue-generators but he knows that the former Montreal team still attracts a lot of sales.

Hochman said that under MLB's revenue-sharing agreement, all 30 teams receive revenue from the sale of Expos merchandise.

"With its unorthodox, pinwheeled cap paired with a classic rouge-blanc-et-bleu colour scheme, it's a logo that's guaranteed to stand the test of time and live forever in the hearts of baseball fans around the world," Creamer said.

"A quick walk through any shop throughout Montreal will quickly reveal its lasting impact on the city today, over a half century after its unveiling. Entering any of the city's sports shops, you'd be forgiven for thinking the Expos were still taking the field at the Big O, rather than having been hastily shuffled off to Washington over a decade ago."

Stewart would be looking down from on high with a smile on his face in admiration.

"At first, I thought that the merchandise was selling out of nostalgia. But I guess that the design's still considered cool," Bronfman said.

And on the top of the logo and the memorabilia associated with it, Harvey Stone for years was the biggest collector. He was the Expos equipment manager for years so he had an 'in'. He was one of the first employees hired by the Expos on October 26, 1968. He held the position until the early 1980s when John Silverman took over.

Over time, Stone had begun to sell off his huge collection, much of it to Herb Pearo of Burlington, Vermont. Stone was a bachelor, who lived in a Days Inn in the Montreal area when he wasn't holed up at Jarry Park or Olympic Stadium.

"He was a story teller. He knew all the secrets," Pearo said. "I remember him saying that he would go up to players and know who was ready to play. He knew the ones who wanted to play, who was lazy."

Stone was also a heavy gambler and would often call Pearo and tell him to come to Montreal to buy some of his memorabilia because he needed money to pay bills.

"Bad day at the racetrack," Pearo remembered Stone saying. "Come on up, I've got something for you."

One such transaction left Pearo with one of his most unusual treasures: long underwear worn by Expos pitcher Steve Rogers.

"They're autographed," he said with a smile on his face.

He's also quite proud of a bat used by John Boccabella, a backup catcher with the original 1969 Expos. This was a rare find, Pearo said, because bats are usually discarded only after being broken, and the weak-hitting Boccabella didn't usually swing hard enough to make that happen.

"I think I had to sell the wheels off a car" to pay for that bat, Pearo said. Pearo had begun his own collection in 1969 when the Expos began operations. He'd find stuff disposed of in dumpsters at spring training and he'd get a lot from Stone. But when the Expos departed for Washington following the 2004 season, he began to divest much of his stash of goodies, which included all of the media guides from 1969-2004 plus uniforms, bats, balls, you name it.

At one point, Pearo sold a good portion to an unknown banker in Montreal.

"He made an offer I couldn't refuse," Pearo said of the banker.

So as he went to press, the unofficial No. 1 collector of Expos' memorabilia in the world is former Expos batboy Daniel Plamandon of suburban Montreal. He has been collecting since the late 1970s.

Up there with a vast amount is Perry Giannias, who told me he began collecting the year the Expos left town. His stash includes stuff he acquired from Pearo, a large quantity of Gary Carter valuables when they were consigned to auction with Heritage Auctions by Carter's family in 2016 and even negatives from photos taken by the late Expos photographer Denis Brodeur.

Giannias turned his love of memorabilia into organizing autograph festivals involving Expos players. He began Exposfest in 2016 and it remains a constant annual extravaganza where former players show up to sign autographs with the proceeds going to the Montreal Children's Hospital and Giannias' Kat D Foundation in memory of his niece Catherine Demes, who died very young of a brain tumour.

Plamandon has the on-deck circle from the 1969 Expos season, bats, balls, uniforms, bases, shin pads, chest protectors, all the pine tar you can think of, seats, travel bags and so on.

Plamandon is an introvert about his collection, Giannias an extrovert.

"I have 20 years on Perry," Plamandon said. "Perry never saw my collection. I sent the photos of my den to him. I like to keep myself off the radar when it comes to people knowing about my collection.

"It got to a point when I wanted to buy Expos equipment, the prices were two to four times the price. It got to a point where my friends bought items for me on the internet so that my name was never seen. It took almost 18 years for me to get off the charts with Expos equipment.

Fortunately for me, Perry is now in the spotlight."

Among the other huge collectors of Expos stuff is Clay Marston, who lives in a community east of Toronto. He sadly told me that a portion of his stash of several thousand items were stolen when thieves intercepted a truck carrying his loot from West Palm Beach back to Toronto. That was in 2014.

And think of the two passionate illustrators from Montreal, who took advantage of the Expos 50th anniversary in 2019 to pound out some wonderful illustrators and portraits.

One hails from Iran, the other from Quebec's Eastern Townships. Dariush Ramezani and Josée Tellier have fascinated former Expos players and a host of fans across Canada and North America with their scintillating art work. Ramezani is acclaimed for his full-length sketches while Tellier is drawing rave reviews for her portraits.

Ramezani immigrated to Canada five years ago with his wife Farnaz from Rasht, a town located on Iran's Caspian Sea Coast, not knowing anything about Montreal's sports teams but he sure got up to speed quickly. You will see some of his work elsewhere in this book.

"Walking around in Montreal, I've noticed clothes with different sport logos are so popular among people of all ages," Ramezani said in an interview. "As a sport fan, I started to spot logos, one after another: CH for Montreal Canadiens, NY for Yankees, B for Red Sox and after a while I could realize the Montreal Impact and Montreal Alouettes.

"Among those, there was one logo, something like a M to my eye, which I didn't know yet. I asked one of my Montrealer friends about it and he told me about the Expos. The most interesting thing for me was the fact that there have been no Expos since 2004.

"I did a lot of research and watched old videos on Youtube," Ramezani said. "My only source was to watch some games. Because it was something new, it took me 2-3 hours to do one sketch when I first started but with the last players, it only took one hour."

Detail by detail, Romazeni gets to share your favourite Expos players and their stances, gestures, windups, deliveries and other idiosyncrasies right down to a T from head to toe. Tim Raines is Ramezani's favourite Expo of all time. His sketches present his Expos subject matters with ballerina-like feet. He explained that as a child, soccer players were heroes with very long legs dancing in the field like ballerinas. He used that imagination to draw the Expos.

Tellier works full-time as an art designer for a Montreal clothing company and on the side, she's a freelance illustrator, working another 30 hours a week. She's been up in heels with her love for the Expos since she was eight years old. She declined to give me a portrait to use in the book in return for free publicity for her with this blurb.

"I thought it would be great to celebrate the Expos 50th anniversary. I was looking for a project to light up my heart," Tellier said. "I did Gary

Carter first. Carter was bigger than the Expos. It snowballed from there. Then I did Andre Dawson, my childhood idol. Oh my gosh, since I was eight or nine years old, he's been my idol. When he was at bat, I was freaking out. I loved Andre Dawson."

Sealing spot in Cooperstown

Dave Dombrowski's place on a plaque in Cooperstown was sealed Oct. 28, 2018, as far as I'm concerned. That's when the Boston Red Sox won the World Series.

Dombrowski's induction won't take place this year, next year, the year after or anytime soon but it will likely happen closer to 2030.

The former Expos general manager was at the helm of two World Series championship teams: one with the Florida Marlins in 1997 and then 21 years later with Boston. He also was the head of the Tigers when they won a few divisional titles.

Those successes cement Dombrowski's future election into the National Baseball Hall of Fame.

One World Series title wouldn't seal an executive's place in Cooperstown but two would. Long-time Royals and Braves GM John Schuerholz became a Cooperstown inductee in 2017 following a career that spanned 50 years and World Series titles with Kansas City in 1985 and Atlanta in 1995.

Former Blue Jays GM Pat Gillick was inducted into Cooperstown because he was at the helm of three World Series champions: the 1992-93 Jays and the 2008 Phillies.

Dombrowski is far from finished as a decision-maker, although as of press time, he had not been hired in a decision-making role for the 2020 season.

Dombrowski surfaced in the Expos front office as director of player development for the 1987 season under Bill Stoneman. Then on July 5, 1988, Dealer Dave became, at age 31, Montreal's wunderkind GM, the youngest in MLB at the time.

Dombrowski left the Expos in the middle of the 1991 season to take over as GM of the expansionist Marlins.

50

Walker was a six-tool player

It was 1987 and Larry Walker, Randy Johnson, Nelson Santovenia and Rich Thompson were chatting in the bullpen outside their Jacksonville Jaxpos clubhouse.

"Do you really think we have a chance to get to the big leagues?" Santovenia asked.

So Thompson, as he told me, jumped in and said, "As a matter of fact, all three of you are going to the hall of fame. You don't realize how good you are?"

As Thompson and I chatted in late January of 2020, he added, "The three of them were tremendous athletes. I was misled on Nelson. Larry and Randy just looked at me when I told them that. I think Larry already knew how good he was. He had about the best arm I've ever seen."

Can you imagine how dead on Thompson was, except for Santovenia.

Thompson was chuckling when he told me another story about Walker when he was playing in Triple-A Indianapolis when Tom Runnells was the manager before he joined the Expos staff. Walker hit a pop-up, took a couple of steps and decided to jog to the dugout. Runnells was pissed off and took Walker out of the game for not hustling but not before Walker gave him a few choice words.

"Larry thought he didn't want to run it out but Tom put him in his place," Thompson said. "So two minutes later, I went to Larry and said, 'What's up?' He said, 'I deserved it.'"

Thompson roomed with Walker in the minors and in 1989-90 in the majors and found Walker to be just a "regular guy."

"Larry wasn't just a baseball player, he was a tremendous athlete," Thompson said. "He was very confident. He never got too high or too low."

When Walker was on his conference call about his election into Cooperstown, he said the phone call giving him the good news was a "surreal moment." When the legendary outfielder recognized a familiar number showing up on call display from someone that would tell him the news, he said, "oh, shit."

It was "disbelief" when Baseball Writers Association of America

Denis Brodeur photo/author's collection
Larry Walker played for the Expos from 1989-1994

honcho Jack O'Connell called him to say, "I wanted to let you know you didn't come up short this time."

I must admit my eyes got misty when I saw the cell phone video of Walker dabbing his eyes when he got the call.

Walker told reporters that when he was 17, he decided to give up hockey and then along came baseball to take him on a journey. He had told me in the 1990s that he didn't know how long he would be able to play baseball because of knee problems caused by playing so much hockey.

"It's a decision I made and then baseball found me and away it went," Walker said on the conference call. "Just a couple of no's and some good eyes that were watching me at the time and then the Montreal Expos signed me and I got that chance. I rolled with it."

Two of those "good eyes" belonged to a waterfront worker in Portland, Oregon for the International Longshoremens and Warehousemens Union by the name of Bob Rogers. On the side, he was a baseball scout. Rogers, an American, discovered and recommended Walker, a Canadian, for the Expos, watching him in the Pacific Northwest and in Western Canada at various tournaments.

"First time I saw Larry, he was 14," Rogers told me in the 1990s. "He was a good sized kid. I used mannerisms, how he handled himself, what he did when he got off that bus for tournaments. He had the size and the body build. I knew he would make it, if he kept his head straight. He lived up to everything I expected."

Rogers told me that he had last seen Walker play in 1987 when he was with the Jaxpos. Rogers passed away in the late 1990s.

Three years after Rogers first saw Walker and tipped off Expos executives Jim Fanning and Bill Mackenzie, Walker was signed for $1,500 after he was further evaluated while he was playing shortstop at the world youth baseball championship in Kindersley, Saskatchewan in July, 1984. That's right, he was a shortstop in those days. And in one game, Walker also pitched an inning, giving up two bases on balls.

As reporter Darron Kloster noted in the hometown Kindersley Clarion newspaper, Walker, wearing No. 16, started the tournament 0-for-8 before smashing a single to the outfield wall. According to clippings from the Clarion I saw, Walker added a home run, triple and double throughout the tournament.

"Some of these players in the tournament became real good ballplayers but at the time, you don't know," said Glen Johnson, who umpired in the tournament. "When they're 16 and 17 years old, what's going to happen?"

Johnson pulled out the rosters for the world tournament and sent them to me. We noticed that future Blue Jays pitcher Juan Guzman was throwing for the Dominican Republic and Jack McDowell, Gregg Olson and Albert Belle were among the Team USA players.

Interestingly enough, Walker was the only Team Canada player from that roster who made it to the big leagues. How about that? So when he was elected into the Hall of Fame, Glen Johnson sent him a tweet, offering congratulations and tagging it by saying he had umpired him in Kindersley. Even musician Jim Stafford of Spiders and Snakes fame showed up in Kindersley.

Lloyd Mack, a reporter alongside Kloster for the hometown Clarion paper at the world tournament, dug into his files to reveal to me for the book that Walker was 7-for-33 in the tournament with a .212 average with a homer, four RBI and eight strikeouts. Omar Linares of Cuba was the tournament MVP.

"It was a pleasure to play with Larry in Kindersley," Team Canada teammate Barry Petrachenko told me in an interview. "I have reflected on it numerous times over the years. It really seems like yesterday – including watching him hit BP bombs off the dugout roofs of the secondary field, 50 feet beyond the primary stadium. The balls hitting the roof of the dugout on the other field were so loud we could hear them over the hum of the pitching machine. Took us a while to figure it all out.

"I remember mostly the stories and laughs we shared on the bus back to our billet community in Kerrobert after games. It was clear from how excited the Expos got while watching him that he was on his way, even though at the time he was more interested in playing goal for the Regina Pats.

"I am certainly filled with pride for Canada and for him for all that he has been able to accomplish since that terrific summer we spent in Saskatchewan."

As time went on for Walker, there were more "good eyes": people who nurtured him, taught him and kept him on the right track. Two were Ralph Rowe and Tommy Thompson, both now deceased. Rowe worked with Walker in his role as Expos minor league hitting instructor in the mid-1980s and Thompson was Walker's manager in Jacksonville.

I watched Walker play with intensity and bravado from 1989-1993 as a beat writer at spring training, regular-season home games and several road trips. He was a pleasure to watch, a pleasure to interview, a pleasure to see him behave like a kid in the clubhouse, farting, belching, burping, breaking up interviews with teammates.

And I learned that he loved to play this card game Pluck with Mike Lansing, Moises Alou and others, right up to within 10 minutes of game time. How they did so close to game time astonished some of their younger mates but it was something to do for entertainment and as a stress buster before they had to go out and face 95 m.ph. fastballs and nasty sliders.

Walker was a slick fielder, had a strong arm, he could hit, hit for power and run. That's what made him a five-tool player. Remember him throwing out some runners at first from his right-field perch, taking singles away from them? The 9-3 putout in the boxscore came up a few times.

Walker boasted that sixth tool, a mental apparatus: instincts, extra-sensory perception and an on-field IQ almost unparalleled. He had the vision and ability to read the field and think far ahead of the play. He didn't have a degree in education but he had a degree in life.

Walker got a hit and walked twice in his very first game as an Expo on Aug. 16, 1989 and went on to hit .313 during his career which took off after he began playing for the Rockies.

Near the end of the 1989 season, though, Walker was really scuffling and struggling and finished with a mere .179 average. He did make improvements at the plate in 1990 and in the first half of 1991 but he told me years ago that he made a change with his batting stance around the all-star break in 1991.

"I was watching television and looking at a lot of players and how they stood at the plate," Walker said. "I saw that Jose Canseco had a pretty open stance. I tried it and it worked. Before I had a closed stance and I was barely striding. Now I'm straight up to the pitcher. Both my eyes are on the pitcher. Before, it was one eye."

One of the most hilarious moments of Walker's career was April 24, 1994 in Los Angeles when he went into foul territory in the third inning to catch what he thought was the third out hit by Mike Piazza. Walker handed the ball off to a kid in the stands as a souvenir and starting trotting to the dugout, only to be told that there were only two out. So he grabbed the ball back from the kid and threw it back into the infield.

With Jose Offerman on third for the Dodgers, former Expos third baseman Tim Wallach hit a two-run homer and the Dodgers went on to win easily 7-1. For the record, Walker was assessed an error on the play. It will go down in lore for being one of the funniest moments in the game.

Back in 1997, I wrote something about Walker in my first Expos book and so this is what I'm doing 23 years later: I screwed up. I implied that Walker had an affair with Expos marketing employee Claudine Cook. I was given this information by someone and published it when apparently it wasn't true. I apologize to both Larry and Claudine for this indiscretion and for the inconvenience it has caused.

The dates of July 24-27 in Cooperstown this year could see a record crowd attending induction weekend with Jeter attracting the most fans. Some say the 2020 crowd may surpass the figure of 82,000 in 2007 when Cal Ripken Jr. and Tony Gwynn were elected.

Walker's presence alone in Cooperstown will attract thousands of Expos fans from around North America, especially Montreal. For those who don't know, Jeter almost became Expos property in June, 1992 but the organization decided to pass on him in the annual June draft of amateur players. Then several picks later, the Yankees took him. He played 19+ seasons in pinstripes.

Walker's induction will mark the end of an era. He's the last home-grown Expo to go to Cooperstown. The others drafted, groomed and tutored by the Expos in the hall of fame are Randy Johnson, Gary Carter, Andre Dawson, Tim Raines and Vlad Guerrero.

For years, when people would tell Walker that he should be in the hall of fame, he would say, "I'm already in the hall of fame." And he was talking about the Canadian hall in St. Marys, Ont. Not only is he an inductee there but he won so many Tip O'Neill awards as the top Canadian each year.

"With Larry Walker going to the Hall, all told we had a pretty good run on Hall of Famers and baseball in general," said former Expos managing general partner Claude Brochu. "Too bad we never got much credit in Montreal. It might have saved the franchise."

Wallach rarely took time off

Tim Wallach was a quiet, out of the limelight kind of guy, who was hard-nosed, fiery and exemplified what a true leader is by his inspired play at third base and at the plate.

He averaged close to 155 games per season over a span of 12-plus seasons with the Expos. He was the franchise's first captain when he got the nod in the early 1990s.

Wallach felt much indignity when he was told/asked during the off-season of 1991-92 that the Expos wanted him to switch to first base after a long career at third. This scenario didn't sit good with him.

Very reluctantly, Wallach did play first base through part of the 1992 season before Tom Runnells was fired. When new manager Felipe Alou took over in May, he immediately put Wallach back at third.

Ironically, 1992 season was Wallach's last in an Expos uniform. He fell to .223 with nine homers and 59 RBI, a way off his normal statistics. It was the impetus for general manager Dan Duquette to think about exposing Wallach in the expansion draft that took place late in 1992 involving the Colorado Rockies and Florida Marlins.

Instead what happened was that the Expos worked out a trade to send him to this home-state Dodgers but it was a complicated procedure. He could have vetoed the trade because of his 10-and-5 rights, 10 years in the majors, the last five with the same team.

Wallach eventually agreed as long as the Expos sold his house in the Montre-al area but a stumbling block, too, was that the Dodgers wanted his contract re-negotiated so that he would earn less money. Wallach agreed to take a cut in pay.

So on Dec. 24, 1992, he was traded to the Dodgers for unknown Tim Barker. I will never forget that. It was a freezer-cold day and I was in the Vermont resort town of Stowe for a Christmas break when I tuned into the conference call with Wallach.

One of the greatest honours for Wallach came when he was inducted into the Canadian Baseball Hall of Fame in 2014.

"The stark reality is that fair-weather fans, the separatist PQ government in Quebec, an unstable economy, bad ownership, labour conflicts, dishonest Bud Selig, inappropriate playing facility, negative media, lack of corporate sponsorship, Jeffrey Loria, Canadiens' 23 Stanley Cups, limited TV/radio exposure, disloyal players, Blue Jays' two successive World Series wins, questionable managers, Rick Monday and plain bad luck have all played equal parts in paving that long and arduous road to Washington. Pity. To borrow from Joni Mitchell in her Big Yellow Taxi demi-anthem, the baseball world won't know what they got "till it's gone."
– Expos fan J.P. Allard of Ottawa.

51

The Expos and the Nationals

The topic of the Expos and the Nationals brings out sensitivity that is more negative than positive.

It has been an issue ever since the transport trucks started moving stuff to Washington from the Expos office building at Olympic Stadium on Ave. Pierre-de Coubertin in east-end Montreal during the winter of 2004-2005.

When the Nationals won the 2019 World Series, the sensitivity took on a new life.

Most Expos fans, if you look at posts on Twitter and Facebook, aren't thrilled at any mention of the Nationals since the Montreal team moved to Washington for the 2005 season, knocking out that long-standing Expos switchboard telephone number of 514-253-3434.

Officially, the Nationals are the successors of the Expos, according to Major League Baseball, but that is where it all stops. I don't see why MLB can ascertain the fact that two separate cities, one in Canada, the other in the U.S. can be the same franchise.

Washington should really have been listed as an expansion team, not a relocated team that took over Montreal. The idea of the Nationals sharing Expos records makes no sense. The Nationals should have their own record books and not even mention Expos records.

If Tim Wallach holds the all-time Expos record for most games played, then the Nationals shouldn't announce that Nationals treasure Ryan Zimmerman has overtaken him.

"To share a history is utter nonsense," Expos fan Ron Rosen said.

"The Nationals have absolutely nothing to with the Expos and I resent that organization trying to adopt the Expos for themselves," chimed in Curt Duckworth, who lives in a trailer park in Alabama. "They can cre-

Courtesy White House Flickr account

Melania Trump and her husband U.S. president Donald Trump pose with Washington Nationals pitcher Stephen Strasburg, manager Dave Martinez and GM Mike Rizzo at a White House reception shortly after the Nationals won the 2019 World Series. Martinez played for the Expos from 1988-1991.

ate their own history instead of adopting the Expos history. They didn't earn the right."

There are some very outspoken Expos fans who even criticize people because they have the gall to cheer for the Nationals. This criticism has reached the absurd where even some people have been kicked off Expos Facebook pages because they cheer for the Nationals. That's people pouring their hearts out on social media, some of it vile and disgusting.

Yet, there are some who admire the Nationals.

"They win in the year they brought out the Expos' throwbacks. That's actually pretty cool," said John Mancusi of New Hampshire.

The Nationals wore Expos uniforms July 6, 2019 for a game in Washington and the Nationals went all out to show their love for their background and heritage. Canada's deputy ambassador to the U.S. Kirsten Hillman spoke in French and English prior to the game.

"Mes dames et messieurs, ladies and gentlemen, your Expos," Hillman said to the crowd.

Between plays, Expos scenes from 1969-2004 were shown on the scoreboard. In the concession stands, you could find Quebec food favourites poutine and smoked meat.

The Nationals win was especially gratifying for manager Dave Martinez, who played for the Expos as a part-time player from July, 1988 until midway through the 1991 season. He was an industrious player, not a home run hitter but a singles hitter, who was solid defensively. He was packaged with Scott Ruskin and Willie Greene to the Reds in exchange for reliever John Wetteland on Dec. 11, 1991. We think the Expos won that trade hands down but that's another story.

I tried to get City Hall in Montreal and Montreal mayor Valérie Plante interested in playing host to Martinez and Nationals bench coach/former Expo Bob Henley at a reception and autograph session last November shortly after the World Series ended. I suggested those two only, nobody else from the Nationals. But it landed on deaf ears.

I even emailed Martinez and Henley but got no reply. I never did get talking to Plante and city spokesman Jimmy Zoubris did finally get back to me after a series of automated emails came back to me from City Hall.

"You do know that many Expos groups are completely opposed to the idea but time heals wounds," Zoubris said in his email.

Expos Nation founder Matthew Ross led the bandwagon of fans, who really have no use for the Nationals even after they won the World Series.

"Our official position is that the Expos were paused in 2004," Ross said in an Expos Nation tweet. "The overwhelming majority of our base is indifferent towards the Nationals. Congrats to them on a great season, but they're not our team."

William Jegher, a member of Montreal's prospective ownership group headed by Stephen Bronfman and Mitch Garber, said hosting Martinez and Henley wasn't something they were interested in.

"Thanks for the idea but we wouldn't be interested in taking the lead on this. For us, it's all about looking forward," Jegher said. "I just personally don't think any of those two guys represent much of a connection to Montreal. I think interest in such an event would be limited to a group of diehards."

It's funny that in all the years the Jays have been staging exhibition games at Olympic Stadium from 2013-2020, the Nationals haven't been the opposing team. And it won't happen anytime soon.

"Baseball book-ended my life as an eight-year-old child living in the Villeray area of Montreal. Jarry Park was in my back yard. I used to see all the stars of the day. I was even at the game when Claude Raymond made his Montreal debut in the early 1970s. I hung out in the players' parking lot. When the team started to contend in 1979, I attended late season crucial games in Pittsburgh, driving through the night to get there. I lived in Toronto as an adult but was back for some key games, including Carter's return and final game in 1992. So at the last home game in 2004, it was like a funeral, emotionally draining a slow death. When Claude Raymond at game's end grabbed the microphone to address the fans, his words echoed what many of those attending felt: why were there no Montreal businessmen wanting to take the leap of faith to rescue this team and save the proud legacy of Montreal baseball? When I saw the emotion of Brad Wilkerson barely keep it together, it contrasted with what I observed 10 years previous in 1994 when the players strike was announced. I was so upset at the players for going on strike, ruining our and my dream season. In 2004, I saw that the players as shown by Brad Wilkerson truly did care and love our city. When Warren Cromartie, who was the catalyst to bring back baseball to Montreal, organized a screening of Jackie's Robinson's movie at a downtown Montreal theatre, I saw Claude Raymond and I told him personally how much I appreciated his words at the last home game. I see in Claude Raymond a type of elder statesman of Montreal baseball in much the same way I saw hockey legend Jean Beliveau with the Canadiens: a classy gentleman." **– Expos fan Alex Hankewicz**

Epilogue

As we remember the past with this book of memories, we look to the future regarding the return of baseball to Montreal.

We see some hope, we see some despair.

Can you wait until 2028 or 2029 before the Tampa Bay scenario is fixed and there is a possibility that the Rays will be relocated to Montreal? Oh boy, it's a long time. I don't think Major League Baseball will allow Tampa Bay to play close to another eight years at barren Tropicana Field.

My guess is that Rays owner Stuart Sternberg will somehow be allowed to sell his team to Stephen Bronfman and his group long before 2028. The Tampa-Montreal proposal is better than nothing but it's flawed and weird anyway. The MLBPA has major concerns about such an experiment because players would have to find lodging in Montreal while also renting or owning a place in the Tampa area.

When I asked former commissioner Bud Selig recently what he thought of the proposed experiment with Tampa Bay and Montreal, he demurred, saying "you will have to ask Rob Manfred." It's obvious Selig isn't fond of the idea.

Expansion is another possibility for a new team in Montreal but that may be a few years away. There are solid U.S. cities looking for a franchise. That causes competition for Montreal. Expansion is not a guarantee for the return of baseball to Montreal. MLB owners may vote for U.S. cities.

At least Montreal has some hope. If former Expos outfielder Warren Cromartie hadn't begun beating the drums back in 2012 with his Montreal Baseball Project and ensuing fund-raising reunions for the 1981 and 1994 Expos, the fever exhibited in Montreal would be subdued. Remember that for eight years from 2004-2012 until Cromartie got the ball rolling, there was nobody showing any interest in resurrecting the Expos.

Without Cromartie, there would likely be no Exposfest, no Expos Nation, two vital organs that comprise the current Expos fever.

We are encouraged by the strong ownership group headed by Stephen Bronfman and Mitch Garber and we are enthused that this group has earmarked a patch of land south of downtown that will involve Devimco in what would be a joint ballpark and condominium/commercial complex.

Denis Brodeur photo/Linda Breault collection
Gary Carter poses with daughter Christy back in the day

There are few details about this project to share but it's all part of the hope and fever that goes along with trying to return baseball to Montreal.

Even Chantal Bunnett is getting in on the fever with a script called Out of Left Field, something she's hoping will end up on HBO or Netflix some day. It's all centered on her true-life career as an Expos scoreboard operator.

We should note that the great Pedro Martinez, the Expos' only Cy Young award winner, reached out to remember the franchise during the 2019 World Series in a segment aired on the MLB Network. In his spiel, Martinez talked about the 1994 team that was robbed of possible glory with the season-ending players' strike.

Back in 2004 after he helped the Red Sox win the World Series, he did something similar in a champagne-soaked clubhouse. He praised the Expos as he was surrounded by microphones.

Go Expos go!

Acknowledgements

With a project like this, a lot of cooperation is required,
especially from former players and executives involved with the Expos
along with people not connected to the franchise.
These people make the memories so important for the reader
with their nuggets, quotes, anecdotes and unlocked secrets.
Special thanks to commissioner emeritus Bud Selig
for taking the time to talk with me and expressing his thoughts
about some of the events involving the Expos.
I especially thank all those who I reached out to more than once
for follow-up interviews. And kudos to those who supplied photos.
Special thanks to graphic designer Dawna Dearing of First Wave Grafix,
whose splendid work is seen in this product.
It was a pleasure working with her.

Appreciation to individuals, publications and organizations

Catherine Gallagher
Jim Gallagher
Sherry Gallagher
Lesley Taylor
Peggy Bougie
Wikipedia
retrosheet.org
Canadian Baseball Network
Baseball Reference
Montreal Daily News
Montreal Gazette
Montreal Star
Kindersley (Sask.) Clarion

Toronto Reference Library
Oshawa (Ontario) Public Library
Pickering (Ontario) Public Library
Canadian Baseball Hall of Fame
Houston, Texas police department
White House in Washington, D.C.
City Hall in Montreal
Rideau Hall in Ottawa
Baseball Almanac
Pittsburgh Pirates
MLB Productions
Exposfest

Interviews

Kavin Adams
J.P. Allard
Bob Armand
Pierre Arsenault
Rosso Atticus
Jack Billingham
Mark Bouchard
Peggy Bougie
Tom Brady Sr.
Claude Brochu
Charles Bronfman
Chantal Bunnett
Tim Burke
Larry Christenson
Stephen Dannhauser
John D'Acquisto
Andre Dawson
Billy DeMars
Don DeMola
Dave Dombrowski
Elroy Face
Jeff Fassero
Mike Fitzgerald
Barry Foote
Joe Forget
John-Patrick Foy
Orrin Freeman
Doug Frobel
Perry Giannias
Brian Gerstein
Bill Gullickson
Russ Hansen

Gary Hughes
John Hughes
Tommy Hutton
Pete Jensen
William Jegher
Jeff Juden
Glen Johnson
Wallace Johnson
Sally Johnston
Rontae Jones
Mike Kozak
Pierre Ladouceur
Ken Macha
Bill Mackenzie
Kevin Malone
Bob Mann
Dennis Martinez
Ron McClain
Bob McClure
Sharon Milner
Michael Ng
Bob Oldis
Al Oliver
David Palmer
Larry Parrish
Stephen Pickford
Ross Porter
Dustin Puckett
Tim Raines
Dariush Ramezani
Claude Raymond
Jeff Reardon

Nikco Riesgo
Jimmy Ritz
Gary Roenicke
Bob Rogers
Steve Rogers
Abe Rotenberg
Cathleen Sanderson
Scott Sanderson
Nelson Santovenia
Bill Seagraves
Ken Singleton
Vin Scully
Bud Selig
Tony Siegle
Firmin Simms
Terrmel Sledge
Bryn Smith
Michel Spinelli
Chuck Staub
Sam Staub
Joyce Taylor
Lesley Taylor
Josée Tellier
Jay Tevan
Rich Thompson
Dave Van Horne
Bill Virdon
Larry Walker
Tim Wallach
Jerry White
Brad Wilkerson
Bobby Winkles

Denis Brodeur photo/ Scott Coates collection
Terry Francona back in the day before injuries derailed his career

'Bataille de coqs'

As former Expos managing general partner Claude Brochu looks back at what happened with the Expos, he's fond of the good things but feels sad about the end of the franchise, zeroing in on his tenure.

"John McHale used to say to me, 'It was always the Expos against the world' and in spite of that, we had one hell of a history, players that were talented and interesting people in their own right, an excellent coaching staff, and a scouting and player development staff that was second to none. We had an all-round good run," Brochu told me.

"We just ran in to a bad situation at the end and lost it all. In French, we would say we lost because of a "bataille de coqs", a fight between roosters in the chicken coop, egos that got in the way, and everybody backing the wrong horse. The franchise could and should have been saved.

"I had a deal with Bernard Landry, the then Deputy Premier and Minister of Finance for the new stadium. I had the Feds on board and we were doing very well getting community participation in the funding. Remember the $100-million naming rights to the ballpark? But a certain number of my partners thought running a baseball team and getting a new stadium was easy and convinced the Premier, Lucien Bouchard, that they had a better and cheaper plan and urged him to reject my plan."

Furthermore, Brochu said some of those partners ganged up to "get rid of me" because they thought he "was the problem."

As for Montreal getting another MLB franchise, Brochu is skeptical.

"It will be very difficult to get a team back in Montreal," Brochu said. "The shared franchise concept (with Tampa Bay) will never work and all talk of this is a set up and manipulative. It reminds me of the locals here (in Montreal) getting eaten alive by (Jeffrey) Loria's New York lawyers, except this time it is Tampa. They never understood the politics and they were out of their league and it's the same again. The local group will never be able to bring together the $3-billion U.S., that I calculate is required for an expansion franchise. They've admitted as much."

Manufactured by Amazon.ca
Bolton, ON